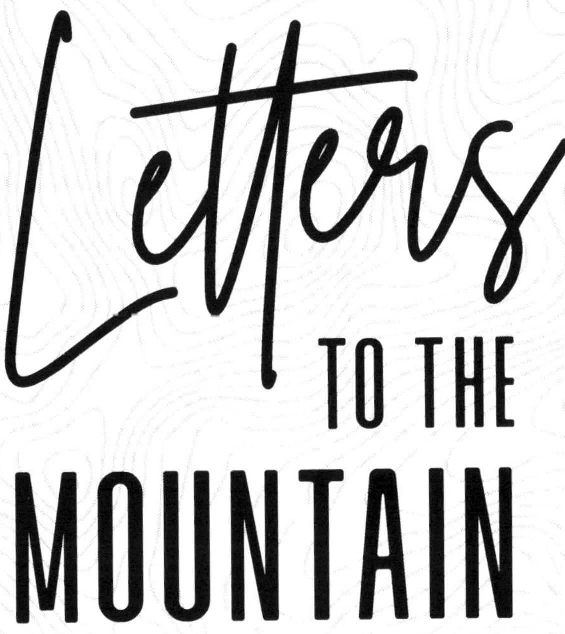

Letters TO THE MOUNTAIN

ANYA WYERS

Anya Wyers
Letters to the Mountain

ISBN: 978-1-9990831-0-6

Manufactured in the United States of America

Editor: Kristin van Vloten
Cover and Interior Design: Laura Wrubleski
Publishing Support: The Self Publishing Agency

Stay in touch with the author at anyawyersauthor.ca
or @anyawyersauthor on Instagram.

For Rachael
My First True Love

Author's Note

I have written the following memoir in the form of letters to Rachael. It is based on true events.

Foreword

September 21, 2010

Dear Rachael,

I miss you. And I love you. I always will.

I am sad and confused and still a bit hopeful. I had this idea to write to you since you are not here to hear all of the things I want to share with you and I have had a hard time getting started. A lot of stuff has been hard lately. Sleeping, waking, eating.

It just doesn't make any sense.

I have so much more I want to tell you but I am going to go to sleep for tonight. It's getting late.

I'm just so tired.

Anya

Chapter One

August 7, 2004

Dear Rachael,

I have a feeling that you would remember exactly how it was that we met and how we became best friends. Then again, it could very well be something that we would just laugh about as we reminisced and admitted that neither of us actually remembered how it all started. Just that it was our first year at O'Grady Catholic High School, and that at one point you went home to your mom and told her that you had met a new friend (me) whose hair was even curlier than yours! I should note that your hair was always curlier than mine, a fact that I was always jealous of.

We had gone to separate elementary schools but came together at O'Grady for grade eight. The only memories I have of high school that don't include you are when I went to Kelly Road for our graduating year after O'Grady closed down. Even then, we still hung out, though less frequently than when we went to school together and saw one another every day.

That first year apart in our last year of high school was the first of many years that we would spend on different life paths. It gave us our first taste of what adult life would be like. Still, I never questioned your friendship or support when I needed you the most. There aren't a lot of people that grew up with me and knew me in those times and saw what my childhood was like or could understand why I am the way that I am.

I'm finding it hard to put into words what it is like for me to reflect on the times we shared, good and bad. I know that you were just always there, no questions asked. I was always invited along on your adventures, and made to feel included as a part of your family and inner circle. It's a very special thing for me because I didn't always feel that way in my other friendships, or even in my own family at times. You were always surrounded by other people that treasured you and thrived in your light. And while I wasn't always friends with the same people as you, we seemed to always make it work when we all got together.

For that and so much else, I will be forever grateful.

When I started school, my parents sent me to the local public elementary school. By the time I was in third grade, my parents thought it was in my best interest to attend Catholic school in downtown Prince George. I was being excessively bullied and my mom wasn't happy with the administration at the public school, so I started taking the bus every day to and from St. Mary's Elementary School. The natural progression from there was to attend the only Catholic High School in town, O'Grady.

You had attended the Catholic elementary school closest to your end of town, as you came from a religious family and there was a school in your parish. The logical choice for you was to attend O'Grady after elementary school.

In our first year at school together your locker was just outside the classroom where our grade eight Religion classes were held. We spent a lot of time with our friends on lunch breaks in the Religion room, cozied up on Mr. Brock's couches or wandering the halls or school grounds, hoping to run into whatever boys we had crushes on at the time. The Religion room is where we practiced routines for the talent shows, including choreography for our stints as back up dancers and karate masters. Eye of the Tiger. Thrill of the fight.

I don't remember spending a lot of time with you one on one when we were at school. At least not in the early years. The fact that there were always people around us is something I can attribute to the person that you always were. Social, loving, welcoming and just a joy to be around. Your birthdays always involved everyone you considered close, as did other special occasions around Christmas and in the summertime.

I remember spending the night at your house when it was just the two of us, watching movies in the dark of your basement. I remember huddling in your room listening to music and talking for hours about our respective revolving doors of crushes. I could really use a good gab session with some tea, cuddled with you underneath a blanket with no agenda and nowhere to be. Some things will always be so nourishing for the soul. We've done this, or something similar, countless times and I hold the memories so close to my heart.

Our maturity progressed over the years. In the summer between grades eight and nine, we all camped out in a tent in your backyard. We lay out in the sun, played your Aqua CD on repeat and chit-chatted until the night was pitch black.

On one of those summer days, we set up a tent in our friend Cass' back yard. We gravitated there with our friends because her mom usually turned her head when we wanted to have a few drinks.

"Okay, what else are we missing?" Cass asked. "I'm going back in for the watermelon!"

"I think we're good," our friend Stef said. "I'll come with you."

"Me, too!" the rest of us replied in unison, following Cass across the yard.

We all headed up the front steps into Cass' house together to get the watermelon she had somehow spiked earlier that afternoon. When we got inside, we found her mom standing there, eating watermelon.

"Ummmmm mom?" Cass asked. "We were just coming to get that!"

We all stood behind her snickering.

"Ah, there's another watermelon, girls! This one was all cut up anyways."

Cass turned her head to us, laughing along. "Wellllll, I cut it up for us."

"Is there anything you want to tell me about the watermelon, Cass?" her mom asked.

"Nnnnnnnooooo..."

"You put vodka in the watermelon, didn't you?"

At this point we were all giggling, shocked that an adult could be so cool about it.

"I injected it!!" And we all burst into fits of giggles, her mom included.

"Be safe, girls," her mom told us, handing us the rest of the watermelon on a plate.

We all went back outside and got settled in the tent with the watermelon and a cooler full of drinks.

"I have to peeeeeeee," Carla whined, just as it was getting dark. "Someone come back inside with me!"

"No way!" Cass replied. "Just pee outside."

"I can't do that!" she screeched.

"Go on," you told her. "It's easy."

"No, seriously guys," she said. "I don't know how!"

"Oh, come on!"

We all laughed.

"Just give it a shot!" Cass told her.

Carla put her game face on and stepped out of the tent. "Someone show me then!"

"I'll come," you told her. "Pass me my shoes!"

The rest of us stayed behind in the tent. There was a commotion outside of branches crunching underfoot and giggles traveling through the soft fabric of the tent.

"Okay," you told her. "It's easy. Just squat and pee like you're sitting down. Just keep your pants out of the way."

Carla giggled. "I can't let it go!"

"Just do it!"

By this time, we were all giggling inside the tent too.

"Ahhhhh!" Carla screamed. "I got it all over my pants! My leg feels warm!"

We all burst into laughter. I was smiling so much my cheeks hurt.

This was around the same time, in or around ninth grade, where things changed slightly. Not between us, but *for* us. The school dances meant pre-drinking, lying to our parents, stealing alcohol and before and after plans that meant we could have a few drinks and really let loose without getting caught. Being at my house when my mom was working made it easier for us to have a few drinks and not worry too much about the adults catching us. We had a lot of fun together, just goofing around, whether we were drinking or not.

I choose not to have a strong opinion about the underage drinking that took place, not to mention the stealing and waiting outside the liquor stores to have older kids boot for us. It is what it is at this point. I think that my family and I were bad influences on you, though I know that you were your own person who made your own decisions. Sure, they were questionable explorations, but each one of us ended up being well-rounded adults with homes, good jobs and families to show for ourselves, so our foolish choices in adolescence couldn't have been that bad, right? (Okay, so I'm not doing a very good job at not having an opinion. But that's something I can always be counted on for...my opinion, un-sugarcoated and forthright. Right?)

We didn't always need an occasion to have a girls' night where we had a few drinks and just acted like crazy teenagers. I say crazy, but by many standards we were very, very tame. There were several times where we slept over at Cass' place, just you, me, Cass and Stef. We hid ourselves in Cass' room, stealing coolers from the fridge.

"Get me one more while you're out there, please!" I asked Cass.

"I'd tell you to get it for yourself you wise-ass," she replied, "but I think you'd give us away for sure, you're so wasted!"

We all responded in giggles. I'm really not sure who we thought we were fooling. Cass' parents never said anything to us about what we were up to, even when it was clear that we were underage drinking. We didn't need to pretend like we were hiding it.

"We're going to be friends forever, right?" Stef asked when Cass returned with the drinks.

"Absolutely!" you replied.

"Obviously," I added. "I think we should be each other's bridesmaids in each of our weddings!"

"Friends forever!" We all agreed.

"Is it glow stick time or what?" Cass asked as she opened the package of green glow sticks.

"I pick Madonna!" Stef said as she chose a CD and Madonna's "Like a Prayer" started playing in the background.

"Our anthem! Now somebody turn off the lights," Cass said as she handed each one of us a glow stick.

We all stood up, started shaking the glow sticks as hard as we could and then pulled them apart. In the dark of Cass' room, the green solution from inside the glow sticks shone neon on every surface. We danced across the floor and over the bed, singing as loud as we could, adding green to the walls, the ceiling and each other.

We collapsed together as the song ended, laughing and smiling, out of breath. Our innocent promises for the future were never kept, but in those moments, we didn't know any better. We were just teenagers living in our explorative bubble together, happy to do nothing and everything all at the same time.

Things changed again when we started driving. We were responsible kids who had been raised right and would never drink and drive. We were forced to be a little more responsible, but it really just meant more sleepovers at whatever place hosted us for the evening. Sleepovers were perfect occasions for experiments like LARM.

"My mom is on graveyard shift this weekend!" I told you and Marie at lunch one day.

"I'll ask if I can sleep over!" you said, excitedly.

"I'll be there! Are you going to invite Lisa, too?" Marie asked of my cousin, who hung out with us and got along well with my friends.

"Sure!"

"I'll see if one of Claire's friends can boot for us," Marie said.

"Sounds good," I replied. "There's always my dad's stash of homemade wine, too!"

Your parents dropped you off on Saturday afternoon. When Marie and Lisa showed up together and shortly after my mom left for work, we brought out our respective hauls.

"I grabbed a bottle of red wine from downstairs," I said as I put it out on the picnic table in our back yard.

"And we got some coolers," Marie said as Lisa pulled out some drinks from their backpacks and added them to the table as well.

"Just wait until you see what I got!" you said as you giggled, pulling a water bottle out of your bag.

"What on earth is that!?" I exclaimed.

Lisa picked it up. "It looks like mud!"

We all giggled.

"Well, I didn't want my parents to notice anything missing," you said. "So I poured just a little out of each of their bottles of liqueur!"

"Rae!! That's so gross!" We all laughed, but we each took a sip and somehow managed not to spit it out.

"We should name this mix of awfulness," Lisa suggested.

"Hmmm, after ourselves maybe?" I asked.

"LARM!" you shouted, rather excitedly.

"LARM?" Marie asked.

"Lisa, Anya, Rachael, Marie!"

Whether we finished it or not, our namesake drink was born. Never to be replicated. Thank god.

I recently read a saying that really resonated with me: "Choices are the hinges of destiny." I believe that this includes the bad choices right alongside the good. We made the same "bad" choices into our adulthood. Over-drinking, inviting boys we didn't know over to our places for sleepovers when we should have known they had *other* ideas in mind, gallivanting in downtown Vancouver and just putting ourselves into unknown situations that really wouldn't be considered all that safe. And yet we're okay. None of these choices, whether we made them as kids or young adults, meant that either one of us would become unsuccessful or unhappy. These experiences that helped us develop into the people we were as young adults. (Side Note: at what point did I stop being a *young* adult? Don't answer that.) And while I don't believe that these small choices helped craft the responsible and successful parts of our beings, I don't think they hindered us either. They're just part of life. Of growing up in a small town, within an even smaller community where as impressionable kids we followed the leader more than I would necessarily hope my own kids would.

Your background was a religious one, having attended church every Sunday and Catholic school since kindergarten. I, on the other hand, only started at Catholic school because it was the only other option for me outside of the local public school. My family had never been overly religious, though I was baptized in my dad's home country of Croatia when I was just a baby. My mom was baptized as an adult after I started attending St. Mary's but there was never a time when we routinely attended church as a family. My mom still likes to go to church on Christmas Eve sometimes, but I have not carried any of the faith I had in my school years forward to my adult life. The only times that I have been to church in adulthood are tied to you, mostly when we went to mass together. Other than a few weddings, that's the extent of my current association with the Catholic church. It just isn't for me. But I know that you found strength in your faith as an adult and I respect you tremendously for it.

There were times when you questioned your faith with me,

challenging the principles of what you had been taught growing up. You wondered why you believed and practiced things a certain way. Was it just because that's what you were told to do? Or was it because you learned to follow and respect the sacraments of your religion and what your family had always done? I could never answer that for you, but I have an eternal respect for the fact that you questioned it at all, especially given your background. You were your own destiny; the life your parents taught you to lead helped you prepare for whatever came your way.

My involvement in sports, both in and outside of school, was something that I maintained separately from you. You played volleyball but never shared my love for soccer. That was always something that I shared with our friend Marie. I only began to share your affinity for music and the arts when I picked up scrapbooking, painting and now writing. I always wrote in journals, but kept those close to my heart, while you were always sharing the beautiful art you created with everyone.

I always admired the fact that your parents never had cable tv; you and your brother and sister were encouraged to explore the outdoors, exercise your creative abilities and help take care of things around the house, including your family's small farm animals. Watching movies with your family was a special time together. I was in figure skating before I met you and then I played soccer through most of my childhood, but I don't remember being very good at anything or passionate about things like you were. I was not a bad soccer goalie, and I had a pretty great throw-in, but it wasn't until recent years that I learned to recognize and appreciate when I'm good at something. Your modesty about your abilities made me jealous. I wish I had had that for myself when I was growing up; I think it would have made a lot of years more tolerable.

By our grade eleven year, our class size had decreased, as had the overall size of the school. We were told that O'Grady would be closing at the end of the school year, leaving us to find a new school from which to graduate. You went with the bulk of the students from our class to Prince George Secondary School and I went by myself to Kelly Road High School. I wanted desperately to go with you and our friends to PGSS but my dad said no. Instead, I walked by myself to school every day and spent the majority of my lunch hours reading or doing homework in the library. It wasn't until close to the very end of the school year that I made a few friends who I started to hang out with on a regular basis. Sadly, it wasn't long enough for me to forge the friendships that would last a day past our graduation. I graduated with my cousin Lisa, whom I still keep in contact with, but other than that, I have nothing except for the memories of missing out on all of the grade twelve milestones that I should have had with you.

While I can wish that certain things were different, I am where I am meant to be, having experienced the paths that my destiny set out for me. But I am still a bit sad when I think about why we never got to stand on the same stage when we graduated or attend our last high school dance together. It's the good and bad experiences that have shaped me to become who I am today. I, too, am my own destiny, after all.

Just because we didn't stand together at graduation or ride in the same limo to prom doesn't mean that we didn't know each other inside and out. There were things I never had to say out loud to you. You were there.

My dad is an alcoholic.

I never actually said those words out loud until well into my adult life. I was so ashamed and even afraid at times. I hid my dad's alcoholism from people who were close to me, even though it would have been clearly obvious to anyone that I grew up with. It really isn't that big of a deal to my friends when I tell them now. It has no reflection on who I am as a person, though it definitely helped shape me into who I am today in a lot of ways. I carried the burden of his alcoholism on my shoulders for far too long.

You knew me the best. You knew me at my worst. There are so many things that you knew and were a part of; so many pieces of my inner being that you were privy to. I never had to tell you that my dad drank a lot or that it meant unrest at home more often than not. You were there. You were there for me and sadly you were there through some of the incidents yourself. If I could have protected you from anything negative you might have felt when you witnessed my dad's drunken outbursts, I would have. But it wasn't my place and it means more than I could ever explain to anyone that you were a part of it. That I didn't need to speak the words for you to know what I was going through. Growing up wasn't easy for me, but having you by my side as my support helped tremendously.

I was always aware of other family members being uncomfortable around my dad when he was drinking. Sometimes they would leave our house early after a family dinner. Or we would stay home when we'd planned to go out if he had already been drinking. I was too young to know the extent of it, but I understood more than I was given credit for.

The only time my dad would come right out and criticize me was when he had been drinking. The unsavoury moments from my childhood blend together in my mind. I see them all as flashes of time.

Flash.

Police lights were shining through my bedroom window.

I couldn't have been more than eight years old.

I sat up in my bed in the dark, holding back tears as I watched the red and blue lights reflect through my room.

I rocked myself back and forth, hugging my knees close. "Please don't take my dad," I said out loud. "I love him. Please don't take my dad."

We had been at my uncle's house for dinner. He and my dad had both had way too much to drink, as had my uncle's crazy wife.

"Please don't take my dad."

I heard the front door of our house open.

"Good evening sir," I heard a deep voice outside. The police were on our front lawn, almost directly outside of my bedroom window.

"Can I help you?" my dad asked.

"We received a complaint that there was a disturbance at your brother-in-law's place?"

"Yes, but we left," I heard my mom interject. "They all had too much to drink so we came home."

"We're following up because there was an allegation of assault."

"Assault?" my dad replied.

"Yes," an officer responded. "By, I believe it was your brother's wife?"

"There was no assault while we were there," my mom said first.

Please don't take my dad.

"We responded to the call there first," the officer went on, "and we were directed here."

"We left before things got out of control." It was strange that my mom was doing most of the talking.

Didn't this qualify as being out of control?

"As long as everything is alright here," the second officer cut in, "we'll be on our way. We've seen enough."

"We had to follow through on the complaint." It was the first voice again. "Just promise us that you'll stay home for the night."

"Yes, we will, officer." It was my dad this time.

"Thank you for your time." And they were gone.

Thank you for not taking my dad.

Flash.

"Come into the big bed with me."

Flash.

"I think I need to call 9-1-1," I told my friends. I couldn't have been more than 13. We had had a sleepover at my house. My mom was at work. We walked into the kitchen to find my dad slumped on the floor, his hands fallen out to the side, his chin resting on his chest. His eyelids drooped over his eyes.

"Dad!" I called to him and touched his shoulder gently.

His eyes were open but they were completely glazed over.

"Dad, wake up!" I was afraid. My friends stayed out of the kitchen.

I calmly walked over and dialed 9-1-1.

"9-1-1, what's your emergency?"

"It's my dad. He collapsed."

"What's your name and where are you calling from?"

"Anya. I'm calling from my home," I said and proceeded to give them our address.

"Okay, Anya, how old are you?"

"13."

"Okay. Can you tell if your dad is breathing?"

"Yes. He is."

"Can you tell me what happened when you found him?"

I took a minute to think about it. "He was cooking breakfast and then he collapsed against the kitchen counter. He let out a big long moan and when I went into the kitchen he was sitting on the floor."

"Has he been taking any medications?"

"I don't think so."

"Okay, Anya. Help is on the way. Can you stay on the line with me?"

"Yes, I can do that."

"Is there anyone else there with you?" the operator asked.

"Yes, my friends."

"Where is your mom?"

"She's at work."

"Okay. You're doing a great job at staying calm, Anya. She would be proud of you."

Silence. I didn't know what to say. It felt like ages were passing, but I soon heard the distant call of sirens. Help was there.

"The ambulance is just pulling up, so I'm going to get you to go answer the door and I'll hang up, okay?"

"Okay."

I hung up the phone and went to the front door. In what seemed like mere seconds, the ambulance attendants entered the house, assessed my dad and took him away in the ambulance.

I called my mom to let her know what was going on and my friends called their parents to be picked up. My aunt was on her way to be with me while we waited for my parents.

After the ambulance was gone, I looked in the garbage. There was a tall empty glass bottle lying at the bottom. I didn't mention it to anyone. I'm sure they knew.

All I was told in the wake of this incident was that my dad had suffered a stress event. No one mentioned the booze. No one ever does.

Flash.

"It'll be our little secret, okay? Don't tell anyone."

Flash.

I was a teenager. My mom was working again. My dad was drinking again.

We were just finishing dinner and my dad got up to get himself another beer. He swayed as he returned to the table. I did my best to keep quiet. I didn't want to say anything that would provoke him.

I could smell the warmth of the beer on his breath and I ached inside. I wished I was anywhere but in my own childhood home. At least he hadn't gotten into the wine.

"I was thinking to see if Auntie Kelly could come pick me up?" I said to him gently. "I could hang out there until mom gets off work."

"You don't want to spend time with me?" he slurred back at me.

"No, it's not that."

"It never is. You and your mother never want to spend time with me anymore." He could get so self-deprecating after he had had that one sip too many.

"I just want to go and play games at their house," I said as I cleared the table. I was trying anything to get him to just agree and get over it.

He took his beer into the living room and sat down on the couch, muttering to himself. I couldn't understand him but I didn't want to interrupt, nor did I want to say anything to further upset him. I took a seat at the opposite end of the couch.

'Why don't you love me?" he said quietly, his head hung low.

I didn't respond. I have recognized as an adult that I sometimes have a difficult time making eye contact with people. I think that stems from not wanting to see the tell-tale glaze over my dad's eyes when I knew he was drunk. I would avoid looking up into his eyes with hope that maybe things would be okay. That I wouldn't say something to set him off or make him angry. That maybe he would look at me with love instead of just looking right through me all of the time.

"Why do you hate me?" he asked.

I stayed silent, waiting for the perfect time to get up from the couch and retreat to my bedroom where I felt somewhat safer.

"You just want to spend time with Kelly and Steve."

At least in there I could block the door if I got too scared.

"It's like all I'm good for is the roof over your head."

All reason had left his words. It was going to get bad, I could feel it. I stood...

"Sit down!" he yelled at me.

I stayed standing.

"You can stay here with me, you little bitch. You're not going anywhere!"

I silently wished that my mom was there with me. She was never much help when my dad went off, other than by trying not to add fuel to the fire, but her presence was always comforting. It meant that I wouldn't have to be the only victim.

"Just sit down!" he yelled again.

We had a low-backed sectional sofa at the time and as my dad yelled, I stood up on the seat of the sofa and climbed over the back rest, just to get away from him.

"Is that how you want to play it?" He was getting angrier and angrier.

I was scared. I was standing by the front door with nowhere to go but outside in the middle of the frigid northern winter. All I was wearing were jeans, socks and a light sweater.

"What do you want me to do?" I cried.

He stood by the couch. "If you don't want to sit, then just get out!"

"Where do you want me to go?!" I cried harder. My hand reached for the doorknob.

He took another step towards me.

I opened the door. "Where the fuck do you want me to go!?"

The silence was worse than the yelling.

I stepped outside, repeatedly asking him where he wanted me to go. I looked out into the street. It was quiet and cold. I cried. I didn't know what to do.

The door was never closed behind me. A minute passed, at the most, before I looked inside. He wasn't there. He must have taken himself to bed. I will never know whether he was just too drunk to function or whether maybe he felt bad about how things had escalated. My bets are on the former.

I stepped inside and closed the door behind me but didn't bother locking it. I picked up the phone and called my auntie to come and get me. There was no way I was staying in that house alone with him any longer.

Flash.

"Are you sure you're okay to walk home?" my mom asked.

"Yup," I answered her. We were down the hill from our house at a family gathering.

"I can take you home quickly before I leave for work if you want me to," she said.

"No, it's okay," I assured her. "I'd like to stay for a bit."

I'm sure that someone else in my family would have given me a ride but I was at an age where I was beginning to gain some independence. I felt good about walking myself home. Even if it was only a couple of blocks.

I stayed a bit longer before I started to walk home up the big hill. When I got home, I called out to my dad. "Hello?"

There was no answer.

Strange. It was only 4:00 pm on a Saturday afternoon. The familiar shameful feeling came over me when I saw a can of beer sitting on the coffee table.

I could have turned around, gone back to the party and went home with one of my aunties. I should have. But I foolishly wanted to make sure he was okay.

I walked through the kitchen and glanced out the window into the back yard.

My dad was standing there, relieving himself off the side of the patio into the flower bed beside the house. He was leaning against the railing with his head tilted back, swaying slightly.

My head snapped back instantly and I froze.

Why did this have to happen to me? Why did the first time I saw a naked man as a young woman have to be my drunk dad?

I turned around and walked back out of the house, unnoticed.

Flash.

I was ready for the day, having showered and gotten dressed. My mom was already at work and I knew my dad wouldn't have gone to bed yet after his night shift. They went quite a long time where they didn't see each other much, working opposite shifts.

"Good morning," I said gently to my dad. He would have been home for a few hours already, but always took time to wind down before going to bed.

There was no response to my greeting. I inhaled slowly and hoped that he was asleep and not just at the point where he was ignoring me already.

He was sitting on the couch with his back to the kitchen. I noticed a few empty beer cans on the table. They weren't there when I went to bed the night before.

I quietly prepared my breakfast, moving as quickly as I could. If I timed it right, I'd be able to get out of there before he woke up. There was no way of telling how much he'd had to drink without checking for bottles in the trash. The bottles were the real tell. My heart raced as I packed my lunch for school, tucked my breakfast into my bag and snuck out the door, holding my shoes.

I let out the breath I had been holding when I got outside. Was it from fear, or was I just being smart?

Flash.

"I'll pick him up, mama," I told my mom.

"Are you sure?"

"Yes, I have to go back up to the University to get some books from the library anyways. I can just go later and pick him up on my way back when he's done work."

"Thanks sweetie, that would be so helpful!" she said. "I'll see you when I get off work then. Bye."

I hung up the phone, thinking to myself that this was the perfect opportunity to finally share my news with my dad. I had been accepted into the Paralegal Program at Capilano College in North Vancouver. I would be moving away for school the following September.

On my way back from the library at school, I stopped to pick my dad up from his co-worker's house. Unsurprisingly, there was no thanks for the ride or even any niceties exchanged about our days. There was a reason why I hadn't yet told him about my new adventure.

"So, I have some news," I started.

Silence.

I knew I had to tell him eventually, so I got as straight to the point as I could. "I'm going to be going to school in Vancouver. I got accepted into a program to become a paralegal."

More silence from both of us.

Only the radio broke the stillness and while I felt good for having finally told him, I was sad that he couldn't even muster a "congratulations" or pretend to care and ask me something about the program.

When he finally spoke, I immediately wished he hadn't.

"I don't know why you would want to push papers for someone else for the rest of your life."

September couldn't come fast enough to get me out of there.

Flash.

I love you and miss you every day,

Anya xoxo

Chapter Two

November 2, 2008

Dear Rachael,

I have been thinking about how even though we ended up graduating from different high schools, we were lucky enough to go to the University of Northern British Columbia together for a couple of years. We even ended up in one of the same classes!

To be honest, I felt like I was forced to immediately continue with my post-secondary education and UNBC was the most logical choice. My parents told me I could live in their house rent-free as long as I went straight into post-secondary school and didn't take a break. Coming out of high school at 18 years old, I didn't know what I wanted to do with my life. Which is fair, I think!

Anyway, we both started at UNBC straight out of high school. I originally wanted to work towards a degree in psychology. That meant I needed to take a core class in the arts to balance out a degree in science. You were working towards your undergraduate degree in the sciences as well, so we ended up taking an arts class together. To date, it has been the only time I have learned anything to do with music. You were so much more suited to this type of class. I have never held an instrument with the intention of playing it properly whereas you were a beautiful pianist and learned how to play the guitar. Our professor was actually a member of the Prince George Symphony Orchestra, so we all took a field trip near the end of the course to see him play. It was my first time seeing a live performance of professional classical music, the second time being you, of course.

I decided pretty quickly that the sciences weren't for me so I didn't actually need the art class as part of my degree. But I have fond memories: sitting next to you in the dungeon-like classroom, listening to our prof teach us the difference between chamber music and symphony orchestra. (I still couldn't tell ya. No surprise there.)

I changed my major to English before eventually finding the paralegal program offered through Capilano College in North Vancouver. I was accepted to start attending Cap in the fall of 2004.

When I shared my news with you, I was met with nothing but support.

"Tell me all about it!" you said with excitement as we found a seat in an alcove at the University where we usually sat to eat lunch.

"Well, I'll be moving to North Vancouver," I explained, "which is not too far from downtown. The program is two years and has really high academic standards. But they have a great reputation and help you find a practicum at the end of it."

"Wow! That's great! When do you go?"

"It starts in September, so I'll likely move at the end of August. My mom and Auntie Laura are going to help me find a place and then make the move."

"Are you nervous?"

I hesitated. "No. I think it's going to be really good to move away."

You nodded. "It'll be so different living in a big city!"

"Ya. I'm looking forward to that, actually! Apparently North Van has a similar population to PG, but in 1/8th the land size or something crazy like that."

"Wow! I can't wait to come and visit you!"

"For sure, though I'm sad we won't get to see each other like this."

"We'll still hang out when you come home. And I promise to write!" You reached over and gave me a warm hug.

You were one of my biggest supporters when it came to making such a big life change. My mom was also very supportive of my career choice, though I know that she wouldn't have chosen to have her nest emptied that soon. My dad's lack of support was not surprising to anyone, and was only foreshadowing what I could expect in the future. His words were hurtful but I didn't let them stand in my way. It never crossed my mind to change my plan or find out what would make my dad happy and do that instead. I was going to become a paralegal and I was going to be damn good at it, thank you very much. I would hope for my own future children that instead of bending to fit someone else's ideals that they would stand strong, as I did, and do what they want to. My choice to enter the paralegal program was not made consciously to defy my dad. But it was the first time I had done something completely for myself without taking anyone else into consideration. It was a move that would shape me positively as a person and lead me forward without looking back.

I was only two years into a degree that I didn't know what I would do with, but I felt a little sad that I was walking away from UNBC without a piece of paper in my hand in recognition of an undergraduate degree. I have always placed value on a good education but there was nothing that I was really eager to learn or that would be beneficial to my future for me there. I truly believed that the paralegal program was my path and I was thankful that it was leading me away from the town where I grew up.

I have no regrets about leaving because I can recognize now how pivotal this choice was. I chose to make myself a priority. I started my life of independence by walking away from everything I had been and done in Prince George to start fresh.

Living by myself in a city where I didn't know anyone was an adjustment. I adapted quickly and even made some friends whom I still have today. I went back to PG during the summer between my first and second years at school and worked in a law firm there while I stayed with my parents. I had a hard time going back to North Van for my second year but I went back to PG for almost every long weekend available in both of the years I was at school. I missed my family, but being away from home made me realize which family members and friends were better suited to be a part of my life only when we lived in the same town. Rae, you were never one of those people who let me fall to the wayside. We were always there for each other, regardless of where we lived.

One of the years that I was at Cap you did an exchange to Germany, which extended your degree by one year. I admired you for making choices that would bring adventure into your life. There was never a time when we lived apart that we lost touch. Sure, we went for longer stretches of time without talking on the phone or seeing each other in person, but we wrote many a good old-fashioned letter and managed visits and phone calls when we could. It was never not enough, and it would never be too much either.

For my birthday while you were overseas, you sent me a pair of earrings and some hair clips in a German birthday card. The envelope ripped open in transit and one of the hair clips fell out but somehow the earrings stayed inside! I actually want to wear them as my "something blue" to my wedding. They are one of my most precious belongings and remind me of you every time I wear them. I have always been a bit oddly sentimental and feel like I carry you with me whenever I wear jewelry from you.

I remember when you told me that you were planning on going to medical school and applying to UBC Med. One of the toughest med schools to get into! It came as no surprise; you had always wanted to become a doctor and even mentioned specializing in the effects that high altitudes have on the body in relation to climbing. You were preparing to sit the MSAT; your mom was making sure you ate blueberries every morning before you studied. Everyone was immensely proud when you passed the test. As part of the application process, you had to sit for an interview at UBC and you came down and stayed with me. I drove you out to your interview. I felt very honoured to be able to be there for you.

Words cannot begin to describe how proud I was of you for making it into medical school. Though I never would have expected any less from one of the most intelligent people I know. One hundred percent selfishly, I was most excited because this meant that you would be living near me again, right out at the campus where I already played soccer every week. It had been at least three years since we lived this close to each other, the last time being in PG before I moved away to North Vancouver for school and your adventures took you to Europe and back again.

I never attended UBC, but we spent a lot of time out there together in your first year when you lived in the residences on campus. We would hang out in your room, drinking there before attending dances or using it as a jumping off point for going downtown or to the beach. It's special to me to have that time since I have never actually lived in the city of Vancouver, just the British Columbian Lower Mainland.

I look back on this time fondly. It was so special to me that you always made the effort to spend time with me; I think that's why I honour quality time so much now. Spending time together means more than any material gift ever could. I know that the fates intervened but it doesn't stop me from wishing that we could go back to a simpler time, together. I can feel your arm slip in behind mine, walking arm in arm together wherever we went.

After I graduated from the paralegal program, I moved from the bachelor's suite where I lived during my second year of school and made my home in a one-bedroom apartment located just off of busy Lonsdale Avenue, still in North Vancouver. It will be a sad day when I move away from this neighbourhood. I know that if I ever want to buy a place, I won't be able to afford to live in North Van. Everything I needed was walkable: my favourite hole in the wall sushi place, small produce shops and a drug store, the fields where I played on a softball team with my friend Jaimie, and the bus stop whose bus took me straight downtown to work or to the Lonsdale Quay and the sea bus. Rent was reasonable and I lived there for two and a half years. I was living the single life and not thinking too much about my future just yet.

Ever since I moved away from PG, I embraced my independent life. I finished school with above-average grades, which were a requirement of the paralegal program to begin with, and had done my practicum plus a few extra months of work as a paralegal at a medium-sized personal injury law firm. I moved around a bit in my career, but found myself settled at another medium-sized law firm, this time doing personal injury defense work.

I was happy to be living my life, doing what I wanted, making my first attempt at being a grown up with responsibilities and extra-curricular activities that pretty much centered around alcohol and meeting people. I may not have been slaying life as a twenty-something, but I was enjoying my days. I spent most of my time alone and even when I had relationships, they were never defined or serious. They were just fun while they lasted.

When you finally moved to Vancouver, of course, we were both more than a little busy leading our own separate lives. You were in your first year of med school and I was still early in my new career. Still, I cherish the times that we were able to spend together, whether relaxing at one of our places or partying at the Medical Student & Alumni Centre (MSAC) with your fellow med students. In my mind we were still just kids, but to the outside world we were doing quite a good job entering adulthood.

Whenever we hung out with your friends, I was the only one who wasn't a student. But I always felt welcome. There were martini parties and games nights at my place and dressing up with your sister for dinner and a show.

The Halloween that I dressed up as Pippi Longstocking, complete with a coat hanger through my pigtail braids, was a big one. We met at your place on campus to get ready and have a few drinks before the MSAC party.

"I brought this coat hanger," I said, "and I thought we could just bend it over the top of my head or something. Then braid my hair around it?"

You laughed. "I'll see what I can do."

You were dressed as one of the characters from the musical *Cats*, which I knew nothing about. Our outfits were homemade and definitely did not follow the trend of sexy Halloween costumes. My mom had sewn the dress for me especially for Halloween; it resembled a paper bag, which was fitting for the costume. Not so much for femininity or sex appeal.

"How's the new job going?" you asked as we put on our makeup.

"I really like it so far," I said of the job I had started just that week. "It's insurance defense instead of plaintiff work so it's a bit different, but I like it so far. The people are nice."

I poured us each a glass of wine in coffee mugs. Res life.

"How about you?" I asked. "What's new and exciting at school?"

"Same old, really, lots of studying and long hours. It's not until next year that we get a bit more practice in the field." You turned to face me. "How do I look?"

"You look great!" I said, even though I wouldn't have known the difference if you looked out of character. Your cat ears and little painted-on whiskers looked on point to me.

"Alright," you said, "let's tackle this hair!"

"So, is there anyone cute we should be on the lookout for tonight?"

"Hmmm." You bent the coat hanger to fit the shape of my head. "Let's see. There's tall smart guy that's in my class, but I wouldn't go for him. I'll point him out to you if I see him."

"And what about for you? Any crushes?"

"I don't think so," you said as you started to braid my hair. "This is going to look great!"

"Thanks!" I said. "But, really? No guys for you?"

"Well, there is one guy that isn't in any of my classes, but I don't know him well enough to say anything to him."

"Drink up!" I refilled our glasses. "Liquid courage!"

We had finished the bottle of wine between us by the time we were finished getting ready. "I think we're all set!"

"Let's do this!" I said as I gathered my coat and we set out for the night.

We passed many other costume-clad students while we walked out of the building. As we stepped out into the cold night, you hooked your arm through mine, a huge grin on your face, and said, "Let's make this a night to remember, Pippi!"

"You got it, kitty cat!"

I have no idea what any *Cats* reference would be. That was the best I had.

We took the bus into the city and made our way over to the MSAC building. The place was packed. We danced, we drank, we flirted, and we had so, so much fun.

"Anyaaaaaaa," you said to me, a tad wobbly, as you made your way over to me after being separated for a time. "I made out with him!"

"Him!?" I said, feeling pretty good myself. "Like him, him?"

"Him who?"

"The guy you needed liquid courage to even talk to."

You paused, grabbing onto both of my arms as you faced me before you said, "No," followed by a giggle.

"Kay?" I questioned. Was I only confused because I was drunk?

"Just that guy," you said, pointing to Dracula.

"Nice!" I said, laughing back. "He's cute! Minus the fangs. Unless you're into that."

"How about you? Where have you been?"

"Just dancing," I said.

"Shots?" A voice came from behind us.

"Heyyyyy!" You said excitedly, introducing me to a fellow student who was also from PG and whom I may have even met once or twice before while sober.

"Hi!" he said, grabbing us each for a hug. He was cute.

"Yes!" you said, pulling my arm as we followed your PG friend back to the bar.

"I don't know, Rae," I started to say. "I think I've had enough to drink."

"Never!" the PG friend said as we joined a group including a mummy, a doctor (so original), and a couple of girls dressed in matching school girl uniforms. He forced a shot into my hand, and even though I knew I shouldn't, I drank it quickly with everyone else.

"Now, we dance!" he said and we all followed him back out to the dance floor. We danced until I couldn't tell if I was spinning from too much dancing or too much drinking. The music pounded and the room filled up with even more people, all in costumes. I stepped to the side of the room to catch my breath. I couldn't stop spinning.

"Hey," I said to you, over your shoulder. "I'm gonna go."

"Okay!" you said cheerfully. "Are you sure you're okay?"

"Yes, I'm just going to grab a cab." I could do things like this now that I was a working woman. It felt great. "Are you going to be okay?"

"Ya, I'll get the bus back to res with some of the other students," you said as you turned to hug me. "Be safe!"

"You, too." I walked out of the building, trying to steady myself before figuring out where I had to go to catch a cab. I looked up and down the dark street, wondering which way I should go when I heard someone throwing up behind me. I turned to see a bumble bee getting sick in the bushes. Gumby was holding her antennae.

"Happy Halloweeeeeeen!" Gumby shouted in my general direction. I needed to get out of there.

I refocused my attention back to the street just as a taxi van turned the corner. I waved and the driver pulled over to pick me up. I climbed into the front seat, buckled in and told him my address. He said nothing; sometimes it was hit or miss whether you would get a driver who would actually take you across a bridge.

I swapped the spinning room where the dance had been for a spinning, moving vehicle. I rested my head against the cold window while the driver took us through downtown on our way to the north shore.

The spinning just wouldn't stop. I think we all know what comes next when that happens.

"I think I'm going to be sick," I told the driver.

"I'll pull over, hold on," he said.

I felt the van slowing to a stop and I reached to open the door before I lost control and vomited all over the inside of the vehicle. I leaned out, thinking that the seatbelt would hold me, but I was shocked when it un-clicked and I was sent flying out of the van, head first. The driver stopped just far enough away from the curb that I fell onto my hands and knees before gracefully face-planting directly onto the edge of the cement curb.

I heard the taxi driver's door slam shut as he ran around the back of the van to see if I was okay.

I told him that I was fiiiiiiiiiiine. I think we all know that I wasn't.

The driver helped me back into the van. I did my seatbelt up (hopefully) properly and miraculously I didn't feel like I was going to be sick anymore. I did feel like my head was going to explode, so I resumed my position with my head resting on the cool window.

We crossed the Lion's Gate Bridge and the driver eventually pulled over somewhere that I recognized as not being my neighbourhood.

"The street should be around here somewhere," he said in broken English, consulting his GPS.

"This isn't right," I said. I was so done, but I could tell we weren't at my home yet.

"The computer is telling me this is where the street is," he replied.

"21st ," I said. "21st and Lonsdale is my home."

I remember that it was dark, I had no idea where this man had taken me, and I was too far gone to realize what a potentially horrible situation I had gotten myself into.

"21st," I repeated, over and over.

Eventually, we arrived at my place. The next thing I knew, I was closing my apartment door behind me, leaning over to take off my shoes. Then it hit me again; I was going to be sick. I had made it home safely, though all of the cash that should have been left in my wallet was gone. A small price to pay for my safety, I know.

I put myself to bed and woke again when daylight crept through the windows. I sat up in bed and turned towards the closet, which had mirrors for doors. All I saw were my pigtails sticking out of the sides of my head and a huge mark of what can only be described as road rash on my forehead, complete with a gash across my nose.

I looked away quickly, laid down, and went back to sleep.

I awoke again several hours later. I grabbed myself a tall glass of water and some Advil and then stood and examined my face.

"Good god," I said out loud to myself. I had been very, very lucky to make it home in one piece.

I searched for my phone and dialed your number.

"Hello?" you answered groggily.

"Hi," I said.

"You made it home safe?"

"Ya..."

"What? What happened?"

"It's a long story. Can I come and grab my stuff? I'll tell you then?"

"Sure. Are you okay?"

"Yes." At least I thought I was. "You?"

"Yep. That was so much fun!"

"Too much," I answered. "I'll see you soon."

I left some things at your place the night before. I wasn't planning on going to get them right away, but I thought it was a good idea to get your opinion on whether I should go to the hospital for my injuries.

A little over an hour later, I walked into your place.

"What happened to your face?" you said in shock.

"Is it that bad?"

"No," you said, walking me through the common area to your room. "Well, yes, but no. What on earth happened?"

I retold my embarrassing story, your mouth dropping open in response several times.

"Do you think I should go to the hospital?" I asked when I was done.

"It depends on how you're feeling," you answered. "I don't think you need stitches or anything, but if you start feeling worse, I'd probably go in. Just to be safe."

"Okay, thanks. Did you have a good time?"

"Yes! It was a blast! I made out with a really cute cowboy!"

"I thought the guy you told me you made out with was dressed as a vampire?"

"Oh ya. He was. But I kissed a cowboy after you left."

You made us some tea and we relaxed a bit before you kindly kicked me out.

"Alright," you said, "back to studying."

"Sounds good," I said as I gathered my things.

"Let me know how your face feels when you wake up tomorrow."

The things you think you'll never say, or hear about yourself.

"I will." We exchanged a quick hug and I took off.

When I woke up the next morning to get ready for work, the sight of myself in the mirror was even worse than it had been the day before. My eyes had swollen shut and my nose was twice the width that it normally is.

I picked up my phone and called you right away.

"My nose swelled up overnight," I told you as soon as you answered. It was still early enough that you hadn't left for class. "I don't even look like myself."

"Definitely go and get yourself checked," you told me. "You don't want to risk a head injury."

"I have to call in sick to work," I said. "There's no way I can go into the third week of my new job looking like this!"

"What are you going to tell them?" you asked with a mouthful of breakfast. That habit always bothered me about you, but I never said anything.

"Not that I got drunk and face-planted out of a cab," I said with an eye-roll.

"Probably a good idea. Let me know what the doctor says."

"Talk to you later," and with that I hung up.

I was able to get in to see my doctor that morning. Before my appointment, I called the office manager at my work. I made up some bullshit story about being kicked in the head playing goalie at soccer and waking up with a swollen face this morning. I highly doubt they believed me, even for a second, but they were understanding when I told them I had an appointment at the clinic.

I went to the doctor and had to explain that I had face-planted into the cement following a night of heavy drinking. That yes, I did vomit following the injury but it was more likely related to the copious amounts of alcohol I had consumed that evening than it was due to the head injury. I ended up at the hospital for a CT scan and called in sick the following day as well. It was a very obvious penance that I had to walk around as the wounds scabbed over; there was no way I would have been able to cover it with makeup, but I did my best to act normal and ignore the millions of questions everyone asked about my trauma that was most obviously not a soccer-related injury.

Rounding out this story was a joke award that my law firm gave me at the Christmas party a couple of months after the incident. They called it the "Kick in the Head" award and presented me with a kid's bicycle helmet. There was no way that anyone believed that's what had actually happened to me, but I didn't tell any of them the real story until I was set to leave the firm years later. I needed the helmet for my drunken adventures and not the ones on the soccer field; looking back on it I can laugh, but it was a serious incident that could have turned out a lot worse.

That year progressed rather uneventfully in comparison to our Halloween debacle. There were countless other dances at the MSAC, including one in the spring of 2008 that was memorable for other, non-alcohol related reasons.

"He asked me for my phone number!" I told you as we left the MSAC building together.

"AD?" You asked. The Almost Doctor.

"Ya!"

"That's a new one for either of us!"

"I know! Actually, I think it's a first for me."

"Woah!"

"Well, other than really drunk guys at the bar that never call," I said, blushing.

AD was a fellow med student of yours, tall and handsome. He definitely had a way with the ladies, though I thought I was something special at the time.

"Is that okay?" I asked you.

"What do you mean?"

"If I go out on a date with someone you go to school with," I explained. "I don't think you're really close or anything, I just don't want it to be weird."

"Not at all," you replied. "We're definitely not close, I think you should totally go out with him!"

"Okay! If I even hear from him."

We were walking to the bus stop; you would head to campus in one direction, and I would continue through downtown to get to the north shore. Before we parted, we talked about our plans to meet again soon.

"Do you think you want to come to the Gala then?" you asked, referring to the UBC Spring Gala, an evening celebrating the arts put on jointly by the medical and dental students.

"Definitely," I said, "especially if you're going to perform!"

"Ah," you said in a modest tone, "it's not for sure yet. Even if I don't, you should come."

"Alright," I agreed as we approached the street where we would go our separate ways. "Just let me know how to get a ticket and all that."

"I'm not sure, but I'll ask around."

"Okay, thanks!"

"That was fun!" You said as we turned to hug each other.

"For sure," I said. "Be safe."

"You, too."

When you called the following weekend, I had happy news to report.

"He texted me!" I told you right away.

"Woohoo! Are you guys going out?"

"Actually. I wanted to talk to you about that. He asked me to go to the Gala with him. He's away for a couple of days and said when he gets back, he wants to go out and suggested that I go with him to the Gala."

"Ohhhhh."

"Is that okay?"

"For sure. I'm performing so that works out well because I won't be able to sit with you anyways."

"Yay! I haven't seen you play the piano in a long time. I have two reasons to be excited now!"

You laughed. "Well, it's a group thing, so don't get too excited. I haven't even had a chance to practice much."

"You'll be great."

"Thanks," you said before you paused.

"What's up?"

"Well, is it going to be awkward if you're there with a date? Should I come say hi?"

"Of course," I replied immediately. "I'd be mad if you didn't! Just act natural."

"Haha, very funny." Act Natural was our phrase for each other when we had too much to drink and were acting obviously intoxicated.

"I don't think it'll be weird if you come and say hi," I told you. "It's just a date!"

"A first date. No big deal!"

"I can't believe I'm going on a date!" I said. "I never really had an official 'first date' with what's-his-pickle."

"He who must not be named," you said with a laugh.

"He who isn't worth it to be named," I agreed, referring to a guy I had briefly dated the previous Christmas.

"Are you nervous?"

I thought about it. "I don't think so. Do I have reason to be?"

"Nah," you said, brushing it off. "But what are you going to wear?"

The Gala came quickly; between work, soccer and the gym, it had snuck up on me. It wasn't set to start until 7:00 pm on the last Saturday in April. AD lived in residence on the UBC campus as well, so I planned to go by your place before meeting him at 6:00 pm. That way we had time to walk over to the Chan Centre.

I still hadn't decided what to wear so I packed a couple of options in a bag before heading to your place.

"What time do you have to leave?" I asked as we walked into your place.

"In about half an hour," you said. "We have one more run through of the performance, thank goodness."

"Are you nervous?"

"A little. But I always get a little nervous getting up in front of all those people. Including you first date kids!"

"Haha. Now help me pick a top!"

I tried on the different options I had with me.

"Wear the black one," you said. "Not too much boob that way."

"Thanks," I said, putting it back on. "Is there even such a thing as too much boob as far as guys are concerned?"

"You wouldn't want to give him the wrong impression, is all."

"True. We should get going. I'll walk out with you. You have to show me where to go."

We parted ways outside your building with a quick hug. "Break a leg!" I said as I turned to go.

"Have fun on your date!"

I shook my head as I watched you go. It was still so weird to hear that. I walked along the path you showed me that would lead over to AD's building. I texted him to let him know I was on the way.

He was just walking out of his building as I got to the front door.

"Hi," He said, leaning to give me a hug. He was really tall. Taller than I remembered.

"Hi," I replied. "Lead the way; I have no idea where I'm going."

"So, how's things?" he asked, leading the way back towards where I came from your place.

We walked and talked about the normal things. Me about work, him about school. He thought it was interesting that I already had a career. Working downtown, living on my own and all that adult stuff. I thought it was fascinating that he was in medical school.

The Gala was beautiful, especially your performance. AD and I went for a late dinner afterwards to one of my favourite restaurants at the time. It was nice. I drove and then dropped him back at his residence building afterwards. I wasn't sure if we would see each other again; I couldn't tell if he was interested in me or not.

The following weekend, he texted me to ask me out again. This time, I picked him up and we went for a long walk at Kits beach. He held my hand, and we made out on a park bench. He made me feel really special. Sadly, he called me the day after our second date to tell me that he liked me too much and didn't want to get into a relationship that he didn't have time for. I had liked him, but not that much, so I really wasn't all that upset when he called it off. But I did realize that I liked having someone to spend time with.

It was then that I decided to give the online dating world a try.

Enter: the thirty-year-old pot smoker.

We started to get to know each other through text and eventually I gave him my number so he could call me. Our rapport over the phone was quick and witty. We talked several times on the phone before we decided to meet. He was going to pick me up at my place one Sunday afternoon and that was the extent of the plan.

I was always taught not to get into a car with people I didn't know, but I threw caution to the wind and hopped into his car outside my apartment building after saying a quick hello on the sidewalk.

"So," he said, "we're in your neighbourhood. What would you like to do?"

"Let's go out to Ambleside," I suggested, "and go for a walk. Or we could grab a coffee and sit and talk."

"Just tell me where to go," he said as he started to drive.

"You'd like that, wouldn't you?" I teased.

"Ha," he said.

I felt comfortable with him right away, which was a good sign. It was a sunny afternoon, so my back-up plan had been to just get out of the car and take the bus home if things went poorly. But he had a great smile and a personality that brought out my funny side; I felt at ease and it seemed as if we had known each other for much longer than however long it took us to drive to the beach.

We made our way to Ambleside in West Van, found a spot to park his car and walked along the seawall. The conversation flowed easily and we eventually settled on almost opposite ends of a bench overlooking the ocean. He was straightforward and to the point, a quality I had myself and found attractive in him. Until he started to ask me about sex. On the first date.

"You're much younger than me," he said, "and it concerns me that you're, uh, less experienced."

I knew what he meant but his words put me off. I have always been one to wear my emotions on my sleeve, so I sat up straighter, crossed my legs away from him and folded my arms. "What exactly do you mean?"

He turned his head to look at me when he asked, "Are you a virgin?"

"Ha," I laughed. I couldn't even look at him. "Really?"

"What?"

"You're seriously asking me that?"

"Ya." He stared at me with a serious look on his face.

"No," I said sharply.

"Really?"

I turned to look him square in the face. It wasn't even so much that he was asking, but now he was implying that he didn't believe me.

"You don't believe me?"

"If you say you're not, then I guess I do," he said with a shrug.

"You guess?" I said. "Alright then."

"You're mad."

"And I hate when people tell me what I'm feeling. Should we head back to the car?"

"Don't be mad," he said. "It's just that I had a bad experience with someone before who lied about it. And then it was really obvious and uncomfortable when I found out she was lying."

I looked right at him as he spoke, my jaw tense.

"I don't want that to happen again."

He sounded like he was being honest. I felt myself calming a bit.

"That's fair," I said. "But I don't appreciate you thinking that I'm a liar. Not cool."

"I'm sorry," he said. We sat for a bit, staring out at the ocean, people walking by. "Do you want me to take you home?"

"That's probably a good idea," I said as I stood.

"I don't want you to be mad," he said.

"I'm more irritated than anything," I told him. "I was having a really nice time."

I moved to go around him and he stepped forward at the same time, his foot landing on the back of my sandal.

"Ah!" I said as I stepped forward before I realized what had happened, breaking my sandal. "My sandal is busted!"

"Oh no!"

"Well," I said, taking the other one off and looking for the closest garbage can, "these are toast."

"Sorry," he started to apologize.

"It's all good, they weren't in the greatest of shape anyways," I said as I threw them away.

"Do you want me to go get my car?"

I rolled my eyes. "Don't be ridiculous, I can walk."

"If you're sure."

"I'm not made of glass," I said as I turned to lead him back towards the parking lot. I was still put off a bit, but it was nice of him to offer to go get his car.

The conversation remained on the surface as we made our way back to my place.

"You shouldn't ask me to come in," he said as he pulled his car over to let me out at home.

I just laughed and turned to face him as I unbuckled.

"I mean, I want you to ask me to come in," he said with a smirk, "but it's not a good idea. I don't kiss on the first date."

"Ya," I said quickly, "me neither."

I reached for the handle and he reached for my left hand before I could leave the car. "Seriously, I'm sorry. Don't stay mad."

"I'll think about it," I teased. "I did have a nice time."

"Good. Me, too. I'll talk to you soon?"

I got out of the car and leaned over to face him before I said, "If you're lucky and I forgive you for making me walk in bare feet back to the car!" And with that, I closed the door and walked into my building without looking back.

The nerve of this guy! To first not believe me when I told him

I wasn't a virgin, then to tell me not to invite him in! Who did he think he was?

Okay, fine. I had kind of wanted to invite him in and I definitely wanted to see him again. I wasn't mad any longer about the sex thing. His reason for asking seemed valid. And he had apologized, twice.

And I couldn't stop thinking about him.

He texted me later that evening to ask me out again and from then on, we started seeing each other a couple of times a week. He continued to challenge me with his questions and his intelligence; I was intrigued and frankly I loved the attention. I was happy not having to spend all of my time alone, knowing that there was someone willing to get out and do things with me. We went to the movies, walked around my neighbourhood and checked out different restaurants. He was picky, so we weren't going for sushi or other ethnic foods as much as I would've liked, but it was fine. He was pretty high strung, except when he was smoking weed, which was pretty much every day. It took a while before he started smoking around me or before we got together, but he was always up front about it and it never really bothered me.

When my birthday rolled around, I was comfortable enough with him to ask him to come to dinner with my friends to celebrate. We had been seeing each for about a month but hadn't discussed our relationship or what we were doing together even once. I was completely fine with it. Things between us didn't feel serious; I figured we were more friends with benefits.

It was probably a bigger deal than I realized to bring him along to meet my friends, especially you, but I had a few drinks and let all my cares go along with my inhibitions. It wasn't until after I had stopped seeing him (and before I started seeing him again, haha) that you told me that you didn't actually care for him.

Want to know a secret? I didn't really either! I cared about him and enjoyed our time together, but if I really thought about it, he just wasn't my cup of tea.

It was the attention that got me. He made me feel wanted, something that I had never felt from a guy before. Still, there came a time a few months in that I realized I hadn't committed to this guy, and I didn't particularly feel like I wanted to. So when I was out with friends one night and met someone else who paid attention to me, I said yes to him almost immediately when he asked me out. Whether it was the drinks, or whether he was actually a sincerely kind guy, he made me feel special. Another feeling I was not familiar with.

"Wait," you said to me on the phone when I told you I had a date with someone new. "A date?"

"Yes! And I'm really excited about it!"

"Oh good," you replied with a sigh, "I didn't really like the thirty-year-old pot smoker anyways."

"Come again?" I said abruptly. "I'm seeing him Saturday, actually."

"Uhhhh..."

"Rae!" I said as I shook my head. "Why didn't you tell me that you didn't like him!?"

"I don't know," you said. "This is all new. I thought you liked him so I didn't want to hurt your feelings!"

"It's not that I don't like him," I explained, "we just haven't talked about only seeing each other. I wasn't going to say no to a date with someone else!"

"Makes sense, but why are you still seeing the thirty-year-old pot smoker if you're also seeing this guy?"

"The new guy. We'll call him the new guy. And I don't know. Cause I can?"

"Fair enough. You're dating enough people for the both of us!"

"Okay Dr. B, but I'd say you're a little busy, what with med school and all."

"I know, I know. But still, have fun!"

"Thanks."

And I did. But the relationship with the new guy didn't go anywhere and, somehow, I ended up right back at square one with the thirty-year-old pot smoker. It's like I was the one with the addicting habit that really wasn't very good for me.

When summer approached and your classes ended, I offered for you to store some of your belongings at my place before you went off on an adventure. It meant that you wouldn't have to waste money on storage and gave us an excuse to see each other at either end of the busy summer. The only time it worked out for you to drop off your things at my place happened to be after my firm's summer party at the Hastings Race Track. The thing with law firms is that there's always an open bar—at least there was at the firms I worked at.

Your friend Jan had loaded up her car with your belongings and you met me at my place after the party.

"Thanks for meeting me here, girls!" I shouted at you when you finally arrived at my place.

"Oh, Anya." You smiled at me. "Have you been drinking?"

"Nooooo," I slurred as I placed a wedge under the front door of my building. We all went up the stairs to where Jan had parked her car.

I missed the last step and tripped slightly, somehow managing to land on my feet. "Well, maybe..." I admitted.

"I actually couldn't tell," Jan said flatly.

We trucked boxes and bags of your things down the hallway to my apartment. I thought it would be a good idea to take a box of random belongings along with the front tire from your bike in one trip.

"Are you sure you can handle all of that?" You asked me. You knew me and my klutzy ways so well!

"I totally got this!" I assured you.

I made it around the corner and was only steps away from the door to my apartment before I gracefully tripped and tumbled on top of the box. Kitchen goods and bathroom accessories went flying everywhere.

"Anya!" You exclaimed. "Are you okay?"

All I could do was giggle in response.

"Who packed this?" I wheezed between laughs, picking up a tampon. "Tampons? And a can of soup?"

You just laughed as you started to clean up. "They fit in the box!"

I'm honestly surprised that none of my neighbours complained about the racket.

"Come on and help me clean up this mess!" you said.

"No, pictures first!" I exclaimed, grabbing my camera. I went to pose and fell over the box again. You got a good one of me there!

When you went to take another picture, you managed to press the record button instead.

"Why is the button not working?" you asked.

"Just press the big one on the top," I tried to help, waiting, posed with one hand on my hip.

"Your camera is very confusing. I can't figure it out and I'm sober!" You handed me the camera.

"It's recording!" I laughed as I stopped the recording.

That video was a mistake that I am very grateful for. The twenty-one second clip brings you back to me: your voice, your laugh, us. It makes me smile to know that I can hear your voice whenever I want to. Even if it is just a silly video, I cherish the memory.

When you returned after your summer away, I helped you find a place to live. We drove around and looked at places everywhere: Kitsilano, across from Vancouver General Hospital and downtown. You finally settled on a place near West 16th Avenue and MacDonald Street. You rode your bike everywhere you could, even in the rain, so the proximity of your new place to the

UBC campus worked out very well.

"Celia is in town this weekend," you told me on the phone one night, a few weeks into the new semester. "Do you want to see if we can get together?"

"That sounds great," I replied. "I've had quite the week, I would love to hang out. And I haven't seen Celia in ages!"

"I think she's going to be at the hospital on Friday," you told me. "Could you pick us up there around 7:00? I'll coordinate with her."

"I can do that, for sure. Then we can grab food and go back to your place?"

"Sounds good, I'll see you then!"

You were always so cheerful, even when just making plans.

I got to Vancouver General Hospital just before 7:00 pm. It was dark and raining and I saw you standing with Celia where we had agreed to meet. I only saw one problem: your bike. I drove a two-door Chevrolet Cobalt at the time, which is not exactly a large vehicle.

"Well, I guess I didn't think that one through," you said with a giggle after I had found a spot to park and we said our hellos. "But I'm sure we can make it fit!"

"Does the trunk open into the car?" Celia asked.

I went around back and pulled the latch that released the seats into the back of the car. "I don't think that's going to help," I said, standing back to look.

You grabbed the bike and slid it in behind the passenger's seat. "Nope," I heard your muffled voice from inside the car with the bike, "not gonna happen." You went to push the bike back out of the car and one of the pedals scraped against the roof of the car. The mark it left was still there the day I sold it.

"Pull!" You said with a giggle.

Celia and I tried to pull, knocking you in between the front seats in the process.

"Are you okay?" I said, biting back a laugh.

"I'm good!" You replied with a giggle.

"Here," you said, climbing back out of the car and grabbing the bike, "let's put the back wheel in first, and kind of stick it in the trunk."

We flipped the bike over and did as you suggested. It fit!

"That's great and all," I said, "but where are you going to sit?"

We all just stood there and looked at each other before bursting out laughing.

"I'll make it work," you said with determination as you climbed into the back seat of the car with your bike.

Celia pushed the front seat into the upright position against your legs. "You okay?" she asked.

"I'm good," you replied, "let's go!"

"Is it okay if I put my leg here?" you asked, moving it so it poked out between the two front seats.

"Fine by me," I said as I buckled in. I turned and looked at you. You had somehow fit your bum between the bike and the trunk opening. Your legs were bent up and over the bike. I couldn't help but let out a laugh.

"You sure you're okay?"

"Yup." I'm not sure if you had convinced yourself or me, but we didn't have that far to go. We giggled the entire way.

"Stop laughing," I said between breaths as I pulled up to a stoplight. "I'm not going to be able to drive!"

"Don't stop the car!" I heard between laughs from the back seat. "I'm not exactly comfortable back here."

We finally pulled up to your place, maybe ten minutes later.

"Help me get out first!" you called from the back seat. "I'm gonna need a hand."

Your little hand reached out and Celia and I each grabbed on. I gave a yank and out you came, falling into us as we all laughed together.

"Miss us?" I asked Celia once we gathered our composure.

"Absolutely," she answered. "Some things never change!"

"We aren't always a disaster like this!" you remarked.

"I just meant the laughter!" she said with genuine care.

We got the bike out and I leaned in to take a look at the mark on the ceiling.

"Did it leave a mark?" you asked.

"Just a small grease stain," I said. "Not as bad as the ding in the door."

"Whoops."

"Ding in the door?" Celia asked as we made our way into your place and out of the rain.

"Ya, this one opened the door into a sign post last week when we were walking the seawall," I said. "The first, and now second, bit of damage to my new car."

"Awww," Celia said.

"Ummmm thanks for the ride?" you said with a smile.

"It's okay, shit happens," I said as I took a seat on the couch.

"Wine!" you said, holding up a bottle. "Makes all things better."

I used to be over-reactive when things happened to me or my belongings. But when you dented my door it was the first time that I consciously decided not to be angry in a moment. I've always led with my emotions, something that has most definitely been tested at numerous points in my life. I remember looking at you as you apologized for hitting the door and I just couldn't be mad. I swallowed my anger, wrapped my arm around you and we headed to the beach.

"That it does," Celia said as she raised a glass.

We sat and visited, leaving our responsibilities behind and getting to know each other as adults. It had been a while since we saw each other last, but some things never change.

A few hours later, we were full of love and food and I was ready to call it a night. "I think I'm going to go," I said, turning to Celia. "Do you need a ride?"

"That would be great, thanks!" she said, grabbing her coat.

"Are you going to make it to the Halloween dance?" you asked before I left. "Or do you have a date?"

I laughed and said, "No date. I'm all yours."

"No date?!" you teased.

"I had two dates back to back one weekend and now I'm some sort of a hussy or something!"

"Always," you said as you hugged me. "Drive safe."

"Thanks," I said, "good night, Rae."

"I don't have a costume," you said as soon as you walked into my apartment one afternoon, the Saturday before Halloween. "I can't believe I don't have a costume!"

"It's okay," I said. "Don't panic! I'll see if I have anything around here."

You put your bag in my bedroom and flopped down on the bed. "It's been so busy, and I just couldn't come up with anything to throw together," you said.

Before I could answer, there was a knock at my door.

"Just a sec," I said and I went to answer the door. It was Leah, my friend from soccer who lived upstairs.

"Hey Anya! I just wanted to bring this back before I forgot," she said as she handed me a bag with a couple of board games she had borrowed.

"No worries. Do you want to come in?"

"Sure, just for a minute though," Leah said.

"You remember Rachael?" I asked as you came out from the bedroom.

"Hi, nice to see you again."

"You, too," you said as you came into the living room.

"We're just trying to figure out a costume for Rachael. We're going out for Halloween tonight," I told Leah.

"You don't have a costume?" she asked. "I have something upstairs you can borrow, if you want."

"Really?" you asked, excited.

"Absolutely," she said, "I'll be right back."

She returned a couple of minutes later with the perfect costume. "Rainbow Bright!" She said as she handed it to you.

"Amazing!" I said.

"Thank you so much, Leah!" you said.

"No problem," she said as she stepped towards the door. "I should be going; you girls have fun!"

We put your hair in pigtails, tied in the ribbons and you were all set. I had borrowed a long red cape from one of the girls at work, tied my hair up and put on a cute little black dress. My last accessory was a wicker basket.

"Little Red Riding Hood and Rainbow Bright!" you exclaimed when we were ready to go. "Perfect friends!"

"Friends forever!" I said as we left for our first party. We met up with some of my work friends for a party in North Van. I haven't dressed up too often for Halloween, but these memories with you of the innocent fun we had together really stand out for me. We weren't at the first party long; we didn't want to miss out on too much of the dance at the MSAC. You looped your arm through mine as we made our way to the bus, my basket hooked in the crook of my other arm, my smile acres wide.

"Do you think we'll run into AD?" I asked, offhand.

"Why??" She asked in a sing-song voice. "You really leaving the thirty-year-old pot smoker in your dust?"

"Well," I said as we climbed aboard the bus between a zombie and a very tall, masculine nun. "If he's not going to man up, it's his loss!"

We giggled together. It was true. I pushed pot-smoker into the far reaches of my mind and walked into the MSAC with my head held high. I didn't particularly want to run into AD but I wanted to make sure that if he saw me first, I looked like I didn't care to see him. He was the one that broke it off, after all. Sense a theme here?

"I need a drink," I said after we walked through the dance floor and past the bar. We squeezed between someone in a gorilla costume and a very scantily clad nurse.

"Original," you said, rolling your eyes as I pulled you next to me and ordered us a couple of drinks.

We made our way back onto the dance floor, in awe of the costumes. These medical and dental students really went all out. I was glad I had borrowed the cape and did my makeup a little more than usual or I would have felt very out of place.

The gorilla was back. I saw him dancing behind me with a different group of people.

"Hey," I motioned to you to come over for a chat. "I think that's him."

You pointed past me in the general direction of the large ape. "AD?"

"Ya, he's been hanging nearby all night, and I'm just getting this feeling from him."

"Are you going to go say hi?"

"Nah, let's just dance."

And dance we did. We had a blast dancing together with your group of friends. When a slow song came on, my intuition was proven correct when the gorilla made his way over to me. He had the top half of his costume pulled down around his waist. I'm not sure what had happened to his head.

"Dance with me?"

"Sure," I said, with a glance in your direction. You exuded

absolute discretion and gave me two thumbs up as you paired up with the devil. Literally.

"How have you been?" AD asked as he put his hands around my waist.

"Good," I said, "really good, actually."

"I'm glad," he said, looking straight into my eyes with his chocolate brown gaze.

I was still attracted to him, but it felt different. I knew he didn't want to date me and if he wanted to go home with someone, he was better off finding the nurse he had been chatting with earlier.

"And you?" I asked, feeling like I needed to fill the silence.

"Oh, you know," he said in a flippant tone. I had a hard time reading him.

"I don't," I said. "That's why I asked."

"Now, now, no need to be like that."

I rolled my eyes.

"Nothing is new with me," he said. "Just busy with school. I don't have anything going on tomorrow, though. Not in the morning anyways."

He definitely just wanted me to go home with him.

"Actually, I've been seeing someone." It wasn't untrue. He didn't need to know that that "someone" was non-committal and that there were even multiple "someones" at times.

"Oh, really?" He pulled his hands closer to my hips and moved slightly farther away from me.

"Ya," I said. "Nothing serious."

He didn't say anything.

This had to be the longest song in the history of all slow songs.

"If it's not serious, do you want to get out of here with me?"

Called it!

"No," I said, being straight with him. "I'm leaving with Rachael tonight."

"Ahh, okay," he said pulling even further back. Dr. Thinks-with-his-other-head. At least that night.

The song was ending, thankfully. "It was good to see you."

"You, too," he said, leaning down to kiss me. I let him. "Are you sure you want to stay?"

"Yes." I said confidently.

He said nothing and left as fast as he could. I was happy. I have never really liked small talk anyways.

"So?" you said, racing over as soon as the horny ape man disappeared.

"He may be dressed as a gorilla," I said, "but he is 100 percent horndog."

"No way!! What did he say to you?"

"It doesn't matter. Are you ready to go?"

"Yes! Just let me go say goodbye to a couple of people."

"I'll grab the coats and meet you at the door."

"Don't think this means you're off the hook," you called to me as you walked away. "You're gonna have to tell me what he said!"

I laughed and wandered over to the coat check.

I now knew what it was like to be wanted for only carnal reasons. I knew what it felt like to be in a relationship where I really just wanted commitment but was too afraid to ask for what I wanted. And I knew what it meant to date casually. None of these options were working for me. I wanted someone who respected me and wanted me enough to tell me that. I wanted someone to love.

Little did I know it would only be a little over a month before I met the man I would one day call my husband.

I love you and will miss you forever and for always,

Anya xoxo

Chapter Three

December 18, 2009

Dear Rachael,

Do you remember what it was like when I met Brad? Do you remember that as soon as I got back from the trip that I took to Mexico with my mom, I told you that I had met the man I was going to marry one day? Who would have ever thought that this random trip would end up bringing me my destiny?

I was 24 years old. Nothing had changed between the thirty-year-old pot smoker and I. I had been seeing him for almost eight months and had yet to spend a whole night with him. We still hadn't defined anything about our relationship and neither of us made any effort to become part of each other's lives. It was fruitless, really.

While I spent the majority of my days outside of work alone or at the gym, I was very happy. I had taken time to learn about myself, what I liked and how I wanted to spend my time. I had realized that while I didn't need to be in a relationship to be happy, I longed for a partner. Someone to build a life with. Someone to love.

In the back of my mind and heart, I knew that the thirty-year-old pot smoker was not the one. As much as I secretly wished there was more there, I would have never been proud to introduce him to my family or dream of the day that we would walk down the aisle together. We were just too different. It could have been the weed thing, but I think it was more that we just had different views of what we wanted out of our relationship and what we wanted for our respective futures. We had fun, but it was never anything more than that for me. I may not have been honest with myself about that at first. In fact, it took meeting a man worth my while before I recognized that. But it was worth the wait.

Sometime in the fall, I received a call from my mom that changed everything.

"Hi sweetie," she said.

"Hi Mama. How are you?"

"I'm good. Do you remember Stacy?"

"Like Matt and Stacey?" I asked her about my cousin and his longtime partner.

"No, Betty's daughter Stacy. She's getting married!"

"Oh, right on! I know who you're talking about. Congrats to her."

"Yes, her and Jason are getting married in Puerto Vallarta in December but your dad won't come with me because they're staying at an all-inclusive resort."

"Oh no! That's nice that they invited you," I appeased her. She always likes being included in everything. But I hadn't realized she was close enough with them to have been invited to their wedding.

"Well, your dad and I were talking about it and if you're able to get the time off from work, we'll pay for you to come with me. If you want."

"Sure, I'll just have to check at work!" It sounded like a pretty sweet deal to me. A free trip to Mexico with my mom and all I had to do was book holidays from work! Sign me up! This was one of the perks of being an only child with generous parents who like to travel. I was all in.

My mom came down from Prince George to stay with me for a couple of days before we were set to leave. Our flight was leaving before the sun rose so we stayed at a hotel close to the airport the night before. It was lovely to spend some time with my mom. I looked forward to a week of relaxing with a wedding thrown in for good measure somewhere in the middle of the week. I knew who my mom's friend was, but I honestly cannot recall if I had ever met her daughter or any of the other people who were going to be at the wedding prior to our departure. This was mainly about time with my mom.

I still can't believe that Brad had been living in my hometown PG before our fateful trip to Mexico. Quite frankly, he didn't have a lot going for him before he met me.

Kidding. My wonderful husband may have been nourishing himself on a diet of McD's and Stag Chili before I came along, but he was definitely making a good go of his first attempt at being a grown-up. He had purchased his first home on his own earlier that year. He started to put down roots close to his family and was settling into adult life a little more so than I was at the time.

Brad's friend Reid invited him to Mexico in a similar way that my mom had invited me. Reid's dad was unable to make the trip and since it had already been paid for, his dad suggested that Reid invite a friend to go with him. Since it was a free trip and Brad had never been out of the country, he had a hard time saying no.

Fate intervened. We were both freeloading wedding crashers destined to meet that first week of December 2008; our lives would never be the same.

When our alarm went off before the crack of dawn the day we were leaving for Mexico, my mom and I were very thankful to be staying so close to the airport.

"Anya," I heard from above my head, which was buried under the covers. "It's time to get up now."

I moaned. I was not a fan of mornings. My mom was not a fan of being late.

"The shuttle will be here in ten minutes," she said as she zipped up her suitcase and strapped on her purse.

"Okayyyyyyy," I obliged. I pulled the covers off and managed to brush my teeth and get myself acceptably ready enough to leave the room.

As soon as we were handed some complimentary rum punches on board, I started to have a lot more fun. We enjoyed some food along with our drinks and once we landed, we were relieved to have left the northern rain behind for the encompassing warmth and humidity.

My parents had taken me to Puerto Vallarta seasonally for quite a few years while I was growing up, but we always traveled in the early new year or spring time, never around Christmas.

"Wow!" I said to my mom when we got to the resort lobby after a quick shuttle ride from the airport. "It's so weird to see a Christmas tree in Mexico!"

The resort was decorated beautifully; in the lobby stood a 15-foot tall Christmas tree shining in red, gold and green. It was like entering a whole new world.

"I know, right!" my mom exclaimed. "Decorated Christmas trees seem like such a northern tradition."

I took in the twinkling lights and ribbons, the sound of the ocean's waves crashing nearby and the salty air permeating my understanding of where I was. The tree stood tall next to the lobby, which opened up to the resort grounds, welcoming us warmly to our home for the next week. There were several people in front of us in line, but I didn't mind the wait one bit.

"I'm excited to be staying at an all-inclusive resort!" I told my mom.

"Me, too!" Neither of us had ever stayed at one before. "Imagine, we don't have to worry where our next piña colada is coming from!"

"You would say that!" I told her as we laughed and stepped up to the counter to check in.

"Want to drop our things and find a drink?" I asked my mom after we were given our keys.

"Sounds good to me!"

I opened the door to our room and went in. "Look, Mama!"

I said, pointing to the swan towel laid out on the king size bed. "The staff decorated for us! There are even rose petals!"

She laughed. "It's so romantic!"

"This is going to be a great vacation!"

"I'm definitely ready to eat and drink to my heart's content!" my mom replied. And with that, we set off to explore the resort and find the rest of the group that was there for the wedding.

As it turns out, I graduated high school with the groom's sister, Crystal, so I actually knew a couple of people from the wedding group. I was able to get to know the bride, Stacy, and her family and friends, and while my mom and I weren't exactly party animals, we had a great time together. We were in bed routinely earlier than the rest of the crew, which meant that we enjoyed the buffet breakfasts sans hangover and felt rested at the end of our week away. I was happy to relax by the pool or the ocean with my mom, books in hand. To me, it was what a vacation should be: hot, sunny, relaxing, free-flowing drinks, good company and not a care in the world.

On our first full day at the resort, I was laying by the pool with my mom reading *PS: I Love You*. I have always loved reading and really enjoy my fluff books as I call them: romantic, feel-good stories where nine times out of ten the girl gets her love. Mom and I were sitting near the people in the wedding group when Reid and Brad were brought around to be introduced to us.

"Sandy, Anya, this is Reid and his friend Brad," someone who knew all of us started the introductions.

Always the social butterfly, my mom went first. "Hi. Nice to meet you both."

She was happy to meet some new people, including potentially a young man for me? I hadn't mentioned much to her, if anything at all, about my romantic status back home.

I, on the other hand, was a little less interested. I lifted my nose out of my book only long enough to say a quick hello and then returned to the world between the pages. I will likely never live this introduction down, but I have to cut myself some slack here. I was just being true to who I am. Even now, if I am reading and Brad is talking to me, I listen. I pay attention. But I also keep reading. So, in remaining loyal to my true self, I feel like I was just letting Brad see the real me, whom he clearly fell for! So, he may complain about how hard he had to work for my attention, but let's be real. Everything worth having is worth working for. At the time I didn't think anything of it. I met a couple of new people, took another sip from my piña colada and returned to the only dose of romance I had ever known in my life. Fictional or not.

The wedding was scheduled mid-week, so on one of the days before the big day I signed up to go zip-lining with the girl I knew from high school, her boyfriend and their friends. It was a great opportunity for us to get to know each other. On the bus ride to our zip-lining adventure, we started chatting.

"So, Anya, do you have anyone special back home?" Crystal asked.

I had honestly never been in a position where I could have answered yes to that question, so even though it was only partially true, I jumped at the chance to tell them I had a boyfriend.

"Ya, my boyfriend is back home," I lied. Why?

They carried on the conversation naturally. "How long have

you been dating?"

"Almost eight months," I said. "Not too long."

At this point the words were rolling off of my tongue with ease. But pot-smoker would have probably screamed "fire" and bolted in the opposite direction if I broached the subject of commitment with him or if he heard that I was calling him "my boyfriend".

Why I felt like I had to tell white lies about my romantic status is beyond me. I really should have just been honest. But instead, I set myself up to be judged for having a boyfriend at home and cultivating a relationship with Brad while off in Mexico alone. I can't explain it, but I think I can pinpoint why I may have exaggerated. I was 24, single, with no prospects in sight who were potential husband material and I wanted to present a better front for myself to these people who were my age and in committed relationships. They had what I wanted and I wanted them to think that I had it, too. Little did I know "it" was actually right in front of me the whole time.

The zip-lining trip was great fun. It was especially nice to get away from the resort and spend time with some people my age. My mom spent the day relaxing and when we got back to the resort, I found her with her friends.

"Hello," I called to them as I walked up to where they were sitting and relaxing with some drinks.

"Hi sweetie," my mom said. "Did you have a nice time?"

"It was great!" I recounted the day's events to her briefly. "I'm just going to go back to the room to have a shower and get ready before dinner."

"Okay. But first, we were just talking about the wedding.

Stacy's dad said he brought their video recorder to tape the wedding ceremony but he doesn't really know how to use it!"

"Well," I told the bride's parents. "If you can figure it out and teach me how to run the thing, I can record the ceremony for you so that you don't have to."

"That would be great, thanks Anya!" Darryl replied.

What was I getting myself into? I didn't even know how to work a camcorder. I still don't. But the wedding group was small and I really felt like it would be better for the bride's family to be able to enjoy the ceremony and not have to worry about recording everything while trying to enjoy their only daughter's wedding. I had no attachment to either of the people getting married, so when I was presented with their predicament, I couldn't help but offer my assistance. Slap a camcorder in my hands and call me a videographer! I heard reports after the fact that I did a good job, but videography is not something I will be adding to my resume any time soon.

The night before the wedding, my mom and I went down to the pool after dinner to take in the nightly show put on by the resort. The entertainment was a fun way to end most evenings and included different dancers and light shows. Chairs were set up conveniently close to the pool bar, which helped encourage the crowds to take in the show.

Following the show, a group of people including Brad, his friend Reid and another guy they called Bird were sitting around having drinks.

"I think I'll go," my mom said, standing.

"Oh?"

"Ya. I'm a bit tired today."

"Okay, I think I'll hang out for a bit."

"See you later, sweetie." And with that, she left.

We sat around with our drinks as the staff cleared the chairs that had been set out for the show. It was obvious that we should relocate, but not before the guys went back up to the bar for another round.

They somehow convinced the bartender to fill us a pitcher of beer and we headed down to the beach, glasses in hand. We pulled a few beach chairs up to the crest of a hill overlooking the water's edge. We sat there in the moonlight, the ocean visiting the sand in the darkness in front of us. We were all feeling pretty good at this point and the flirtatious connection between Brad and I started. Wherever the conversation had taken us, I found myself in a chair next to him, overlooking the crashing waves of the ocean that we couldn't see. Brad was talking animatedly with his hands and he kept pointing at me to punctuate his sentences.

"Stop pointing your finger at me like that," I told Brad drunkenly.

"Why?" he asked, pointedly gesturing in the direction of my face.

"Because I asked you to?" I replied. "It's rude."

"What are you going to do if I don't stop?" he teased.

"I'll bite your finger," I told him, seriously.

"Ya, okay," he said, rolling his eyes. I really don't think he believed me, but on our conversation went and his pointy little finger did not go away. When his finger got a little close to my face without him noticing, I snapped and bit firmly onto his finger.

"Ouch!" he yelped. "What the hell, woman!?"

"I warned you!" I countered, shrugging my shoulders and

laughing to myself.

"I didn't think you would *actually* bite me!" he exclaimed as he nervously started to laugh with me.

"And, hey," I added more seriously, "don't call me woman."

Add that to the list of things I will not live down from this trip.

We were running low on beer, so when someone went up to refill the pitcher, we relocated to the upper pool deck, relaxing on a couple of lounge chairs, chit chatting about life. The breeze coming off of the ocean was making me chilly, which Brad noticed.

"Hey, are you cold?" he asked me.

"No, I'm fine," I tried to convince both him and myself. "I'm always cold."

"Don't be silly," he said as he got up from his seat. "I'll go get you a sweater."

Wow, I thought to myself, he was so sweet. I didn't think anything else about it. Why else would a man go out of his way to get a woman a sweater than to make sure she's not cold! Surely not to show her what a sweet guy he was because he was romantically interested in her. Certainly only because he was a nice human being. End of story.

A short time later Brad came back and placed his sweater gently around my shoulders.

I smiled up at him. "Thank you."

He winked. "No problem. Did you forget your sweater at home, or just in your room?"

"I have a light one in my room. But it's not as cozy as this one."

"You only brought one sweater with you?"

"Well, ya. We're in Mexico. It's supposed to be warm!"

"The sun goes down at some point! I thought you would know that; you've been here before!"

"That I have. But I told you, I brought a sweater, it's just upstairs. I got myself a nice new souvenir now anyways," I teased, snuggling into his sweater.

"Hey now," he said with a laugh.

"Don't worry, I'll give it back."

"You can keep it if you want!"

"Nah, you can have it back eventually. I don't usually go souvenir shopping anyways."

"What do you mean? You've been to Mexico how many times and you've never gotten yourself something to remember your trip by?"

"Not really," I answered honestly. "My dad bought me a dolphin statue and some blankets from here before, but I don't really have anything special that I bought for myself, no."

"Well, that just won't do!" he remarked.

As the grounds crew rearranged pool chairs and cleaned up around us, we sat listening to Bird go off about one complex subject or another. I was sitting beside him, listening as attentively as I could, having had more beers than I usually do in one sitting. Reid was sitting across from me and Brad was beside him.

I innocently glanced up at Brad. I can still see his eyes as they locked with mine. I can feel his soul looking deeply into me, past my eyes, further than what he could physically see. I had never felt anything like it before, and haven't felt it with anyone else since. Time passed and my heart swelled before we broke eye contact.

I took a deep breath, settling my rapid heartbeat and re-entering the present conversation.

Looking back, I can see that my soul and my perception of Brad would never be the same after that moment. Yet at the time, I somehow still didn't realize what was happening between us.

Bird was still talking to the group and I was trying not to pay too much attention to what Brad was saying or doing.

"I think I'm going to call it a night," I said, following a yawn.

Brad stood as I gathered myself to make my way to my room. "Good night," he said.

"Good night," I said as I breathed out and quickly turned to walk back to my room. I felt different but I didn't take the time to recognize why. It had been a long day. I attributed the funny feelings to the drinks and the sun and didn't think twice about what was starting to happen with Brad.

The next day was the big day. My foray into videography.

The ceremony wasn't until closer to sunset that evening so I headed down to the pool bar after breakfast with my mom. I was just settling down with my book when Brad and Reid came over.

"Good morning ladies," Brad said. Reid said a quiet hello.

"Morning," my mom and I said in unison.

I took a sip of my first drink of the day as Brad asked, "What are you drinking?"

"A piña colada."

"I don't think I've ever had one of those," he replied.

"Grab one at the pool bar and pull up a seat," I said.

"Sure thing."

My mom got up and went into the pool for a dip, so I was alone when Brad and Reid got back with their drinks.

"Man, there are so many drinks listed up there that I have never tried before," Brad mentioned as he took a seat. "This cola-da thing is really good!"

"I bet you couldn't try all of them," I replied.

"There's only one way to find out!" he challenged.

"There are almost 20 drinks up there!" I exclaimed, but regardless of the number of drinks on the list we soon found ourselves working through a combination of at least 15-20 cocktails involving Kahlua, Tequila, Rum, fruity blended drinks and everything else under the sun. Literally.

"What are you kids up to?" my mom asked when she got back from the pool.

"Brad thought it would be a good idea to drink all of the drinks on the menu at the pool bar," I told her.

"Oh, that sounds fun!" my mom said with a laugh. "Except I would never have any of the ones with tequila."

"Mom, you can't pick and choose what you have! You're either in or you're out!"

"I'm in," she sighed. "But no tequila! I'll end up dancing on the tables if I have tequila and I really don't need to hurt myself."

"Whaaaat?!" Brad said. "You dance on tables?!"

"Well, no," my mom tried to backtrack. "Only when I was younger."

"Sounds like there's a story there, Sandy! This I have to see!"

Brad teased her.

My mom just giggled. She was in and out of our drinking challenge throughout the day. Brad and I took turns going up to the bar for the next round. It didn't take long before we were feeling pretty darn good. We relaxed on the pool loungers, went for a swim and dried off with our feet in the pool. We stayed pretty close to that pool bar for the whole day.

"I think we already tried this one," Brad slurred as he walked back from the bar and took a sip of the most recent cocktail off the menu. He sat down next to me. My feet dangled in the water as a volleyball game went on nearby.

"Yup," I replied after he handed me my drink and I took a sip. "We've definitely had this drink before. Do you need someone to cut you off now?" I giggled as I set my drink down and nudged his shoulder with mine.

"Very funny," Brad replied and before I knew it he nudged me just a little harder and I went flying (probably not very unexpectedly) into the pool.

I landed with a big splash and when I came up for air I saw him sitting beside the pool with Reid, both of them laughing at my expense. As shocking as it was refreshing, I knew I had to get him back, but this guy was swift. Just pushing or pulling him into the pool wasn't going to be good enough for me.

"Hilarious," I told Brad when I had made my way out of the pool and came back around to where he was sitting. He flinched as I sat down. "I'm not going to make it that easy! I promise you won't see it coming!" I said of my eventual retaliation. "Silly."

We continued to make our way through the drinks, my mom

skipping the tequila as promised. We got to one that tasted like chocolate and had some sort of cherry liqueur drizzled through the glass, garnished with a maraschino cherry.

"Now that's good," I said as I drank half of mine in one sip. Brad was busy chatting to Reid about something and had nonchalantly placed his drink down between us. I finished mine quickly, reached down and swapped my empty glass for his full one without him noticing. I finished his, too.

Brad picked up his glass and looked up at me quizzically when he realized it was empty.

"What the..."

"You should learn to drink faster!" I laughed.

"Huh!" he exclaimed. "Unfair!"

"Well, in case you were wondering, it was really good. You should go grab us a couple more!"

"I should?! You go get them! You're the reason why I didn't get to try that one!"

We laughed and smiled. We had already had too much to drink, but I headed back up to grab us two of the next drink on the menu.

"Hey, this isn't the same!" Brad remarked as I sat down.

"I know," I said cheekily. "You snooze, you lose."

"Oh, I see. Is this your way of getting back at me for pushing you in the pool?"

Up until that point, I had been patiently waiting while contemplating my retaliation. And then it struck me. I wasn't going to just push him into the pool but rather make him jump in on his own.

"Nope, this is!" And in a move that is normally reserved for kindergarteners who pull each other's hair to show their masked affection for each other, I grabbed his sunglasses off of his face and I tossed them just far enough into the pool that he was forced to leave his seat in the hot sun. Brad: 1. Anya: 1.

Welcome to my world, Brad; stay awhile.

He dropped his head as he looked sideways at me and laughed. Then he stood up and jumped into the water to retrieve his sunglasses from the bottom of the pool.

Needless to say, we didn't make it through the entire drink list. We also didn't make it to the wedding sober. Speaking of the wedding, the time was approaching when I needed to return to my room to get ready for the ceremony. I drunkenly realized what an irresponsible videographer I was being.

When Brad came out of the pool with his sunglasses, we walked back and had a seat in the pool chairs where we had started our day together. I think it's accurate to say that I was swaying in my seat. Involuntary swaying does not a great videographer make.

"Well, I need to be heading back to my room to start getting ready," I told the boys.

"Wow, already." I'm sure Brad would have slurred if there had been any difficult-to-pronounce consonants in that sentence.

"It takes time to make myself beautiful! I have to put on my face."

"No, you don't," he replied.

And with that, I took my naive little self and what was left of my 100th drink of the day and staggered back to my room, mid-afternoon, well-pickled, to get ready for the wedding. I don't know looking back whether I realized that Brad had just paid me a compliment until well after the fact. He was a very, very sweet boy trying very, very hard to get through my imperviously thick skull. Good thing for me that Brad is nothing if not persistent. Once he is faced with a problem (such as my obliviousness to his interest in me) he will not give up until he has reached a solution.

Even after spending a lovely day flirting with Brad, intoxicated in more ways than one, my head had still not taken my heart's lead to recognize what was going on between us. I was completely clueless to the fact that a human being would be interested in me in a romantic way.

I got back to our room and managed to make myself presentable in time for the wedding. I even responsibly made it over to the suite where the bride was getting ready and grabbed her dad's video recorder to assume my duties as videographer before the ceremony. As far as I remember, my stint in the film industry went smoothly. I came up with a sneaky way to keep the recorder steady by bracing the elbow of the arm that was holding it with my opposite hand and holding my arms in close to my body to avoid wobbling drunkenly. It was a beautiful ceremony, made all the more special by the fact that I was not much more than a spectator allowed to witness and record this special event in the happy couple's life. Technically, I was my mom's date, but as a relative stranger to the couple and their families, I was very humbled to be given the opportunity to witness their vows to each other. I had not been to many weddings up to this point in my life, and I remember it being very special to me.

Also, now that I know the group of people who were there for the wedding, it made me feel better to know that I wouldn't be pegged as the drunk videographer. Rather I would be the videographer who was just as tipsy as everyone else. Maybe even less than some people were.

Following a post-ceremony champagne toast (now there's an alcohol I bet was not in any of the pool bar drinks—don't mind if I do!) there were pictures on the beach and a lovely celebratory dinner. Following dinner, everyone gathered around the pool for the evening show.

"Is this seat taken?" I heard from behind and I looked up to see Brad gesturing to the empty chair next to me.

"All yours."

For one inebriated reason or another, Brad decided to try and go around me and sort of step over the chair before he sat down. In his grace, he upended my pink drink, spilling it all over my dress.

"Whoops! I'm so sorry, Anya!"

"Ahhh!" I stood in reaction to the cold drink that I suddenly found in my lap, causing it to leak down all over my dress, including the white in my skirt. I found myself standing right up against Brad, face to face. We were so close, I could feel him breathing down on me.

"It's okay," I said sincerely. "Accidents happen. But I could use another drink."

"Okay, this one's on me!" he replied. So generous, this one, to refresh my spilled drink at the all-inclusive bar.

Following the show, the bridal group decided they were going to go downtown to keep the party going. The resort that we were staying at only had one night of dancing each week, which had been on the night of our arrival. If they didn't leave the resort, there would be no dancing for their wedding reception. I found myself enjoying a few drinks with a group that included Brad, Reid, a few other wedding guests and Mike and Michelle, a couple that was also from British Columbia but was not there for the wedding. Mike "the big deal" was a riot and Michelle was a beautiful soul; we had had drinks with them on and off throughout the week and I had gotten to know them a bit.

My mom was going dancing and had already left me behind. Brad and Reid were not going downtown. I hadn't thought too much about what I wanted to do as I enjoyed a drink with Michelle. Brad and Reid were with Mike up at the bar, out of earshot.

"Are you going to go downtown?" Michelle asked me.

I hadn't yet decided if I wanted to venture off of the resort or not. "I'm not sure."

"Well I notice that your lover-boy is staying behind," she said with a cheeky grin.

"Lover-boy?" I asked, confused.

"Ummm, yes. Isn't it obvious how much Brad is into you?"

"Brad?"

"Yes, Brad. Or have you been staying at a different resort?" she asked me, straight as an arrow.

I paused. Brad? Into me? Nah. He was just a really nice guy!

Oh.

Wait.

"Hey, Mike," Michelle asked Mike as he returned to our table with her drink. "Isn't it obvious that Brad likes Anya?"

"Ha!" he retorted. "Obvious? If that boy fell over his feet any more than he already is over you, he'd be laid up on the floor for the rest of the trip!"

Oh.

I see.

"Huh," I replied, when the words finally found me. "That actually sounds pretty accurate now that I think about it."

"You had no idea?" they asked.

I thought about it. "No, I didn't."

"Awww, you should totally go for him! He's such a nice guy!" Michelle exclaimed.

"Ya, he's a cool guy. And he wouldn't have asked us to help clue you in if he wasn't really into you!" Mike added. Quite the moves, dear Brad! Just think…if he hadn't tried so hard, I never would have known that he was into me. I probably should have been embarrassed that Brad had to recruit help in order to get through to me, but my mind was too busy playing catch up.

Given the fact that I never had any sort of conversation about commitment with the thirty-year-old pot smoker, I hardly gave him a second thought before turning my mind and my heart completely over to Brad. And so, with the encouragement of Mike and Michelle, I chose to stay behind at the resort that evening.

Brad and Reid took their drinks down to the beach, so I refreshed my drink and followed suit. My perspective had completely changed. Thinking back over the week so far, I couldn't believe that I hadn't noticed that Brad was into me. Man, was I clueless.

I found them on a couple of lounge chairs, drinking their beers.

"Hi," I said.

"Hello," Brad replied.

I sat down at the end of one of the chairs and we chatted about the wedding and reminisced about our drunken day for a bit. I wanted nothing more than to be alone with Brad, but I wasn't going to be the one to ask Reid to leave us. I don't know if Brad finally gave him a suggestive look that said "LEAVE US ALONE NOW" but he finally got the hint.

"I'll leave you guys," Reid said awkwardly, leaving me alone on the deserted beach with Brad.

"Good night, Reido," Brad called to his friend as we watched him walk away.

Brad got up and moved over to the chair I was sitting on. "Come here," he said. I turned and scooted backwards so that I was resting in Brad's lap, wrapped in his embrace. We stared up at the moon, listened to the sound of the waves crashing and just relaxed into each other for a time. I don't specifically remember what was said, but I do recall that at one point Brad started tickling me from behind, which caused me to giggle and turn my body in towards him. He reached for me and gave me the most romantic kiss I could have ever imagined. My insides were electrified and I was lost completely in the moment.

In the span of an hour, I had gone from being completely and utterly oblivious to Brad's feelings towards me, to being absorbed—mind, body and spirit—by my soul mate. While ours was not an instance of love at first sight, it was unlike anything there had ever been. I had finally been captured by true love; there was no greater feeling.

Being roommates with either your mom or your friend was a surefire way to keep any potential for a romantic fling rated PG. We stayed up late at the beach talking and kissing. It was actually likely closer to being early, depending on which way you looked at it. I returned to my room just as the sun was coming up.

I was hooked. After that night, all I could think about was Brad. I wondered where he was and when I would see him again. I spent the last two days of our trip with my mom relaxing at the resort, and when I did see Brad again it was the night before we were set to fly back to our respective homes. We took a stroll along the beach together, holding hands and talking endlessly. When I think back about how we sat and watched the sun set, I honestly wonder whose story this is and what happened to the lonely single girl who had left for a trip with her mom only seven days before. A new me was born when I met Brad and finally allowed myself to fall for him.

When we got back to the resort after our walk, everyone else was having dinner.

"Hey, are you going to be around for a bit?" Brad asked me.

"Ya, I'll come back here once I grab myself a bite to eat."

"Okay, I have something for you, I'll just go and get it."

He went back up to his room and when he returned, I was sitting with my mom having dinner. He was holding something wrapped in the sweater he had let me borrow just a few nights before.

"Maybe we can go for another little walk when we're done

eating," he suggested. "You can open it then."

"Sounds good to me."

Brad went and grabbed himself some dinner and joined my mom and I to eat.

"So, Sandy," Brad said between mouthfuls. "Are you really going to leave me hanging on this whole 'dancing on tables' thing you mentioned the other day?"

"Heehee," my mom giggled. "I don't do it anymore!"

"'Anymore' implies that you used to dance on tables!"

I smirked behind my hands and my mom shot me a look. "Well, I used to leg wrestle at the Salmon Valley Music Festival and when I have a few too many drinks I've been known to dance on the picnic tables."

"This I've got to see!"

"Oh, I don't think so..." she said before interrupting herself. "Maybe at your guys' wedding!"

Brad and I both smiled and looked quickly down at our plates. I rolled my eyes, but I secretly wondered if it was a possibility.

"I'm going to go back to the room. Are you going to be out late?" my mom asked as she finished eating.

"No, I'll come back to pack up in a bit."

"Okay, sweetie. Good night, Brad."

"Good night, Sandy."

After we finished eating, Brad stood up and grabbed my hand. We walked around the resort a bit and settled on a seat in the garden.

"Go ahead," Brad said, handing me his packaged-up sweater. "Open it up."

"Thank you," I told him sincerely. "No one has ever gotten me a gift like this before."

I took his sweater off from around the package and put it on. Surely that's why he brought it?

I pulled the box open and saw the most beautiful hand painted tile. It was the scene of a couple from behind, walking through a village, holding hands. My mouth dropped open as I looked up at Brad.

"Thank you, Brad. It's beautiful."

"You're welcome. I asked the artist if he had anything of a couple holding hands and he painted this. From scratch. Just for you."

Choking up, I thanked him again. "It's so thoughtful."

"You deserve it," he replied.

I smiled at him, feeling more special than anyone had ever made me feel before. His thoughtfulness was unlike anything I had ever experienced. He made me feel loved before I even knew that our love was possible. Before I even knew what true romantic love was.

"Well, we have a long day tomorrow," I started.

"Don't remind me."

I wasn't the only one who didn't want our trip to end, for obvious reasons.

"Good night, Brad." I bid him good night with a kiss and headed back to my room. When I got there, it was almost as if my mom was waiting for me.

"Hi," I said to her.

"Oh, hi. I didn't expect you so early."

There was a tone to her words. Great.

"What do you mean?"

"Well, you've been off doing who knows what with *Brad*." Her emphasis was firmly on Brad's name.

"You know…" I started. I knew exactly why she had the attitude towards me. "I haven't done anything with Brad that I won't tell the guy I've been seeing at home." I didn't need to justify it to her, especially not given that I was in the process of falling in love with my soul mate. But still, I cared about her opinion of me.

"Oh?"

"Ya. You don't need to think badly of me."

"Well, it's just that I really like Brad," she said almost shyly.

"Me, too."

The next day, my mom and I were seated a few rows ahead of Reid and Brad on our way back to Vancouver. I kept stealing glances at them between the seats in the plane, hoping that Brad would catch my eye. Either he was way better than me at not obviously looking my way, or he had more composure and I wasn't on his mind at all.

Brad and Reid were set to take a separate flight to Prince George and my mom and I were headed back to my place before she left for home a few days later.

"Pssst," I said to Brad as he started walking away from me at the departure gates of the Vancouver International Airport. "Come with me for a sec."

I pulled him by his hand in behind one of the closed information desks. I couldn't have picked a more romantic setting if I had tried.

"I want to see you in a few weeks when I'm in PG for Christmas."

"That would be good," Brad said. Always a man of many words when making plans. To this day.

I got up onto the tips of my toes and stole a kiss that had to last me weeks. Then I turned to walk away from my love without glancing back. My heart knew that I would see him again, but I was still very sad to have to leave him.

Aside from the leaving, was this what it was like to be happy? Is this what I deserved? Was I falling in love?

I arranged to see you as soon as I could when I got home. I drove to your place and we went for a walk around your neighbourhood.

We had barely made it out of your driveway and got all of the usual pleasantries out of the way when I blurted out, "I think I met the man I'm going to marry!"

"Seriously?! What about the thirty-year-old pot smoker?"

"You're kidding, right?" I replied immediately. "I think we all know that that wasn't going anywhere, um, ever. Besides, I'm pretty sure I'm going to break up with him ASAP. Before I get to see Brad again!"

"Oh good." Your honesty came out with a sigh. "You know that I didn't really like him anyways."

"I know, I know!" I exclaimed. "Anyways, it doesn't matter. I know you'll love Brad!" And with that I proceeded to recount my fated trip.

I am so happy that you were able to be there for me, to hear about the beginning stages of my fairy tale and hear how infatuated I was with Brad. We walked and talked all about him and I spared no details. You asked me all of the questions and I shared it all with you. We were always like that; it was so easy to talk to you and unload all of what I was thinking. When we parted after chats like these, I felt like we carried each other wherever we went. I gave myself to you in my words; my soul floating to you just as I felt yours coming to me over the years we had together.

I wish we could go back.

I added Brad on Facebook and told everyone who would listen, including all of the people at work, about this amazing, kind man I had met on my trip.

Almost everyone asked what had happened with the other guy I had been seeing but it was one of my bosses at the time who eventually encouraged me take the steps to break up with the thirty-year-old pot smoker for good.

"So now what?" Rick asked when I told him about Brad.

"I don't know," I answered honestly.

"Well first thing's first," he said, "haven't you been seeing someone else?"

"Yes..."

"So you dump him, clearly," he retorted as if it was as obvious as the light of day.

"Clearly? Is it that simple?" I had asked myself that question a million times. Could things actually happen with Brad when we led such different lives? Not to mention that he lived in my hometown and I was happy in the lower mainland.

"Let me ask you this about the old guy. Does he hold your hand when you guys go out?"

I thought about it. "No," I replied. I don't think he had ever held my hand. Not even while watching a movie in the comfort of my own home.

"Why not?"

I simply shrugged.

I don't even think Rick replied out loud. His look alone let me know he thought this guy was not worth the time of day.

"You know," Rick started. "I have always been a firm believer that everyone should break up with someone at least once in their life."

"Oh?"

"Absolutely. It's like reading Harry Potter."

I stared at him blankly. "You lost me."

"You may not have any interest in reading a seven-book series about a teenage wizard with a star shaped scar on his forehead..."

"Lightning bolt," I interrupted.

"Sorry?" Rick asked.

"The scar on his head was a lightning bolt, not a star."

"Okay, nerd. But you get what I'm saying, right? You may not want to initiate a break up but it's just something that everyone should do at least once in their life. It's a learning experience."

I nodded and left his office, not knowing that I would end up taking his advice that very evening. The thirty-year-old pot smoker's ears must have been burning because he called me that evening while I was making dinner.

"Hello?" I answered cautiously.

"So, am I coming over or what?"

He was flirting with me. Oh boy. I didn't respond right away which prompted him to say, "Is something up?"

"Ya," I replied, not knowing exactly how to do it. Do I come right out and say it? Tell him I think he's great and then cut the cord? No need to lie. Plus, he was onto me.

More silence followed, this time on both ends.

"Are you breaking up with me?"

Kinda hard to break up with someone who you were never exactly committed to in the first place.

"Yes." This was good. Directness is good.

I stood in my kitchen, stirring my dinner, waiting for him to say something else. The hard part was done, right?

"So, should I still come over?" He asked, catching me off guard.

I gulped. "I guess, if you want to."

"Well, I think we should talk about things."

He sounded hurt. Great. This was never my intention. I felt uneasy because I had already omitted a few of the details of what happened between Brad and myself in Mexico. (I may have left out the part with the exploding fireworks when our souls collided. Okay, yup. I definitely left that part out.) But given the fact that there was just no meat to the bones of our relationship, it really couldn't have come as much of a surprise to him that I wanted out.

Could it?

"I didn't see this coming," were the first words out of his mouth when I answered my door a short time later. I was in the middle of trying to scarf down my dinner before he got there, hoping that he wouldn't stay long. It was the night the Canucks were retiring

Trevor Linden's jersey and I had planned on relaxing with a glass of wine while I watched the hockey game.

We sat down together on the couch.

"It just wasn't ever going anywhere," I started. "I want more."

"What do you mean, 'more'?"

I thought about how kind Brad had been to me in Mexico. We had known each other for barely a week and he had already swept me off my feet, taken care of me and bought me a present. None of which this supposedly mature man had done for me in over eight months.

"I don't know. Just more." I paused. "I don't see this being a forever kind of thing."

"Oh," he said rather neutrally. I think he was waiting for me to say more, but I was trying hard to pretend I wasn't focused on the tv, where the number 16 jersey was being raised to the rafters of GM Place.

"We've never even talked about our relationship. What we mean to each other." I volunteered.

"Why didn't you ever bring it up?"

"I don't know," I answered honestly. "I guess because it just wasn't meant to be."

We sat on my couch for a little while longer. My dinner got cold. The first period came and went.

"Is this because of that guy you kissed in Mexico?"

See. I was honest about the parts I told him.

"Maybe. I don't know." I owed it to him to be honest but he didn't need to know that I had met the man I thought I was going to marry one day or that I never thought he was going to be that guy for me.

"Okay," he said slowly. "I guess that's it, then."

I had no words.

And with that, and an awkward hug at the door, he left. We didn't see each other again and other than one random email in the new year to tell me that he missed me, I never heard from him either.

All my love,

Anya

Chapter Four

August 4, 2010

Dear Rachael,

For being such strong, independent women, it was always our lot in life to find guys. I am a little ashamed of that. But we were just looking to have a good time. To flirt and create good stories to swap after we left a party together, drunkenly swaying arm in arm. I didn't think that I'd find my soulmate by making out with random guys at the MSAC or while you were waiting for me outside the Cadillac after being kicked out. We had a lot of harmless fun with boys over the years but deep down I know that we both longed for love.

I didn't think I was ever going to be worthy enough to find it. Or at least I thought that by anticipating that I would never find love, I would be sparing myself disappointment. I never had a lot of confidence in myself as a romantic partner for another human being, so when I met Brad and he actually made me feel special about myself, I felt like the luckiest girl in the world.

Later in the same month that I met Brad, I went home for Christmas. I was free from the shadows of my previous relationship and I was really looking forward to seeing Brad again. The mother of the bride who got married when I met Brad has an annual party on Boxing Day and she invited Brad before we left Mexico. My parents were also invited. Knowing that there was even a remote possibility that Brad would show up at her house on Boxing Day, I made sure I tagged along with them to the party.

"Merry Christmas!" Betty said as she welcomed us into her home. "You guys are early!"

"Well, George always likes to get home to bed, and you know me!" My mom said in response. My mom is notorious for her desire to be early, if not precisely punctual.

"Come in, come in!" Betty said. She took our coats and I went into the kitchen to pour us a few drinks. Everyone was sitting around the kitchen table, catching up on each other's Christmas, when Brad finally arrived.

My excitement level shot through the roof when I saw that he was there. He had to have come just to see me, right?

"Hello again," he said to my mom and me. "Merry Christmas!"

"Merry Christmas!" I said back happily.

"Here, Brad," Darryl said as he handed Brad a beer. "Have

a seat."

He sat down at the opposite end of the table from me, beside my mom.

"This is my dad, George," I said, gesturing to my dad, who was seated next to me.

"Hello," Brad said to my dad.

"We met Brad at Stacy and Jason's wedding," my mom explained.

My dad almost immediately stood up from his seat and left the table without saying a word.

"Did you guys have a nice Christmas?" Brad asked as he stood and moved around my mom to take the abandoned seat next to me. As he sat, he put his arm around the back of my chair.

How could such a small gesture leave a girl so completely electrified from the inside out?

"How are you?" he said with a small smile. This time it was just for me.

That smile. I had missed it. I missed that feeling he gave me, just by being next to me. We remained in contact since coming home from Mexico, but I wasn't sure until he walked through the door whether he would show up that day.

"I'm really good," I smiled back at him. "Especially now that you're here."

"Who, me?" he teased.

"How was your Christmas?" Mom asked.

"It was good, quiet," Brad said. "I actually just drove back from Vanderhoof and drove straight here."

"That's a long way!" Mom exclaimed.

That just made me even surer that he was there just for me. Why else would he have driven all that way?

My dad came back into the dining room and stood behind me.

Brad looked up at him and started to stand saying, "Would you like your seat back?"

He ignored what Brad said and left the room again.

"How was your Christmas, Sandy?" Brad asked as he sat down again and turned back to face the table.

"We had a very nice Christmas," she responded. "Thanks for asking, Brad."

There was a small disturbance in the front room that made my mom stand up from the table.

"I think it's your dad," she said. "I'll be right back."

I heard the front door open and close and saw my mom look out the front window. Then she disappeared from sight, the front door opening and closing again.

I didn't need to see or hear what was going on outside to know what was happening. My dad had gotten himself into a huff and was leaving, on foot. This wasn't out of character for him. My parents lived up the hill from the party and he had been drinking, likely for the better part of the day. Who am I kidding? His waking hours since Christmas Eve had likely been spent intoxicated at some level.

My dad had never seen me interact with someone who could potentially have a romantic interest in me before. Not that I can recall anyways. There was one time when I had been home the previous Christmas that a guy called the house to speak to me. My dad hated him right off the bat because he didn't say hello or engage him in conversation. Plus, he worked in his dad's company washing windows, which was clearly just not good enough. (This coming from the man who drives a taxi for a living; you would think a consistent, honest, paying job would suffice.) Never mind that my romantic interest's job is none of my father's business. Brad was earmarked as trouble before he even met my dad.

My face was flushed with a bit of embarrassment, but as soon as I gave Brad my attention, I forgot about the drama with my dad.

"Wow," I said to him, "you came all the way back from Vanderhoof today?"

"Ya," he said, smirking. "There was this girl who asked me to go to this party. I couldn't say no."

"You know what's good for you!" I flirted. "Do you want another drink?"

"I'm good, thanks. I'm driving."

"A responsible one!" I said as I stood to refill my wine glass.

My mom was standing in the kitchen when I got in there.

"Everything okay?" I asked her.

"Fine!" she said with too much effort. "It's so nice that Brad is here."

"It sure is," I smiled.

"I'm happy for you."

"Thanks, Mom, that means a lot."

"Me, too, please!" she said, gesturing to the bottle of wine. I topped up her glass and we went into the living room, where everyone was now seated.

I went to stand by Brad, who was hovering by the Christmas tree.

"I think everyone is going down to another party, if you guys want to come," Betty said.

"What do you think?" I asked Brad.

"I'm going wherever you are," he said.

"Okay," I replied. "Well, I'm not ready to go home yet, so that sounds good to me."

I can't remember if my mom tagged along to the next party. I had my head in the clouds. Brad and I found a spot downstairs in a crowd of people; I was leaning against the wall and Brad put his arm above my head and then leaned in to talk to me. It was as if we were the only two people in the world. I went home with him that night and we just laid there, talking, for hours and hours. When we got up the next day, Brad drove me home. I was finally doing the typical things that I never did when I was in my teen years or earlier in my twenties. This is what it meant to be happy; I felt like I was finally living my life!

"Hello?" I called when I got home.

"Hi sweetie, how are you?" Mom asked. My dad was in the living room, staring at the tv. He didn't even flinch when I came in.

"I'm good. Did you stay long at the party?"

"No, I left shortly after you guys did," she replied.

"It smells so good in here!"

"Dinner's in the kitchen; help yourself. I'll be playing games," she said as she headed down the hall to her computer room.

It didn't take long before I noticed that my dad wasn't speaking to me. It wasn't the first time I received the silent treatment from him. It was his specialty.

The lead up to my dad's alcoholic outbursts were usually accompanied by days of him drinking more heavily. This trend was always more pronounced during the holidays. His moods would change often and he would lose the ability to make sense with his words. Then he would say something that I disagreed with, which would prompt me to either stand up for myself, my mom or something that I believed in. He never liked that very much. This would result in my dad yelling, slamming doors and sometimes throwing things.

My defensive behaviour remained the same even after I no longer lived at home. I would either retreat to my bedroom after realizing that my voice would never be heard through the alcohol, or I would recognize that as an adult, I had the power to leave. These routines would end with a day or two of the silent treatment, followed by his return to perfectly normal behaviour, as if nothing had happened. But there had been a change in me since I had moved away; I wasn't going to feign "taking responsibility for my actions" anymore. I was done following the lead and pretending that everything was okay.

Given that we were in the middle of the Christmas holidays, it was no surprise that the pattern of my dad drinking consistently for days on end came to a peak shortly after Christmas Day. I helped myself to some dinner and took a seat at the kitchen table.

I opened my book to read while I ate. I noticed my dad shift in his seat on the couch.

"You should be ashamed of yourself," he said in the direction of the tv.

I continued to read. I was still coming down from the high of being with Brad. I didn't want anything to spoil it.

"You should be ashamed of yourself," he repeated.

"What for?" I questioned back at him.

"Having anything to do with that asshole who stole my seat."

"Excuse me?" I started, confused. "What are you even talking about?"

"That asshole stole my seat when I got up to go to the bathroom at the party," my dad replied.

I hesitated. "It was a party. That's what people do when they want to talk to each other. They sit down in an empty seat beside someone who they want to talk to."

"He's an asshole and you should be ashamed to have anything to do with him," he said as he stood.

I was getting to a point in my adult life where I didn't want to have to put up with my dad's bullshit any more.

"Please don't talk to me like that," I pleaded.

"Like what," he spat back. "It just shows me who you are if you're choosing to spend time with people like that."

I had had enough. There was no point in fighting back; I had finally realized this. I stood, took my plate to the sink and went to my bedroom. I texted Brad to come and get me and I packed my things. I didn't ever deserve to be spoken to like that or judged so harshly by someone who is supposed to love me.

The next morning, my mom called my cell.

"Hi Anya," she said.

Uh oh. She doesn't usually start by calling me by my name.

"What's up, Mom?" I treaded carefully.

She started to cry.

"I left your dad last night," she said when she was able to quell the tears. "It got…things got…not nice."

"What happened?"

"I…" More tears.

"Go on," I encouraged her.

"I can't talk about it right now," she said as she broke down.

"Where are you?" I asked.

There was silence while she pulled herself together.

"At your auntie's," she replied. "But I don't want you to come here."

"Oh?"

"I'd like it if you could meet me at the house. Your dad is at work and I'd like some help to gather up my things while he's not there."

"Of course," I answered as if by reflex. I didn't want to see my mom hurting. I would do whatever she wanted to help her improve her situation.

We made arrangements to meet at the house I grew up in. I agreed to meet her there, but hadn't truly thought about what it meant to go to the house we had spent so many years in together to help my mother gather her worldly possessions so that my alcoholic father wouldn't destroy them. So that she could continue to live her life in another place, another home that had not been hers for the last twenty years.

Brad agreed to drop me off and then pick me up later. He asked no questions. I told him the logistics of what was going on but hadn't yet branched into the explanation of why my mom was leaving, or what had happened between myself and my dad the night before.

When we pulled up to the house, my mom was waiting in my aunt and uncle's vehicle.

She stepped out of the car when she saw us pull up. I went straight up the driveway to say hi to my family and embrace my mom. She immediately collapsed into my arms in tears.

"I just don't know what happened, Anya," she said between sobs.

"He drives a Hyundai?" I heard my uncle say of Brad as he reversed down the driveway.

The hardest thing I have ever done in my life emotionally was helping my mom gather her belongings that day. I believe to this day that I never should have been asked to help her with the task.

We walked through the front door and I felt as if something just wasn't right. It took a second before I realized that the Christmas tree that had been standing in the front window only the night before was missing.

"So, what happened last night?" I asked nodding towards the front window. I was afraid of the answer but had to know. "After I left?"

"Oh, Anya," she replied. "I have never seen him so mad."

I looked over at her. She was terrified. And that made me scared, too. I was thankful in that moment that she was standing in front of me in one piece.

"He wouldn't stop fixating on how rude Brad was to have stolen his chair at the party. Like it was even a big deal!" She was starting to get worked up over it.

I nodded.

"You know how he gets," she said. "He just wouldn't let it go."

I nodded again.

"I finally told him that he should drop it. That Brad was a nice boy I knew from Mexico. That we should just be happy for you to have found a nice boy."

She went quiet.

"Then what happened?"

"He was just so drunk," she said softly as the tears started again. "He got mad at me for saying anything, of course. And then he took the Christmas tree outside and threw it in the garbage."

"Oh, Mama," I said gently.

"The things he said, Anya," she went on after she had calmed herself enough, "were so mean. He was just so mean to me and about you. I can't take it any longer."

I put my arm around her and squeezed her tight. "I'll always be here for you, you know."

"I know."

"No matter what happens," I assured her.

We sat together in silence for a time before we stood. We were the only people who actually knew what it was like when things with my dad escalated. We never spoke about it; we never have. But in that moment, all she needed to know was that I understood. I guess that's why she wanted me to be the one to help her gather her things.

I was surprised that my mom was able to hold it together

while we went, room from room, packing things in bags and boxes. The scrapbooking stuff stayed. She was taking the truck, which made it easier to have a place to put everything she was taking with her. She packed her clothes and personal items on her own.

I gathered the rest of my belongings and anything that I had left in my childhood room that I actually wanted to keep or didn't want destroyed. I remember taking this pair of little ballet slipper flats that had belonged to my mom. I have no idea why I did it. They weren't mine. I didn't think she ever wore them so I put them in my bag. Did I think I was pulling one over on him? Ha, take that! I'm taking these slippers so you can't have them! Did I think he was going to put on my mom's little black slippers and sit in the house moping in her absence? I have no idea. I wore them infrequently and ended up throwing them out. I sure showed him.

What happened to my psyche that day has taken a long time to undo. My mom relies on me far too much. For her happiness and in this instance as her number one supporter. This has been an ongoing problem in my relationship with her. I am supposed to be the child in the relationship, but given the co-dependence of my parents' relationship when I was growing up, I don't recall really being allowed to just be the kid.

Yet, as we pulled away from the house, I glimpsed at the strong woman that I know my mom to be deep down. She'd had enough of my dad's bullshit, too, and I was proud of her for leaving it behind.

I spent the rest of my time in PG with Brad. I spent New Year's Eve at my aunt and uncle's place because Brad had plans to attend a big party in Vanderhoof with his friends and family. Ringing in the New Year with a man by my side would have to wait another year, I suppose!

Brad still hadn't asked about what was going on with my family. It wasn't until we were out for dinner one night and my phone rang that the truth finally made its way out to him.

I grabbed my phone to see who was calling. "It's my dad," I said as I looked up at Brad.

"Are you going to answer it?"

"I don't think so," I told him honestly.

When my phone buzzed with the alert that I had a voicemail minutes later, I was shocked.

"He left a message," I said to Brad. "He never leaves voicemails."

"Are you going to listen to it?"

"I feel like I should."

"Would you like me to?"

"You would do that?"

"Well, ya," he replied. "I don't have any idea what's going on with you guys, but if you want me to see what he said, I can do that for you."

"I haven't told you what's going on yet?" I asked, surprised.

"Nope."

"And you haven't asked?"

"I thought you'd share with me when you wanted. It seems pretty serious, so I didn't want to press."

"I didn't realize I hadn't said anything about why I needed a place to stay," I told him honestly before I proceeded to tell him the whole story.

When I was done, he asked me to load the voicemail. I waited while he listened to it.

"It doesn't make any sense," he said.

"What do you mean?"

"Here." He handed me the phone. "Just have a listen; it's fine."

The string of words that lasted five seconds at the most didn't make any sense.

"Huh, he must be drinking again." I paused. "Still."

"Are you going to tell your mom about his call?" Brad asked.

"I don't think so. Not unless she asks."

We went on to have a lovely dinner, just the two of us. I hadn't realized just how much I had left Brad in the dark but confessing to him opened up a whole new level in our relationship. I hadn't thought twice about telling him the truth. I didn't hesitate and I certainly didn't sugar coat it. It felt right that he know what I was going through, that he had the opportunity to run as fast as he could in the opposite direction. Instead, he chose to be there for me. He already had been without even knowing why.

The time to return to North Vancouver came quickly. I was so sad to be leaving Brad behind, but my home, my job and the life I had created for myself away from all of the bullshit was waiting for me.

"So, keep in touch?" he said after I had packed up my bags, ready to leave for home.

"Of course!" I said. "You're not getting rid of me that easily!"

For the first time returning to my home in the Lower Mainland, it felt as if I was leaving a piece of my heart behind in PG. I remember wearing a sweater to work that I had worn while cuddling with Brad on his couch. The sleeve smelled of him; I didn't wash it until the scent had disappeared. This was all new territory to me; I had never been this smitten with anyone before.

I had also never felt so damaged, or determined to fix it. I started to open up to my friends about my history and the relationships that I had with my parents. The weight I carried for so many years was lifted, just by admitting out loud that my father was an alcoholic whose drinking problem continued to affect me in my adult life.

Once I started talking about it, I learned that I wasn't the only one. As it turned out, my friend Tara's dad had a heavy drinking problem and she had a strained relationship with him as an adult. She mentioned to me that she saw a counsellor in North Van, not too far from where I was living and gently encouraged me to make an appointment to talk to him. She gave me his name and left it with me. I was inspired that she was strong enough to seek counselling to help herself and booked an appointment with him to discuss what I was going through.

I had never had any experience with anyone who had seen a counsellor before. It was never an option for me growing up. My mom didn't even appear to talk to anyone she considered close about her problems so it would have been a far stretch to think of her talking in depth about her issues to a stranger. I was nervous leading up to the appointment, but I felt like I was going down the right path in putting my mental well-being first. I was finally looking out for myself as number one.

This counsellor's office was located in his house. If he hadn't been recommended by Tara, I would've turned and run in the other direction when I saw that I had to go into the basement of his house to get to his office.

He answered the door and welcomed me inside. I sat down across from this man that I didn't know.

"So, Anya," he started. "Tell me what brings you here."

I wasn't sure where to begin, so I started with the briefest version of my life in reference to the most recent events. "I have an alcoholic father, which presented its own share of difficulties growing up and is continuing to give me problems now, even though I've moved away from home and don't see my parents very often."

I never could have anticipated the first words out of his mouth.

"You were sexually abused."

I froze. I'm sorry? Wasn't I the one who should be talking about my issues so I could get some help working through them? Should a stranger be telling me what he perceived to have happened in my past, five minutes after he met me? I didn't know what to say in return so I didn't say anything.

"Do you want to talk about that?" he prodded.

"Well, no," I said, my face flushed. "Because that didn't happen."

I sat there, traumatized. I somehow managed to finish the hour talking through my life, avoiding the subject that he clearly wanted to talk about. When our time was up, I left quickly and never returned. Here I was being faced with something that, yes, I did remember from my childhood but was choosing not to discuss. Not in the first five minutes anyway. Not only did it scare me, but it also hurt to think about. I had chosen to suppress it and when—and only when—I wanted to discuss it would I allow it to come to the surface. It was my choice when to bring it up, not someone else's. This counsellor was most definitely not a good match for me; I couldn't believe someone who was supposed to be a professional would accost me about a presumption, whether or not it was correct.

However, I was so determined to find peace and work through my problems that I didn't allow that experience to deter my journey to a healthier me. I turned to the internet to help me choose a counsellor more suited for my personality.

I eventually found a lovely yet quirky woman who made me tea and welcomed me into her warm office located on Mountain Highway, also in North Van. I immediately felt at ease with her as she covered her lap with a blanket, her dogs sleeping nearby in their beds. We worked through a lot of things together, specifically my years as the child of an alcoholic father and a co-dependent mother. She helped me recognize my feelings of guilt and loneliness in a way that helped me learn that it was not my fault, nor was I alone. She created a trust between us that allowed me to eventually open up to her about everything in my childhood. I shared with her what I needed to share and moved forward when I needed to. I learned that I had a choice in all aspects of my life. I chose when to share my deepest secrets, and I decided not to explore repercussions for those involved. And that was okay. It was up to me, after all.

It was also up to me to stand up for what I needed out of my relationship with my parents, and to recognize that they're not perfect. But that neither am I. We're dealt each other; that's what family is all about.

Eventually Brad and I were talking on the phone and texting every day. We were becoming ingrained in each other's lives even though we were living in different towns.

I continued dating, as much as I had ever dated anyways, which wasn't much. You, your sister and I spent Valentine's Day together; we had a lovely homemade dinner at your place and went to a local theatre to see a play. I had plans to go out dancing with some friends afterwards where I met "other Brad." We had some fun together, but more than anything it sparked a serious conversation between the first Brad and me.

"See," he said when I told him about going out with other Brad. "You're having too much fun being single to commit to me. I live too far away."

"I'm only dating other people because I'm not dating you," I countered. The logic made sense in my head. "You could be dating, too. You're just not."

"You're right. But I'm in Prince George. No one to date here."

"I don't want to be dating anyone else..."

"But I don't want you to miss out on anything in real life," he said softly.

"You're real life."

"When will I see you again? In real life."

I chuckled. "Easter. I can take a couple of days off around the long weekend and drive up."

"Are you going to stay with me?" he asked playfully.

"If you'll have me!"

"Uh, ya," he replied as if it was obvious. Okay, it was obvious. "But my roommates will be here then. My cousin Scott and Sunny."

"Okay," I replied. "No time like the present to start meeting the family!"

"Haha, very funny."

I had something serious I wanted to tell him. "Speaking of family, my mom moved back home."

"Oh?"

"Ya. I guess my dad asked her to come over to help him with laundry and they got to talking."

"That's good?"

"As long as she's happy, it's good. Sounds like she felt bad for him. But he told her that he stopped drinking. So that's good."

"Yes, it is. Do you want to stay there?"

"No," I answered honestly. "I think I'm done staying there. We have too much to work through. My counsellor actually suggested that I talk to them about how I'm feeling after what happened at Christmas. And over the years."

"So, you'll go up there to see them?"

"At some point, yes. I'm writing a letter to them so that I can say exactly what I want to."

"A letter?"

"Ya. Seems stupid, doesn't it?"

"Not at all."

I was relieved to hear him say that. My counsellor had suggested writing the letter and then either dropping it off for them or going in person to read it to them. That way I had everything I wanted to say in front of me in case things turned or my emotions got in the way. It seemed like a good idea to me at the time. I should have known that it wasn't. Not really.

And so my trip's purpose was twofold as I drove myself nine hours north to PG for Easter. I had four uninterrupted days and nights with Brad and I had the opportunity to work on my relationship with my parents.

I told my mom that I wanted to come by the house to talk. I think she was glad. Being that our family never talked about the hard things, I don't think she expected me to actually make an attempt.

My parents sat down at the kitchen table with me as I read:

Mom and Dad, I have gone through years of being the victim of dad's drinking and I don't want to be hurt by it any more. All of the times that dad has gotten drunk and yelled were so scary for me. It made me happy to move away and not have to deal with it anymore, but I feel like I was just assisting in sweeping our problems under the rug. I don't want to do that anymore, so I'm coming to you to talk about how we can move forward as a family and work on the hurt that lies beneath the surface.

What happened at Christmas was terrible. I felt so judged by my choice in a partner and by my actions. It was hurtful to be told that I should be ashamed of myself and that Brad is an asshole. It's not fair. And he is not an asshole. He is a really great guy.

If I am to come back to see you guys again, I need dad to stop drinking and get some help to deal with his problem. I won't come around if that doesn't happen.

I love you both.

I finished reading to silence. No one spoke.

Then my dad stood. "That's all in the past," he said.

That was it. He left the table. The conversation was over.

Probably even worse, all my mom could manage to say was "sorry".

I had poured my heart out to them, trying to remedy the hurt that had built up over the years and show them that I wanted to move forward as a family. And I was told that it was all in the past; my feelings didn't matter.

I left abruptly.

I was angry as I drove myself back down to Brad's place. Sorry? What did saying sorry really do anyways? The point of the exercise was for me to say my piece. To gain control of my feelings and my status in our family. To prove to myself that I had a voice and that I didn't need to yell or fight to be heard. I had been honest with them and I was not responsible for their reactions. I forgave them for what they had done and I released them with love. We never spoke about it again but rather swept it under the rug, just like everything else involving emotions in my family. I knew that I had done what I needed to do to heal and I made peace with my parents and who they are. In order to be my best self, I was the one who had to work on me. They were my family, warts and all.

I will be forever grateful that I found a counsellor who was able to help me improve my self-worth and navigate adulthood, including my relationship with Brad. Her help over the years has given me faith that talking to an impartial third party about the difficult things is the first step to loving yourself and forgiving life's unfairness.

I believe that the world only throws things your way that it knows you can handle. Call it God or a higher power, if you wish. When I met Brad, I had matured and I was ready to start putting myself first, above all of the bullshit that I grew up with. I was establishing my own life away from home; putting down the roots that would help to grow my family. I was more than ready to stop putting up with the abuse at home. Reading back on my journals from the time, I was excited about Brad and the prospect that I had met my future husband, but I didn't write down anything about what had actually happened when I was home for Christmas that year. It's sad, really. I am sure that I felt ashamed at the time and was choosing to remain positive in my writing. But it makes me sad to think about all of the other incidents that I forgot about because I was too afraid to put pen to paper out of fear that what I was experiencing was actually real. I chose to put the memories out of my mind because they were just so embarrassing and painful. I didn't want to remember the feelings of guilt, of blaming myself for something that wasn't mine to carry. I am glad that I was able to move away from shameful feelings from my childhood and instead focus on my future and build a better self.

I've developed into a pretty respectful human being, one that is more than worthy of love.

After my trip at Easter to see Brad, I was hooked. I offered to fly him down to see me for the May long weekend, after which my heart belonged to him one hundred percent.

He came down on the Friday and we hung out at my place for the evening.

We relaxed on Saturday with no real plans for the weekend other than heading out to Surrey to meet some of Brad's friends that he had from when he lived there.

"Sooooo, what do you want to do this evening?" I asked him. It was the first of countless times this question would be asked in our life together.

"I dunno." This was also the first of countless times I would receive the same answer from Brad.

"Well, I think we should get dressed up and go for a nice dinner. My treat!"

"Okay. Where do you want to go?"

"I think we should just get dressed and see where our feet take us! There are a few nice restaurants down Lonsdale that we can check out."

A short time later we found ourselves at a lovely Italian restaurant about eight blocks away from my apartment. We still go there every once in a while to reconnect and reminisce.

"Do you want some wine?" I asked him. For me, wine was a given.

"Sure, do you want to share a bottle?"

"Absolutely! It's not like we have to drive!"

"And it's not like we're in a rush either. Let's order an appie."

We shared an appetizer and were enjoying the wine when the conversation took a bit of a serious turn.

"So, do you know what kind of a ring you want when you get engaged?" he asked. "You know...one day?"

The marriage talks always seemed to flow easily with Brad, but I had never actually given engagement rings a thought. "No!"

"Really?" He was skeptical. "Don't all women have their weddings planned out from the day they hit puberty or something?"

"Oh, Brad! I'm not like all women. Haven't you learned that yet?"

He chuckled. "Maybe one day."

"Or maybe not," I gave him a wink as the waiter stopped by to top up our wine glasses.

"Another bottle?" the waiter asked.

"Of course!" Brad answered for us. He may not always take the initiative, but when it comes to wine, the more the merrier! Especially when we were having such excellent conversation.

We had already been at the restaurant for over an hour when our entrees arrived, along with the second bottle of wine.

"So, seriously though," Brad brought the conversation back around to marriage. "You don't have your wedding planned out?"

"No!" I admitted. "Though obviously we would go back to Mexico to get married. If you and I, uh, were to get married."

"Naturally," he agreed. "I see. She won't admit what kind of engagement ring she wants but she knows that she wants to get married in Mexico!?"

"Let me guess," I teased back. "You know what kind of a wedding ring you want and have your whole wedding planned out?"

"Given my work," he said, "I probably won't ever wear a wedding ring." He was working as an apprentice to an electrician at the time.

"Oh." I was most definitely a bit upset at hearing that. I always pictured my future husband with a ring on the third finger of his left hand. A display of our love and commitment.

"It just doesn't make sense if I'd have to take it off all the time for safety reasons at work," he went on. "Most electricians I know don't wear them."

"Well, if you wouldn't wear a ring then neither would I," I said one hundred percent honestly.

"Really?"

"Yes." I was starting to tear up at this point. "Why would I if you weren't going to?"

"Well, because it's a girl thing, isn't it?"

"But I wouldn't need a ring," I said as I gazed over the table at those beautiful eyes. "I'd have you."

He stared back at me, searching for my soul with his eyes. I knew he could tell I was being sincere by the way he lifted his glass to take a drink, never breaking eye contact.

By the time we ordered dessert, the mood and the conversation had lightened. When we started our walk home, we realized just how long we had been there.

"Dinner took us three hours!" I exclaimed.

"Time flies when you're having fun!" Brad responded as he

reached for my hand. We walked along the streets together on our way home.

You told me once that you didn't want a traditional engagement ring either. At the time, I told you I thought that a ring wouldn't be an engagement ring if it didn't have sparkly diamonds, but I think I would have wanted to have been involved in the process of helping your future husband design your atypical engagement ring whenever that day came. Sparkly diamonds or not.

After realizing how much I wanted to be with Brad and what I was willing to give up to make that happen, it didn't take me long to suggest to him that I wanted to move back to PG so that we could be together.

This conversation, of course, happened over the phone. We dated before FaceTime or Skype got really popular. Before smart phones took over the world.

"I was thinking," I told Brad one night, "that I should move back to PG. So we could be together."

"We've had this conversation before, Anya."

"Ya, but ever since you were here, things are different."

"How so?" he asked, unsure.

"Well for starters, I haven't been dating anyone else. And I don't plan on it."

"Okay," he said. "But I don't want you to move back here just for me."

"Why the hell not?" I was set on it. "Plus, it's not like I'd be moving somewhere where I don't know anyone. I grew up there."

It's not so much that I had to convince him, but rather prove to him that I was making the move for my own reasons. Not for his. He would have loved to move closer to me, but his ties to Prince George were stronger than mine were to North Vancouver. Hell, my ties to Prince George were stronger than my ties to North Vancouver, regardless of how much I loved it there.

"And what about your Europe trip next year?" he asked, bringing up my plan to obtain my Croatian passport, quit my job and travel Europe.

"So, we go to Europe for a few weeks together instead of me going indefinitely?" I suggested pointedly. "It'll be much more fun to go together and come home than it would be go on my own now that I have you."

"Ya..."

"Plus, you've never been overseas, have you?" I asked.

"No," he responded. "I haven't."

And so, in the summer of 2009, it was decided that I would be moving back to Prince George. A small town that I had eagerly left five years before to start a new life.

I was able to give my work plenty of notice and even though we scheduled the move for the end of October, Brad came down to visit me in August and again at Thanksgiving. Near the end of August, Brad came down with his brother, Gerry, and sister-in-law, Tanya. The four of us were going to see AC/DC on the Saturday they were here, which also happened to be the day of one of my close friends' baby shower.

"Are you sure you don't mind if I go?" I asked Brad. It was

Saturday morning and we were having a slow start to the day.

"Of course not," he assured me. "I have a little surprise for you anyways. So, I'll keep busy. Don't worry about me!"

"Okay," I told him. "Thanks!"

I left him a key to my place and headed off to Becky's baby shower. I got to chatting with a few of her friends and mentioned that Brad had come down from PG for the weekend and was at my place planning some sort of a surprise.

"What do you think it is?" Jenn asked.

"I honestly have no idea! He said that he needed to go somewhere, but that he saw the place from the window in the bus on his way over, so he'd just walk there!"

"So exciting!"

When I got back to my place after the shower, my bedroom door was closed.

"I don't think we have time for the surprise before we have to meet Gerry and Tanya," Brad told me. "Do you think you can wait?"

"Sure," I said. "But the suspense is gonna kill me!"

We took the bus and the sea bus downtown and met Brad's brother and sister-in-law at their hotel. We had a great time at the concert, our first together! When we got home late that night, Brad suggested that I close my eyes before we went into my room.

"Ah, it's killing me!" I told him as I let him cover my eyes from behind.

"Okay, this way," he said as he led me into my room. "Alright, open up..."

I opened my eyes to the most romantic gesture he has ever

made for me. He had spelled out "I ♥ u" on my bed in rose petals.

I turned into his embrace.

"I love you, too!" I told him. I had never said those words out loud romantically before! Hell, I had rarely even said it to my immediate family. "And I had planned on telling you that I'm in love with you before you left this weekend!"

We were in love! And soon we were going to be actually living in the same town, able to see each other regularly and go on dates and everything!

Our relationship was growing so beautifully. I couldn't wait to make the move back to PG to see where life would take us. I started trying to look for work but the market for paralegals and legal assistants in Prince George was much slower than in the Lower Mainland. It was getting closer and closer to my moving date but I had still been unable to secure work. Moving in with my parents was not an option, though things were going okay with them. I chose, instead, to talk to Brad about it.

"I still haven't been able to find a job," I confessed. "I'm looking, even for LA work, and there's just nothing up there."

"That really sucks," Brad replied.

"Ya. I'm starting to think that I'm not going to be able to find a place of my own to live either. Not if I don't have a job to support myself."

"Are you gonna move in with your parents?"

I paused in thought. "I don't think that's a good idea."

"Would you want to move in here?"

"I dunno. We haven't even lived in the same town together before," I replied. "Do you think that's a good idea?"

"I don't see why not," he responded. "But I do have two other roommates. So, you'd have to put up with the three of us."

"Sure," I said, hiding my true level of my excitement. "I'd love to move in with you."

I don't think either of us realized that I was going to move in and never, ever leave.

For Brad's Thanksgiving visit, I took a day off before the long weekend to spend with him.

Our lazy day started out the same as most others.

It was mid-morning before the question popped up this time. "What do you want to do today?" I asked him.

"Let's go downtown," he replied. "I have an idea."

"Okay!" I said excitedly. I didn't have to make the plan! Sign me up! "Where are we going?"

"You'll just have to wait and see!"

We drove into Vancouver and ended up in Kitsilano for brunch at Sophie's Cosmic Cafe. It being a Friday, there was no wait, so we were able to quickly enjoy our meal at the retro diner before heading downtown.

"Just park anywhere along here," Brad suggested as we approached Smithe Street.

I pulled over and parked along Burrard Street where parking was permitted during non-rush hour times during the week.

"You have totally planned this out, haven't you!" I asked as we started walking down the street and I reached for his hand.

"Just you wait," he said in return.

He stopped about a block down the road from where we had parked. We were standing in front of a shiny storefront with glass doors and a button for entry. It was then that I noticed displays of diamond rings near the entrance.

"Are you taking me here?!" I squealed, typically.

"Ya...is that okay?"

"Sure!" I responded, shocked. "But I thought neither of us wants rings when we're married?"

"Come on!" he said, ignoring my comment. "It'll be fun to look."

"Okay! If you want to go here, I'm not gonna say no!"

When we walked in, we were greeted in a friendly manner. "Congratulations!" the shiny Barbie doll-like sales associate welcomed us.

"Thanks," Brad said first.

"Can I help you find anything?"

"We're just here to have a look," he responded.

"Alright," she said and proceeded to encourage us to try on any rings we found.

First, we looked at the antique rings. I tried a couple on. They weren't really my style.

"Is there anything that stands out to you?" Brad asked.

"Well," I started slowly. "Since we talked about it last time, I may have looked at a few rings online...and I am kind of interested to have a look at the solitaire diamonds."

"Okay," he said with a huge grin on his face. So much for not being interested in rings.

I tried on a gorgeous princess cut solitaire diamond set in white gold. I loved the look of it online, but it wasn't quite as lovely when I had it on the third finger of my left hand.

"Why don't we go have a look at the multi-stone diamonds?" Brad suggested.

"Okay!" I was really enjoying myself, wandering around looking at the rocks that are traditionally known as a girl's best friend.

Brad pulled one almost right away. "Here, try this on."

I slipped it on my finger.

Oh my.

It was stunning.

"I love it!" I told him.

Just then, Barbie came back over to us. "Find one you like?" she asked. "It's gorgeous!"

They've got to be trained to say that to everyone about everything.

"It's pretty nice," I admitted. "But I don't think we're going to purchase anything today."

"That's okay," Barbie told us. "Let me take down your ring size and write down the style number. We can keep it on file for the future."

And so, we found ourselves sitting together with Barbie as she took down Brad's name and information about the ring. When we finally left, we were both giddy. We stumbled out into the busy street with no idea that so much time had passed. It's like we had been in a sparkly time capsule for the past three hours.

"What time is it?" I asked Brad, looking down the street towards where we had parked my car.

"3:30."

"Uh oh. I think we got towed."

"What!?"

"Well, I don't see my car, do you?" I asked him as we walked to the spot where I had parked.

"Nope," he said as he glanced up at the street signs. "Huh. Would you look at that! Apparently you're not supposed to park along here past 3:00 pm!"

We looked at each other and started to laugh. It was very typical of us to not pay attention to where we had parked, lose track of time and get towed. Brad called the number on the sign and was given the address of the lot where they take cars parked illegally along Burrard Street. We headed south on Burrard by foot, stopping only for some snacks at 7-11. A nice long walk and $150ish later, we had my car back. We also had some priceless memories involving the diamond store visit that ended at the impound lot.

It was over that same long weekend that we had dinner at your place. A "Friendsgiving" of sorts. It was the first time I got to go to a special holiday event with a date! We got to meet some of your med school friends and we had a really lovely time. It was the perfect time for you to get to know Brad. There was so much to be thankful for: food, wine, friends, loved ones, my big move ahead and your third year of medical school. Life was treating us all so well; I never would have imagined that by the same time next year you would have vanished from our lives.

Moving back to Prince George never would have been my first choice if it weren't for Brad. In fact, I doubt it ever would have happened. I was growing in my career, I had a great base of friends and I was truly happy with my life and where it was going for the first time. Little did I know that I would still end up having my life in the Lower Mainland alongside my love. I just had to endure ten months back in my hometown first. I was a bit apprehensive, given my history with living in PG, but I was in love. Nothing was going to stop me from living close to Brad from then on.

My dad had managed to quit drinking on his own and self-admittedly had not taken a sip of alcohol since my mom had left him the previous January. It was easier for me to continue my relationship with my mom, especially since I was living back in PG, if I reconciled with my dad. Not surprisingly, there was no conversation about me welcoming him back into my life, or him welcoming me back into his. It just sort of happened since we were living in the same town again. It wasn't exactly a joyful occurrence, but it worked. He wasn't drinking and I had promised myself that whenever he said something that was unkind towards me, I would simply ask him to change the subject or I would remove myself from the situation.

Another challenging aspect about being back in PG was finding work. Brad was supportive of me finding something in the legal field and wasn't going to let me resort to finding any old job until I had exhausted all of my options. It wasn't until the new year that I secured employment at a small law firm in downtown Prince George. The cranky old lawyer I was working for was rarely in the office, but his partner and his assistant, who was also his wife, kept me company most of the time. The parking lot out back was gated; walking to the courthouse a half a block away meant passing by the local needle exchange. I locked the door when I was there alone and placed a sign outside asking everyone to call instead of knocking. The environment was clearly shitty and I was doing a job that I was overqualified for at a far lower pay grade, but work was work and earning a living for myself made me feel like I had made the right decision when I followed my heart back to PG.

It was nice to be near family when the holidays came around and we were able to celebrate birthdays with our parents and extended families. I joined a soccer team and Brad and I joined the gym. We were making a good show of settling down together but deep down we both wanted to be in the Lower Mainland again. It just suits us so well.

When 2010 arrived, Brad and I started talking about the Europe trip I had had in the back of my mind before I met him.

"So, Ireland, hey?" Brad asked one night over dinner.

"Ya! My friend Tara lives in Dublin with her boyfriend," I explained. "It would be cool to stay with them and then travel around Ireland, exploring."

"For sure," he said. "How do you know her again?"

"We met at the first law firm I worked at in downtown Vancouver. She was the legal assistant to team MRM."

"Right. Am I going to get along with them?"

"You get along with everyone! Gary is a really cool guy. I'm sure you guys will get along great."

We started watching for seat sales and finally booked our holiday for the last two weeks of May. The thought of travelling the world with my love was so exciting. He would get to meet more of my friends and we would be creating memories of our adventures together.

It was our first big trip together as a couple and Brad's first time overseas. I was still living on cloud nine with my man and was thrilled to have found someone to experience the world with. Brad was only able to take a couple of weeks off of work and since I had started a new job only a couple of months before we left, it turned out to be a good thing that we had only planned a short trip.

Brad and I drove down to Vancouver from PG. It had been cheaper to fly out of Vancouver and we didn't mind the nine-hour drive down from PG before our trip. We left after work one day and got into Coquitlam, where we stayed with Brad's great aunt, late in the night. I called you the next morning to set our plans.

"Hey Rae! We're meeting some friends at Steamworks after they're all off work," I told you. "So hopefully you can make it for dinner?"

"Yes, I can do that," you confirmed. "I won't be able to stay long but I can come by after school."

"Okay!" I said excitedly. "We can't stay too late either; we're going to a concert."

"Oh?! Which one?"

"Our Lady Peace!" I exclaimed. "We're actually going on a double date!"

"Ohh! Very nice!"

"I know, right?! I don't think I've ever been on one. Okay, have a good day at school and I'll see you later!"

"You got it!" And with that, you hung up.

We arrived at Steamworks early and got a big table in the basement. Some of my old friends from North Van were there, as was Jaimie. We were all having some drinks and chatting when you walked in, taking off your helmet. You had ridden your bike over, wearing a dress, which pretty much sums up your care-free, loveable nature right there!

"Anyaaaaaa!" You exclaimed as you noticed me and ran over.

"Hi Rae!" I welcomed you with open arms. "Oh man, I've missed you!"

"I missed you, too!"

I made the introductions to everybody you didn't know and you said hi to Brad with a hug. Knowing that you two were on a hugging basis warms my heart still.

"So, how's things?" I asked as we all sat back down. The guys had migrated to one end of the table so we were left to catch up with my friend Jaimie.

"What's your guys' plan for later?" You asked after you told me all about how med school was going between hospital rotations, studying and classes.

"Well, we're going to the concert with Jaimie and then we'll be coming back to your place!"

"Okay, I'm going out but I should be home after 10."

"Sounds good," I said, "we can catch up a bit more then!"

After dinner we parted ways. Brad and I headed up to the Vogue Theatre with Jaimie and her date, and you headed the other direction on your bike.

We grabbed a couple of drinks before getting settled into our seats before the concert.

"It's so nice to see you, Anya," Jaimie told me.

"Same here, Jaimie!" I replied. "And it's even better that we're able to take in a show!"

She agreed. "It's just like old times!" And we laughed, reminiscing. "It's nice to see you happy."

"Thank you!"

"It seemed to happen so quickly when you moved up to PG," she told me. "None of us down here had even met Brad before you were gone to move in with him!"

"Wow," I thought out loud. "I guess I never thought of it that way." And I hadn't. No one in my North Van life had had the chance to meet Brad or get to know him at all, other than what I told them about him.

"I'm so happy for you," she told me sincerely. "You seem very happy and Brad is a cool guy."

"Thank you. I'm glad you finally got the chance to get to know him." I was bursting with happiness and it was so nice to know that it was obvious to others, too.

We had a great time at the concert and then before coming back to your place Brad and I started a late-night drunken tradition of visiting the Roxy Burger after taking in a show. We had a few more drinks and then walked up to your place. We woke you up when we got there; we stopped for snacks on the way back and were reading your "What's Your Poo Telling You?" book, giggling like little school children in the living room.

I eventually crawled into bed with you, leaving Brad to get cozy on the couch. We lay there with the lights off, chatting just like we did when we were in high school.

"I'm really happy for you, Anya," you told me in the dark. "And I really like Brad."

"Aww, yay!" I said sincerely. "I'm happy for me, too. I have the two people that mean the most to me in this world under one roof."

I could almost hear your smile.

We laid in silence for a while. I wasn't sure if you had fallen asleep yet when the lump in the darkness next to me spoke groggily, "What's it like to have a boyfriend?"

Up to this point in our lives, neither one of us had ever had someone that we would call a boyfriend.

"Well," I answered. "It's not like I can give you wise words from the dating world. Brad is my first boyfriend."

"True," you replied. "But you're totally living with a boy!"

"Haha, I am!" I said excitedly. "I still don't believe it sometimes."

"Why is that?"

"Well, I just never thought I'd get so lucky. He's an awesome guy."

"He does seem really great for you."

"I mean, he let me move right in when we hadn't even lived in the same town as each other before!"

"You're so grown up!"

"Says the one in training to become a doctor!"

"I know, right? But you wouldn't be so impressed if you saw what happened during my maternity rotation in the first birth I attended..."

"Oh?"

"I fainted!"

We burst into giggles.

"You didn't!?" I replied.

"I did! I woke up on the floor after they had finished delivering the baby!"

We looked at each other in the darkness and just laughed.

"I miss this!" I said.

"Me, too. It's been a long time."

It had been.

Had I known that it would be the last time we had a moment like this, I would have let you know, in detail, how great Brad and I are together. How he is an easygoing guy who fits all of the parts of who I am so well. With my friends, my family, my hangry mood swings, my opinions. It all just works. I would have taken the time to tell you how important you had always been to me.

Laying there with you in the dark I felt alive. I was so excited to be travelling abroad with my love and spending time with my best friend the night before such a wonderful adventure. I really didn't think that it got any better than this. Looking back it was fitting to spend our last night together sleeping in the same bed, chatting in the dark. There had been so many times over our years that we spent nights like that together. At your parents' house or mine growing up, in a tent in someone's back yard, in cabins at various retreats over the years, at my first place in North Van or my apartment, and for the last time, at your apartment in Vancouver. These times were so special to me. No one can ever take them away.

The following morning, Brad woke up and ventured out on a coffee run, his treat. Your mom actually told me later that you told her about this act of kindness on his part and how it really solidified him as a good guy in your books. Free coffee with delivery—we all know how frugal you could be!

I had a lazy morning while the first two loves of my life enjoyed their coffees before the three of us took off for the sky train. Brad and I were eager to get our day started, though not at the cost of our time with you.

"I almost forgot," you said as we finished breakfast. "I have your birthday present!"

"Oooooh, yay!" Everything was exciting to me that day, but my birthday was always extra exciting in my books.

"I don't have a card to go with it, but I wanted you to have it before your trip. It's for both of you."

I looked down at the piece of paper you handed to me. "The Guinness Storehouse!"

"Ya," you explained. "Two tickets to tour the Storehouse, including a sample of Guinness!"

"Thank you, Rae!" I said as I stood to give you a hug. "This is amazing!"

"You're welcome! I did the tour when I was there. It's really something everyone should do!"

"What a thoughtful gift!" Brad chipped in. "I'm really looking forward to it, thanks."

"Well," you said, grabbing your helmet. "I'm meeting a friend at the climbing gym in half an hour. Shall we go?"

"Yes," I said. "We do have to go out to Coquitlam to grab our things before we head out to the airport."

It was a sunny morning as you pushed your bike down the street while we walked alongside you. I remember the way the sun spoke boldly and unexpectedly, glinting off of the green of the leaves shading the sidewalks. Brad strolled ahead of us, leaving you and I to walk side by side, which he still does now if we're with one of my friends. I will always remember the smiles and laughter reflected in the day, the trees and the company. And the happiness. I could always count on you for laughter and happiness.

We said our goodbyes and Brad and I got on the sky train, looking forward to our next grand adventure. I never thought twice about seeing you again. I most definitely took it for granted that I would. That your face would light up again when you next saw me and that my soul would be complete upon seeing your happy face.

I have a picture that sits in our hallway of Brad and I at the top of the Guinness Storehouse, enjoying what will likely be the only pint of Guinness I ever drink. It sits next to a picture of you and I before one of the O'Grady dances. They are two very happy pictures that bring me much joy every time I pass them.

It turns out that travelling together is a huge test for any relationship. Especially for a relationship newbie! Brad and I had a wonderful trip, but we definitely learned some valuable lessons. For instance, always carry snacks. And as soon as one person says that they're hungry, the first thing to do is find food. Apparently, we as young adults are very similar to children. Always be prepared in order to avoid meltdowns. There is no such thing as too many snacks!

We took advantage of our time in Europe and grabbed a quick flight over to Paris to explore the City of Love together. We hadn't made any plans before we got to Dublin and booked our flights to France after we had settled in at Tara and Gary's place. We also wanted to travel Ireland as much as we could, especially since Tara and Gary worked during the week, so when we returned from France we booked a train trip to Galway and planned to take a boat to the Aran Islands. It was my favourite part of our trip; just the two of us and our back pack, learning the streets of Galway, touring Inishmore on bikes, taking in too much sun and thoroughly enjoying the best cider we have ever had, Magners.

It wasn't too long after our trip when I talked to you on the phone that you first told me about Jonathan.

"Sooooooo," you said after I told you all about our trip. "I have to tell you about a boy I've been seeing!"

"You're seeing a boy! Tell me!"

"We met at the climbing gym..."

"Wait a second!" I interrupted. "Is this the same 'friend' that you were meeting on our way to the sky train that day?"

"Yep!"

"You didn't say you were meeting a friend-boy!" I teased.

"I know," you said. "I didn't want to jinx it, but we've been hanging out quite a bit!"

"Tell me about him!"

"Well, he's a bit older. And works for the government. He owns his own place and is originally from Montreal!"

"Have you kissed him?" I asked the most intimate questions reserved for such close friends.

"Ya!" you giggled in response.

"And?"

"He's a gooooood kisser! Maybe the best!"

"Wow, awesome!" I was sincerely happy to hear your news.

"He's really into climbing and the outdoors," you went on. "He's into hiking and even though he hasn't done much scrambling, he's willing to go with me!"

"That's great! He sounds like the perfect match for you."

I was so excited that we were both able to feel the love that we had wanted for so long. You and I were in a happy place then. I don't recall us ever having any serious fights or disagreements and those that we did have were either too petty to remember or were resolved on the spot. There was no time for bullshit between us. If you had done something that bothered me, I told you straight away. It was the same for you with me. There was never any concern that you would take my sometimes-abrasive approach the wrong way; you had known me too long and too well for that.

"I actually have some other news," you said, your tone turning slightly serious.

"What's up?" I asked, curious.

"I've decided to take a break from med school before I start my fourth year."

"What!?"

"I'm going to go to South America to learn Spanish and volunteer as a med student in some hospitals and clinics. They really need the help down there."

"Wow! That's amazing!"

"Thanks! I'm really excited about it."

"Is it a big deal to delay your fourth year?"

"Not really. If you're going to do it, now is the time. Fourth year is really heavy with hospital work and then leads right into your internship, so it's better to take a break now rather than later."

"That's really great, when do you leave?"

"After the summer. I haven't booked my flights yet, I'm just waiting to hear back from the hospitals."

It meant that unless you came up to PG during the summer we wouldn't get to see each other again before you left. But I pushed aside my selfish feelings and spoke from my heart, "I'm so proud of you; for taking the risks and following your dreams."

"Thank you."

"You're such an amazing person."

I'm honoured even now to call you mine.

Later in the summer, the next time we spoke, it was my turn to share some news.

"Do you remember this time last year when I had some news to share with you?" I asked, referring to when I told you that I was moving back up to Prince George.

"That you were going to Ireland?"

"Nope." I said. I should have known you wouldn't just guess our news. "Brad and I are moving back to the Lower Mainland together!"

"That's great! You sure didn't last long in PG." you said with a laugh.

I agreed. "None of us thought I would!"

"When is the big move going to be?"

"The end of September," I replied. "Brad is going to go back to a company he used to work for at the beginning of October and I'm still looking for a job."

"Too bad it's not the beginning of the month. I won't get to see you before I leave!"

"Ya, I thought that, too. But that's okay because we'll be nearby when you get back!"

"You bet! What an exciting time."

"So, how's it going with Jonathan?"

"Really well," you said. I could practically hear you blush over the phone. "He told me he loves me."

"Whoah!" I exclaimed. Brad was nearby listening, asking me what you said. I waved him away with my hand. "Did you say it back?"

"No," you said with a sigh. "Not yet. I don't know if I'm in love with him. How do you tell?"

"I'm no expert, but I think when you know, you just know." I told you. "There won't be any question."

"Know what?!" Brad said, loud enough for you to hear over the phone.

"Hi Brad," you said.

"Busted..." he replied as he hit the speaker button on my phone. "Hi Rae. Did Jonathan tell you he's in looooooove with you?"

"Haha, yes, he did."

"And?" Brad was always close by when I talked to you on the phone, pitching in his perspective when he wanted. He was always eager to add his two cents, from a man's perspective, as far as dating advice was concerned.

"I don't know if I'm in love with him yet," you replied honestly.

"Oh, when you know, you'll know!" he said.

"That's what Anya said."

"She's so smart," he said as he grinned over at me. "I think I'll keep her around."

"You know," I chipped in. "It's fine that you haven't said it back. It think it's honourable, actually, that you are taking your time."

"Thanks," you said. "I haven't felt any pressure since he said it. I just want to be sure."

"Totally honourable," Brad agreed.

"Well," you started to wind up the conversation. "I should get going."

"Sounds good," I agreed. "Take care and give me a call before you leave!"

"I will. Bye Anya," you said. "And Brad."

"Bye Rae!" We said in unison.

I was happy to have Brad nearby when we had these conversations. He was able to see how free I was when I was talking to you, how you made me feel loved and happy. I needed that at so many points in my life—to have unconditional love pressed into my hands and my heart. I was so happy that Jonathan had said those three little words. Of course he loved you; we all did. I hope you were able to express yourself clearly to him so that he knew exactly how you felt about him. I think you loved him in your own way. It would have only taken time before you let him know that love was in your heart for him.

Love,

Anya xoxo

Chapter Five

June 18, 2011

Dear Rachael,

WE'RE ENGAGED!!!!

Brad always says that he can never pull one over on me, that I somehow always know what's going on. That may be the case typically, but when it came to my 27th birthday, Brad floored me with this big milestone event. There is no part of me that saw our engagement coming so soon.

I suggested to Brad that we drive to Seattle to see the Vancouver Whitecaps play their top West Coast rivals, the Seattle Sounders. Brad and I have been Whitecaps fans since we moved back to the Lower Mainland and the Whitecaps team joined the MLS (Major League Soccer Club) in March of 2011. We attended their first MLS match at Empire Stadium and in the years since have become season ticket holders.

The game in Seattle fell on a Saturday, the week following my birthday. Anyone that knows me, knows how much I love my birthday, soccer and travelling, and since this getaway included all three, I was as excited as I could be.

I have also been a hockey fan for many years, and it just so happened that our local NHL team, the Vancouver Canucks, were playing in game five of the Stanley Cup Finals on the Friday that we were set to drive down to Seattle after work. Brad is also a fan and decided to grow a playoff beard that year for the Canucks' post-season run. This apparently meant that he was going to channel his inner pirate because let me tell you, his beard was pretty impressive by the time the cup finals came around. And by impressive I mean "please don't ever let it grow that unruly again, okay Brad?"

The night before we left I heard Brad start his electric razor.

"What on earth are you doing?" I asked him as I walked into the bathroom and saw what could have been part of a small, ginger-coloured Pomeranian fall from his face into the sink.

"Shaving."

I promise you, the sarcasm, at points, only gets better from here. (In our marriage; not so much in this story.)

"Yes, I see that. But why on earth are you shaving your playoff beard? The Canucks need all the help they can get!" I exclaimed, likely in a more high-pitched tone than was necessary.

"Ah, the big guys at work were giving me a hard time about not looking overly professional," he said smoothly, giving me no reason to question him.

I will admit, I was a little sad to see the ginger pirate go. I was curious to see just how much red beard my boyfriend had in him, as clearly I was never going to encourage him to grow that creature on his face again. Little did I know he had another reason for shaving his beard and it wasn't related to work.

Late Friday afternoon we donned our Canucks jerseys, loaded up our car and headed south of the border. Our first road trip to the United States together. Our first trip there, actually. This was only the third time that Brad had been out of Canada and the first time he crossed the Canada/US border. And it just plain felt special to be getting away together

We arrived at the hotel in downtown Seattle, all ready to check into our king suite, only to be told that they had given away their last king bed before we got there. (This occurrence started a strain of bad luck that Brad and I have with hotels giving away our king-sized beds, even when we make reservations.) We were given two options: we could take a queen suite at that hotel and move to a king bed the next night, should one become available, or we could move to their sister hotel which had a king bed available in a kitchenette and was just up the hill from the main hotel. Onward and upward we moved, driving up to the sister hotel where we checked in directly across the street from Virginia Mason Hospital. We had an unparalleled view of the ambulance bay complete with the flashing lights and the screaming sirens of incoming ambulances. Never mind all of the oblivious people coming and going from the emergency ward. Not that that's what I heard all night or anything. Whatever. It was still more important that we had our king size bed.

We didn't specifically have plans for our time in Seattle, other than Saturday evening's Whitecaps game, so we followed our feet to a quiet restaurant not too far from our hotel for dinner, grabbed some drinks on our way back and spent a quiet night in. This type of evening was typical for Brad and I, especially given our plans to go out the next night. We've never been partiers by any stretch of the imagination, but we enjoy lengthy dinners out, great food and drinks.

The next morning, I placed a call to the main hotel to secure the king room that we had "reserved" and confirmed that they did have something available for us. There was no way either of us wanted to spend another night listening to the crazy hospital patients or the symphony of sirens. We packed up and moved to our new room, which was also in a better location as it was walking distance from the stadium.

Since it was Brad's first time in Seattle we splurged on a City Pass, which gave us access to many of Seattle's main attractions. We started our morning by grabbing coffee and taking off on foot to find the Pike Place Market, which is a lot easier to find when you have a map or a cell phone with data. Neither of which we had because we were naively confident in my navigational abilities. I had been to the Market once. Surely I could find our way to it years later as an adult who was actually responsible for finding my own way.

The journey is more important than the destination, right? I feel like this could be the motto for our life together.

Once we finally reached the Market, we took it all in, including the famous fish-tossing at the Pike Place Fish Market, and clusters of tourists and locals indulging in the fresh produce. From there, we walked over to the Seattle Aquarium and enjoyed goofing around taking pictures with the fake octopus arms, petting the starfish and learning about the local marine mammals that lived in and visited Elliott Bay.

A section of Waterfront Park had been set aside to host the carving of a totem pole that was being crafted in the memory of a First Nations wood carver who had been fatally shot by a police officer in downtown Seattle. It was very humbling to see the deceased man's brother create such beautiful art that now stands at Seattle Centre, near the Space Needle. Brad chatted with the artist, who was one of several people to carve animals onto the totem pole, all in memory of their lost friend and family member. Letting the day guide us on such a priceless adventure was humbling and unexpectedly enriched our time together.

We eventually found our way on foot to the Space Needle. It was iconic. Necessary. We walked and walked. Then we walked some more. The Space Needle was not exactly walking distance from everything else, but we had a great time. We embraced our time as tourists and it couldn't have been more fun!

We ventured up the Space Needle for views of the city like no other. It had been a tiring day and although I don't specifically remember how we made it back to our hotel, I really wish that we had had time to take a nap when we got back. However, it was almost game time, so we geared up and set off, on foot, of course, to CenturyLink Field, home of the Seattle Suckers. I mean Sounders.

Given that we were new to the MLS and following our team

across the Pacific Northwest, we didn't realize that there would be a supporter's section where Whitecaps fans would have seats together to cheer on their team. Duly noted. We had actually purchased tickets in the middle of the field, Row 8. When we found our seats, we sadly realized that we were blue and white in a crowd of mean, green Seattle fans. This would not do. We were heckled, which we took in stride, but once the match started, we were also left sitting while every single one of the Seattle fans in front of us stood to watch the game.

I turned to Brad. "After all of the walking that we did today, there is no way that I can stand for the match. Not sober, anyways."

"I'll get the beers!" he said, all too happy to try and numb the exhaustion. Ever the dutiful boyfriend, he returned with two beers for each of us, which we downed quickly and followed with many others. We stood alongside the Seattle fans and cheered on our team. Funny, I don't remember my feet hurting much after that.

At half-time, Vancouver was ahead by one goal. We went out to the concourse for another round of drinks and we just happened to run into another fan dressed in white and blue.

"Hey guys, where are you sitting?" the not-so-stranger asked.

"Oh, just down in this section," Brad answered, gesturing towards our seats.

"You should come and sit with us in the supporters' section!" our new friend invited. And with that, we left our grumpy, heckling Seattle friends and joined the rest of the Whitecaps fans in our home away from home.

More beers followed. I actually ran into one of the lawyers I used to work with, Rick. The one I had to thank for encouraging me to break up with whatever-his-name-really-was. He was down from Vancouver as well, celebrating his stag.

We may have moved sections, but we still stood, cheering our team on as loud as we collectively could. I was busy watching the game when Rick turned to Brad.

"So," he said over the noise, directly into Brad's ear, "when are you going to pop the question?"

"I actually have a ring back at the hotel room," he said as he looked proudly at Rick. He glanced down to me with a smile and then took a drink of his beer.

Rick slung a drunken arm around Brad and then patted him on the back. I thought it was a dude thing, completely unaware that Brad had gotten his first congratulations before there was actually something to congratulate him for.

"Atta boy," Rick said to Brad, loud enough for me to hear. I didn't think anything of it.

We went on to tie the match in the 85th minute to bring us to a 2-2 draw. A tie is always less than satisfactory, especially when you're playing your rivals, but at least we didn't travel all that way to see our team lose.

We indulged in so much liquid lubricant for our sore feet and tired muscles that both Brad and I were desperate to find a washroom following the match. Security wouldn't let any of the 'Caps fans leave our sections until all of the Sounders fans had left the stadium, so we waited impatiently with floating teeth while our rivals' fans took their time clearing out of their seats. The lineups for the washrooms were ridiculously long, so Brad and I took off on foot in search of the nearest washroom, with the hopes that they also would serve us some food and more beers. We stumbled, hand in hand, down the unfamiliar streets of Seattle, not knowing where we were going, letting the dark and our inhibitions lead the way.

We randomly found a pub that happened to have some live music and no lineups for the ladies' and gents' rooms. We ordered bucket after bucket of Budweisers that we didn't even finish and enjoyed the live piano music the bar had to offer. We gifted the leftover beers from our last bucket to a nearby table, whose guest of honour was celebrating his stag. The man clearly didn't need more beer, free or not, but neither did we if we wanted to make it home in one piece. We said our drunken goodbyes, congratulated the soon-to-be married man, and ventured off on our feather-light feet to find our hotel.

I remember laughing a lot on our way home. There is also photographic evidence of our escapades somewhere, but we don't really need to go there right now. Those pictures will remain buried along with pictures from my stagette and a real prize photo taken of Brad in his Shamrock tighty-whities from Ireland.

We got back to our room. I removed my jersey and sat on the bed in my undershirt and jeans, looking back on all of the hilarious blackmail pictures we had just taken and the other photos from our day out and about in Seattle.

Brad had been in the washroom for a while when I heard him call out to me.

"Hey babe, can you bring me my shaving kit?"

"Yup," I said, not moving a drunken muscle other than to sway a little in my seat as I chuckled at just how hilarious the pictures of us trying to make the letters of our names with our bodies on our way back to the hotel were. Don't ask. I couldn't even explain if I wanted to.

"Hey babe," came Brad's voice from the washroom again. "I really need it. Like now."

I sighed as I put down the camera and went across the room to search through our suitcase. I found the shaving kit I'm pretty sure Brad inherited from his great granddad following the war near the bottom. I took it over to where he was standing, just in front of the washroom and the door to our hotel room.

"Can you open it for me?" he asked.

"Why?" I wondered aloud while I carelessly tried to hand it to him. He wouldn't take it.

"Just open it."

I unzipped the frayed black pouch.

"What's inside?" he slyly asked.

I reached inside and found a ziplock bag that held a small brown box. I looked up at him through blurry eyes and blinked slowly when I realized what it was.

"Open it up," he said, with a huge grin on his face.

I opened the box from Spence Diamonds with my heart aflutter to find the multi-stone brilliant cut diamond ring that Brad had picked out for me. It seemed like years before that we had fool-heartedly visited Spence Diamonds together. When actually, it had only been about a year and a half.

I don't specifically remember my body language at this moment, but if I was a betting woman, I'd say my mouth was hanging open and my eyes were no longer just blurry from the drinks.

"I want to marry you," my love told me. "Will you marry me?"

"YES!" I said, of course. We hugged and celebrated and Brad placed the ring delicately on my finger. I couldn't believe it! He had taken me completely by surprise! I hadn't seen it coming for miles and certainly didn't think that we would be in our hotel room post-match, celebrating our engagement.

I was elated, shocked and still quite drunk. We lay down on the bed and Brad gave me all of the details.

"When did you pick up the ring?" I asked.

"I went downtown a few weeks ago to order it. Then I was only a couple of blocks away from you on the same day that you were getting your tattoo consultation, picking it up."

He had called me that day after work. He knew that I had taken the sky train downtown and was on my way to the tattoo shop for a consultation before booking my tattoo. He had asked me to clarify exactly where I was walking, which I didn't think anything of at the time.

"You sneak!" I teased him. "I can't believe you were able to pull one over on me!"

"So you were really surprised?"

"I honestly couldn't be more shocked right now!" I exclaimed. "What the fuck just happened!?"

Brad laughed. "Once we started to plan our trip to Seattle, I knew that I wanted to propose while we were here."

"I thought it was going to be a while before you proposed.

Financially, you know?"

"Only for you, babe," he said with another laugh. "We met outside of the country and I wanted to propose to you outside the country as well. So, I went back to Spence and they still had the ring style on file from our previous visit. I ordered the ring so that it would be ready in time for our trip."

"You're so sneaky!" I told him. "And I absolutely love it!"

I began to think about what a big milestone we had hit in our relationship and our lives when my thoughts started to shift. There was only one person who I wanted to share our news with at that moment. I started to feel a knot form deep at the base of my throat. Tears were filling my eyes and I just looked at Brad and could tell he knew.

"There's only one person I want to tell right now," I managed to say.

"I know," he said. I could feel his heart ache as he gazed into my eyes. I knew that he could feel what I was feeling and that our promise to dedicate the rest of our lives to each other was destined. Our souls knew it. Our hearts knew each other.

"Can you tell her?" I asked him, fighting the knot and embracing the tears.

"Hey, Rae," Brad whispered, himself choking up. He hugged me close to him as we lay in bed, resting his head against mine. "I just asked Anya to marry me. And she said yes."

We sat together in a warm embrace, tears flowing freely. I let him hold me while I cried. I knew that he would never let me go.

I glanced down at the sparkle on the ring finger of my left hand.

"What the fuck just happened?"

"Hahahaha, oh babe!"

"Seriously, though," I pondered. "What the fuck just happened?"

"I totally pulled one over on you, didn't I?" Brad remarked.

"You did! I did not see this coming! Hey, is this why you shaved your playoff beard?"

"You caught me," he said. "I wanted to present my best self to you when I asked you to spend the rest of your life with me."

"Where is all this romance coming from?!" I asked him, jokingly. "You're so sweet!"

"And let's face it," he continued, "that beard was gaining a life of its own."

I laughed. "It was a little wild."

"Just a little."

"Hey Brad?"

"Ya?"

"What the fuck just happened?" I said as we laughed and cuddled together, drunkenly basking in the news that was ours alone for a few more hours.

I'm so happy to share our news with you.

Love always,
Anya (soon-to-be Wyers!!)

December 21, 2012

Dear Rachael,

Not too long after we got engaged, we set our wedding date. It was booked more or less 18 months in advance at the beach I found on the Internet while we were still living in Prince George. Our wedding day would consist of a private boat ride for our guests along the coast of Puerto Vallarta in the late afternoon. They would have an open bar and would be greeted by Brad when they arrived. The ceremony would take place on the beach and start shortly after they were handed drinks after getting off of the boat. There was a small bungalow overlooking the beach where dinner would be served. While we were eating, they would set up a dance floor and a small bonfire on the beach for everyone to enjoy while we partied. The boat would take us all back to town after the party was over and we would be bussed back to the resort together.

It sounded perfect to Brad and I; we would have our intimate sunset wedding on the beaches near where we met, in the middle of a week-long vacation with our friends and family. We chose a nice resort for everyone to stay at for the week of the wedding, somewhere we thought that not a lot of our family and friends would choose for themselves if they had booked a trip on their own. We wanted everyone to have a wonderful and relaxing holiday while enjoying their surroundings in a country that many of them had never been to before, and might never visit again. After everyone left, Brad and I planned to treat ourselves to a more luxurious resort for the rest of our holiday and honeymoon.

Before we solidified the plans for our dream destination wedding, Brad and I had quite a serious discussion. We had always planned on returning to Mexico to say our vows. And we knew that it would not necessarily be a popular decision as it's a lot to ask people to travel for a wedding. However, we didn't anticipate the backlash we received from our families for actually going through with our dream destination wedding.

It still baffles me that anyone, regardless of who they are in relation to a bride or groom, would make any sort of comment about how, when or where a couple chooses to get married. Neither Brad nor I believe that it is anyone's place so we struggled with people when they voiced their negative opinions. We had always been vocal about wanting to return to the country where we met and to Puerto Vallarta, specifically, to get married. In my mind, no one should have felt obligated to come. If it had simply been Brad and I on the beach, toes in the sand while we pledged our love to each other, it still would have been perfect. But, sadly, there are people who choose to make everything about themselves.

Oh, how I wish I had had you around to ground me through this time!

Thankfully Brad and I agreed that we were going to plan our wedding to suit our dreams and that whoever could make it, great. All that we hoped for from anyone who couldn't make it was love and support. Sadly, this was too much to ask of some of our closest relatives.

We took some time off for a trip to PG shortly after we got engaged. We stayed with my parents while we made the rounds to celebrate our recent engagement and visit with everyone who was dear to us. I got an odd feeling from both of my parents every time we talked about Mexico and the wedding around them. My mom was so happy for us and supported our choices right from the start. She was going to come to Puerto Vallarta with us; there was never any question. But for some reason that Brad and I just didn't know yet, every time we brought up the wedding in front of my parents, my mom got very quiet and my dad didn't say anything at all. It struck me as odd but I was hesitant to ask them directly about it, given our history. I finally struck up the courage to say something before Brad and I left for home as I thought it was better to have any difficult discussions in person.

"So, dad," I said, figuring that the only way to start a difficult conversation, especially with my dad, was to cut straight to the point. "Are you going to walk me down the aisle at our wedding?"

"No."

It was clear that this was going to be another so-called "conversation" I had with the back of his head as he watched tv.

"What do you mean?" I asked. I felt defensive and angry right away but attempted to stay calm and hear him out.

"I don't believe in destination weddings."

Okay, now the anger was growing, challenging my patience. I glanced over at Brad, who was standing near the hallway with my mom.

"Sorry?" I directed to my dad.

"I don't believe in destination weddings. I won't be going to your wedding."

"I don't believe this!" I lost control of my anger and the pressure burst, causing me to react impulsively to my inner feelings. "You're not going to be there to walk your only daughter down the aisle?"

"No. It's ridiculous that you're asking people to spend thousands of dollars to see you get married. I won't go."

"Well first of all..." I started to try and explain that we understood that people might not be able to make it before I realized that it wasn't worth my breath. He had made up his mind and he didn't even remotely care why we were going to get married in Mexico. He didn't care enough to bring his position up to me first or to turn off the tv when I finally brought it up myself. He didn't even have enough respect for me to have a real discussion about it, never mind to look me in the eyes while he told me that he wasn't going to walk me down the aisle, or be there for a father/daughter dance.

"If you guys get married here," my dad went on, "I'll pay for your wedding. But I'm not paying to go to Mexico for it."

This from the man who has gone to Puerto Vallarta on holidays almost every year for as long as I can remember and would likely be booking his ticket shortly to go to the same place only a couple of months later.

What he really meant but didn't say is that he wanted to have a big Croatian wedding and invite whomever he wanted to the wedding in order to show off to a community that he didn't even have anything to do with anymore.

In retrospect, I can't say I am surprised that he took this

stance. My dad remains the most stubborn person I have ever met and has some very specific and forceful opinions and beliefs about entirely random things. But even though I have never felt especially supported by him in my life's decisions, my heart yearned for things to be different this time.

"Well, we're not getting married here. So, I guess we'll be going," I said in a huff.

I turned to Brad. "Start getting our things together. We're leaving."

"Anya," my mom finally spoke. I think she was crying but I couldn't tell. I was too angry to worry about the impact this conversation was having on her. "Don't go like this. Please."

I ignored her and set off down the hallway, gathering our things from around the house. I shuffled our belongings to the front door and Brad took them out to the car, our bags a mess of half-packed items tossed together from various rooms. My mom stood by crying, saying nothing further than what she had already pathetically tried to muster. My dad never moved from his spot in front of the tv.

I already knew the answer, but once we were ready to leave, I asked my mom anyways: "Did you know that he felt like this?"

She looked at me with sadness in her eyes. "Yes," she answered quietly.

"And you didn't think to say anything to me about it? After all the times I talked about the wedding and how excited I was?" I was so angry. It became obvious why she had been avoiding talking about the wedding when my dad was around. And just as she had stood by while he did and said whatever he wanted to me when I was a kid, she stood by silently now. Her falling tears represented the countless heartbreaking unspoken words of love and support that I longed for and deserved to hear.

She started to reply, likely to defend his actions, but I just turned and headed for the door. We left without saying good bye. I also managed to leave without telling my dad to fuck off, which I think was a victory in itself.

I was overwhelmed by the anger that came from being so disrespected by the people who are supposed to love and support me unconditionally. Deep down I was just a girl who wanted my daddy to walk me down the aisle. I longed for him to want to be there for me in one of the biggest events in my life.

It was all feeling very familiar: my feelings, my reactions and especially the actions of my parents. Was I ever truly going to learn?

When we left my parents' house, I called my Auntie Laura and asked her if we could come over.

"Of course, honey," she told me over the phone. "Any time."

"We'll be there shortly," I told her hastily. "We're just leaving my mom's place."

She opened the door to me when we got there and comforted me with a big hug. "Come on in you two."

"We just left my mom and dad's," I started to explain. "Apparently my dad isn't coming to the wedding. And he didn't think to tell me himself..."

"I know," Laura replied. "Your mom told me when he first told her that he wasn't going."

"You knew?"

"Yes," she replied to our blank faces.

I couldn't think of anything to say in response. My blood had been boiling back at my parents' place, but my insides were starting to feel like they were being crushed.

"Your mom was really mad at him," Laura continued, "and she didn't want to be the one to upset you. She didn't know what to say."

"Well, she could have started with the truth," I replied bluntly. "But no one in this family ever wants to talk about the truth, do they?"

"We're all going to be there for you and Brad, honey," she tried to assure me.

"I'm so embarrassed that you knew," I said as I hung my head. "Who else did she tell?"

She didn't even need to answer. It turns out that pretty much everyone in my family knew about my dad's refusal to go to our wedding before I did.

"It wasn't anyone else's place to tell you what was going on, Anya," she told me.

"I get that, but all it would have taken is a bit of encouragement to talk to my parents, or my dad specifically, about the wedding. A clue that maybe a big event coming up in my life would be impacted by something I needed to talk to my dad about." I paused. "I feel so disrespected."

"I don't think it's a lack of respect thing..." she tried to explain.

"I feel like a fool," I interrupted her. "Everyone knew what was going on behind my back and didn't say anything. I've been going on and on about our wedding plans. I've been so excited."

"And you have every right to be excited," Laura told me. "You're going to be a bride!"

"I know," I told her honestly. It didn't make what had happened any easier, but it definitely helped bring me back to earth. It took some work, but I wasn't going to let my dad ruin our big day.

"I'm so sorry, Anya." Laura came over to give me another hug.

"Thanks," I told her from my heart. Laura has always been there for me when I needed her and this was no exception.

I ended up doing what I have always done when it comes to matters of my family. I got upset, dealt with my feelings in my own way and moved forward without talking to anyone directly involved about how I felt and why. Sure, there were conversations with my aunties and my mom about how unfortunate it was that my dad was acting this way, but there was no real concern for me and my feelings. When the heart of the matter concerns matters of the heart, I am defenseless. When I care deeply about something or someone, I automatically let my guard down and open myself up to be hurt. And I would have been alone in dealing with my disappointment except for my new husband-to-be. The two of us were creating our own family and have made it a priority to always talk things through. To make sure that we face everything together, regardless of how hard it might be at the time.

Following this incident with my family, I saw my counsellor. I was reminded that I didn't do anything to garner my dad's reaction. I cannot control it, nor can I change it. Just as I cannot control how anyone else reacts to any of our choices in life. It was important to remember this because my father's was just the first of several unfortunate reactions to our wedding plans.

We returned home and moved forward with our destination wedding plans without skipping a beat. My relationship with my parents was strained because of it, but the only part of it that I could control was my self-respect. I wasn't going to let myself or my relationship with Brad suffer because of what had happened with my parents. As far as the fatherly wedding traditions go, I decided that I would walk myself down the aisle and surprise my mom with a first dance together. It was fitting, really, given my independence since moving out of my parents' home. Closer to the wedding my mom offered to walk me down the aisle, but it felt like it was coming from a place of protecting me from being disappointed, not because she wanted to be the person supporting me and giving me away instead of my dad. I needed to be the one to walk myself down the aisle to prove that my self-worth would never waiver. I wanted to be the one to give myself to my husband. I was choosing to be my own support as I wasn't getting it from expected sources. We weren't having a typical wedding, so how hard was it to let go of one more antiquated tradition anyways?

Quite a bit of time passed without talking to or hearing from my dad and it got increasingly more difficult to carry on a normal relationship with my mom. I kept in touch with some other family members and following a conversation with my Auntie Laura, I laid it all out to Brad.

"So, I talked to Laura just now," I told him after he got home late from work one night.

"Oh?"

"Ya. She told me that shortly after my blow out with my dad, my mom told her that there was no chance she would be tagging along with my dad on any of his trips if he was going to put up such a fuss about going to our wedding."

"Didn't they just go to Vegas together?" He asked.

"Ya."

"Wow," Brad looked as shell-shocked as I felt. "So much for your mom standing her ground. Or standing up for you."

"Ya, that feels great. Then there's how much he hates going to the states."

"And even though your mom said she wouldn't go anywhere with him. Let alone the country he hates."

"You got it. I guess Laura asked her about that and my mom just told her that it wasn't worth it to put up a fight."

"Oh, man. How are you doing?" Brad slipped an arm around me while we sat on the couch.

"Alright, I guess," I answered as honestly as I knew how. "I mean, it hurts. But they're going to do whatever they're going to do. I know that. I think I just need to find a better way to deal with it."

"With what?"

I paused, thinking.

"It hurts when my mom tells me about her trips with my dad and how happy it seems to make her. I get that they have their life together, but she acts like she'll stand up for me behind the scenes and never does. I wish she wouldn't bother pretending she's got my best interests at heart."

"Well, I do think she has your best interests at heart," Brad responded carefully. "It's just that she and your dad are her number one priority. I don't think she means to hurt you."

"No, I don't think so either."

"She just doesn't have a clue, Anya." Brad hugged me tight and reminded me that I have someone close that does and always will have my back. "What are you going to do?"

"I have an appointment with my counsellor next weekend, so I'll just keep to myself as far as my mom is concerned and see how I feel after my appointment."

"That sounds great, babe. I'm really proud of you for working through this and doing what's best for you."

So was I. I finally learned that I needed support to help work through my issues with my family and that I was never going to get that support through them. I found great comfort in talking through these events and issues with my counsellor. I was beginning to be unrecognizable to myself; who was this mature, soon-to-be married person? A confident, happy, strong woman, that's who.

Sadly, my dad wasn't the only one who gave us a rough time for having our wedding in Puerto Vallarta and made our wedding about themselves instead.

My future brother-in-law made Brad feel so guilty for having a destination wedding that I didn't know whether their relationship would survive. In the end, he came to our wedding and showed us support in his own way, but the road to the wedding was littered with multiple discussions between them about his disappointment regarding our wedding and what he saw as our selfishness. He repeatedly listed the reasons why he didn't want to come or why he wasn't going to make it. It wasn't unlike how he justifies everything else extravagant and materialistic in his life. It was selfishly ironic, really. There would have been no hard feelings if anyone in our family had not been able to make it to our wedding. It would have been easier to hear, "hey, we can't come" as opposed to hearing the reasons why they thought we shouldn't expect them to come. Our sister-in-law and nephews were not in attendance and neither Brad nor I hold that against them in the least. It was almost worse that my brother-in-law chose to show up, cause numerous drunken scenes and mope around because he missed his family at our wedding. I don't remember him being able to muster any words of congratulations, never mind give a speech at his only brother's wedding. Instead he spent hours at our reception standing alone in the ocean (in protest?) because he was sad and missed his family. At least my dad stayed home.

Then there were my future in-laws. When it came to his parents, Brad had to basically fight tooth and nail to get them to admit their disappointment in our choice of wedding venue. And while it didn't stop them from being there for us, it definitely did not stop them from bitching about it either. I get it; people tend to actively care more about themselves than others, even family. Brad's dad was upset that his mom wouldn't be able to come to our wedding, but it's not on Brad or I to make sure that certain people can be in attendance at our wedding. It's. Not. About. Them. Try and tell them that. We just had to remind ourselves repeatedly that we were doing what we wanted to do to celebrate our big day in a way that was most meaningful to us. It didn't mean we loved anyone any less because we weren't doing what they wanted. We were just putting ourselves and our marriage first.

During the year and a half that we were engaged, Brad and I had plenty of time to save and prepare for not only our big day, but also our big trip. There were never any feelings of being rushed while planning and I had plenty of time to create handmade invitations, thank you cards, place holders, tags for the wedding favours and bags for all of our guests. I loved being able to get creative and put thought into making not only our big day, but also everyone's trip, a little more special. I know that everyone who made it to our wedding went out of their way, both directionally and financially, but it wasn't our intention to put pressure on anyone to come. We included a message in our invitations that said that people's presents to us would be their presence, whether in person or in spirit. For those people whom we knew wouldn't be able to come, we sent along another note to acknowledge that we knew they wouldn't be coming, but we wanted them to have an invitation to signify how special they were to us.

Early in the new year—the year that Brad and I would become husband and wife—my mom came to visit us. The holidays had been awkward, to say the least. My parents had gone to Hawaii for Christmas (yes, another trip to the country my dad hates) and were in the Lower Mainland twice on their way to and from their vacation. I still hadn't spoken to my dad, but my mom failed to let me know that they were even coming to town until after they were already back in PG. I let her know how much her actions hurt my feelings, she apologized and we left it at that. I took care of myself and had to be okay with just that.

My mom planned her visit for a weekend, so we were able to go shopping and spend some time together during a day when I wasn't working. When we got back following an afternoon out together, Brad welcomed us home.

"So, ladies, how was your big day out?"

"It was pretty great!" I said, giving him a hug and a kiss. "I tried on a wedding dress for the first time!"

"You did!?" He was genuinely excited.

"Ya. I didn't find *the one* but I think I found a style that I like."

"That's nice that you were able to go while your mom was here!" We had planned on shopping when we went out, but trying on wedding dresses was a spur of the moment thing. "You must have been excited, Sandy?"

"Yes," my mom giggled. "She looked beautiful in everything!"

"I'm sure she did!" Brad agreed.

"Which is nice," I replied. "But not exactly helpful to narrow it down."

We all laughed.

After dinner, we were sitting in the living room, chatting. My mom seemed to get quiet, but I'm sure I'm the only one that noticed because when I asked her, it piqued Brad's interest as well.

"Is everything okay, mom?"

"Oh, I'm fine."

Her automatic response to everything. This was going to take a bit of digging.

"Are you sure?" I asked her. "You seem a bit quiet. Weren't you happy that we were able to go dress shopping together today?"

"It's not that, Anya," she said. She was willing to open up; I could work with this.

"What's going on?"

She hesitated. "It's just that it's really hard looking forward to your wedding when your dad isn't going."

Brad and I sat on the couch together, waiting for her to continue the conversation.

"I'm really sad," she said. "And I don't want you to be mad at me."

"I'm not mad at you," I replied. I was still angry at my dad. I found it difficult, though not impossible, to sympathize with her, but I didn't blame her for my dad's actions. "We don't blame you for what he does."

My mom started to cry, which was her usual reaction in difficult conversations. I was surprised she had already said as much as she had.

"He makes me so happy. We've had great trips lately. I just wish that he would stop being so stubborn and come to the wedding," she said.

We all sat together in our living room quietly. An uneasy feeling passed between us before things took a turn.

"Do you think I should leave him over all this, Anya?"

I hesitated. I wanted to think carefully before responding but

Brad got there first. "Our opinions about that don't matter. We will support you in whatever you want to do."

"You have to make that kind of decision on your own, Mom," I told her sincerely, agreeing with Brad. The wedding drama wasn't reason enough for her to leave him. And then a part of me didn't really want my parents to separate. Either way, it wasn't my place to tell her what to do. It never has been.

She broke down even further, holding her head in her hands while she cried. I got up to give her a hug.

I thought she had settled down a bit but as I sat back down she said, "If it wasn't for you, I would have committed suicide. I just don't have anything else to live for."

I was in shock, though the severity of a comment like that didn't hit me with its full force right away. Even now, I didn't know what to say.

She started to cry even harder.

Brad and I sat there, motionless. I looked over at him and could tell that he felt the same way I did. How the fuck was saying something like that beneficial to anyone? Never mind your own daughter.

In one breath she was saying how much she loves my dad and how happy he makes her and then she tells me she would've killed herself if it wasn't for me? Her logic didn't make any sense, and neither did her telling me something like that. What was I supposed to do? What was I supposed to think or feel? I cannot imagine a scenario in which a child should carry that sort of burden or even know about it. I was lost, but thankfully I didn't have to reply.

My mom continued, "I just don't know what to do."

"We can't tell you what to do, Mom," I told her. There's no way I would even try.

She had calmed herself down somewhat when she realized that neither Brad nor I were going to tell her what to do.

"Have you ever thought about going to talk to someone about all this?" I asked her.

"What do you mean? Like a counsellor or something?"

"Yes. I see someone," I told her. "The same person I talk to about Rachael."

"Oh. Well, I tried to talk to someone once, you know. I didn't find it helpful."

"You have to be open about talking to them about everything," I explained. "I think it would be really helpful for you to have someone impartial to get some advice from. About how to deal with how you're feeling."

"I'll try, Anya. I promise."

"Okay," I said. "We're not going anywhere. You know that, right?"

"I do." She was starting to tear up again. "Thank you, sweetie."

Brad and I got up and pulled her into a big hug together. I didn't know what else to do or say, but we transitioned easily into a card game and didn't talk about it any further.

After she went to bed, I asked Brad if he thought she would actually cause herself any harm.

"No," he said. "I honestly don't."

"Okay. Good. I don't think so either. But if she was likely to, we should definitely tell someone in PG."

"Like who?"

"I don't know. But it doesn't matter because she said she would talk to someone about it."

"Do you really think that she will?"

"No."

We left it at that.

As the wedding approached, so did the traditional celebrations. I really didn't want to have a bridal shower. Brad and I had been living together for years at this point and whenever we needed or wanted anything for our household, we went out and purchased it for ourselves. I have never been overly materialistic and really didn't want to be in a situation where the point was basically to shower the bride-to-be with gifts. When my mom insisted on throwing me a shower, I agreed as long as she wrote on the invitations that I had requested no gifts. Of course, only one person actually listened to that request, but it made me feel better to have it out there that I was requesting presence over presents. We did the same thing on our wedding invitations, knowing it was mostly for our peace of mind and that people were going to do whatever they wanted to do as far as gifts were concerned.

My mom drove down from Prince George for my shower and surprised me by bringing along my Auntie Laura, who had said she wasn't going to be able to make it. I wore a pretty dress and had my hair blown out for the first (and only!) time in my life. My mom had arranged tea at the Wedgewood hotel in Vancouver, which was pretty fancy! It was a mix of my friends, a work colleague and my mom and aunt. My mom did a lovely job planning and even had gifts and games, which I would have also skipped if it were up to me. (I think we both know by now that I tend to go against the grain when it comes to traditions.)

I asked Ashley, who was coming to Mexico with us, and Becky and Jaimie, who weren't, to plan my stagette. The event ended up being the same September weekend as Brad's stag. It was nice for me to have something to do while he was gone. I spent a couple of nights alone at the house while Brad was away before my girlfriends picked me up at our place. I was told to bring an outfit that I would wear for a night out in Mexico as well as an overnight bag. We drove up in a decorated car, listening to a homemade CD of wedding and love songs. We rocked out to tunes, enjoyed some road pops and drove north to Whistler where we spent the night with seven of my closest friends.

The girls did such a lovely job planning. They had a potluck of appies, drinks and games and had decorations put up in the hotel where we stayed. I am sure that they expected me to have a moment of missing you, if not several, regardless of where we went. And their expectations were fulfilled.

I had a few too many drinks before we even left for dinner and I regret a) how drunk I got and b) the unfortunate hairstyle I gave myself before we went out.

"Are you just about ready?" Becky poked her head into my room to ask.

"Yes," I said. "Just finishing my hair."

If only I could rewind time and ask her to help. No?

I walked out of my room and saw that one of the girls was wearing jeans tucked into flat boots.

"Your dress is cute!" she said.

I was too distracted; I wasn't usually the type to wear heels, but we were supposed to be dressing up. "Well, if you're wearing flats, I'm wearing flats, too!"

I came back out of my room in flat black shoes. When Becky spotted me, she gave me a hard time. "Where are your pumps? They looked so good!"

"Let's be real," I said. "I want to be comfortable and it's probably safer for me not to balance any higher than I need to be."

They laughed.

"Is everyone ready?" Becky asked the room. Everyone had reconvened in our living room, all dressed up and ready for a great night out.

"We're going to GLC for dinner," Becky told me as we all left the hotel.

"Awesome!" I said as we walked the chilly streets of Whistler Village. It was nearing the end of September, the crisp air suggesting that the snow was not far off.

We got to the restaurant and were seated at a table near the back, beside the dance floor.

"Have I had too much to drink," I started after everyone had been delivered their drink orders, "or are those miniature sand buckets?"

The girls laughed.

"It's the drink specials!" Rebecca told me. She was sharing with flat boots and jeans girl.

I ordered a burger to share, but no one really kept an eye on how much I was eating. I placed my hand on the table as I stood to go over to the washroom. "Woah."

"I'll come with you," my friend Tina told me, putting a hand out just in case.

"Thanks!" I may have been wobbly, but I was feeling excellent.

I went into one of the stalls, forgetting to lock the door in my inebriated state.

Bam! "Ouch!" I yelled from the stall. Someone had tried to open the unlocked door to my stall while I was in there and the door had slammed into my forehead.

"Are you okay?" Tina called from outside.

"All good," I said as I came out to wash my hands.

I turned to her. "I'm so glad you're here!"

"Aww, thanks," Tina said. "I wouldn't have missed it for the world."

We got back to the table and were waiting for the girls to settle the bill when I started to feel sick.

"I don't think I feel so good," I said to anyone who was listening.

No one said anything. I didn't manage to say anything else before I leaned over under the high-top table and got sick for the first time that evening.

"Let's go," Becky said to me, all business once I was done. "Before they come around again and see that it was us!"

I went outside with Becky and Jaimie while everyone else gathered their coats. It was there, hit abruptly by the chilly air, feeling vulnerable after having been sick, that I began to cry for you. With my closest friends nearby and my senses swimming in cocktails, I finally let myself remember that you weren't there with us. And why.

I remember Jaimie rubbing my back as I cried.

"It's okay," Becky reassured me.

Everyone else slowly made their way outside. They stood with us; no one was talking much but I was so grateful that they were there for me.

"It's not fair," I cried softly.

"It's okay," Becky said again. "It was bound to happen. It'll be okay."

I tried to stop the tears. I didn't want this evening to be about sadness. You wouldn't have wanted that for me.

I can't begin to describe what it was like not having you there. As I stood there and allowed myself to miss you, my heart ached immensely.

"Alright," I said as I straightened up. "Let's go."

I wiped my eyes and lead the charge down the stairs to the village walk.

"Ready to dance?" Becky asked with a smile.

"You bet!" I said. "Though I don't think I should have much more to drink, just between you and me."

"Okay," she said with a laugh.

It came as no surprise to anybody when I *did*, in fact, have more to drink. And it came as even less of a surprise that I didn't handle my liquor all that well that night. I was usually much more responsible, drinking plenty of water and eating properly in prep for a night out. But this time it was different. I allowed myself to go with the flow, to let loose and do what I wanted without actually thinking about it. For one night, I didn't want any responsibility. I didn't want to have to care that I was going to feel like crap the next day, or that I would be sick in the middle of the night. Or under a table in public. I let my friends take care of me and I set out to have a great time.

And that I did. We made it to the club, danced a bit and drank much more. I wasn't able to stay long but I was there long enough to get a lap dance by a random stranger, have more drinks and sadly pose for pictures.

"I think I'm ready to go home," I told the girls.

"I'll take you back," Becky said.

"I'll come, too," Tina said. The other girls stayed behind to party; I was glad. They were all there to have a good time, too. And they deserved it, even if I couldn't manage to stay past midnight. Or eleven. I can't remember.

The three of us left the club. My memories are a bit foggy, but I appreciated the company. They took me back to my room and made sure I was snug in bed before returning to their rooms.

I woke groggily in the middle of the night. I rolled myself out of bed towards the bathroom. I didn't think my roommate had come to bed yet so I crawled straight over top of her bed, the shortest path to the bathroom. I felt a hard lump under the blankets and heard her moan. I didn't have time to stop and apologize before I scraped myself to the bathroom. I hung out in there for a bit, just in case, and when I came back to our room, she was fast asleep. Leave it to me to room with the only person who wasn't going to wake up and help me take care of myself.

I crawled back into my bed and was just pulling the covers up when she sat up in her bed.

"Are you okay?" she asked, her covers going flying as she popped out of bed. "Let me get you a glass of water."

I take it back. Even in her state, in the middle of the night, she got up to help take care of me. I was so grateful for my friends.

I woke up the next morning to find the other girls tidying up our shared living area.

"How are you doing?" Ashley asked as I curled up on the couch.

"I have definitely felt better," I said. And before I could ask, she brought me a glass of water. "Thanks."

"No problem. Did we wake you up when we got back last night?"

"No, why?"

"We made snacks and were hanging out in here after the club!" she said with a laugh. "I'm surprised but glad we didn't wake you."

"I think I was out," I said. "I had a little too much fun."

"No such thing!" She sat next to me. "Do you want to go for breakfast somewhere before we all head home?"

"That would be nice," I replied, considering to myself whether food was going to happen anytime soon. I decided it was a good idea to eat something, so we stopped at the White Spot on our way out of town. I felt so special that weekend to have my girls there to celebrate my last hurrah before becoming an old married lady.

The girls dropped me off at home, where I promptly curled up onto the couch under a blanket and did not move until Brad came home late that night. I peered up at him, not even bothering to stand and say hi, even though we hadn't seen each other in four days.

"Hey babe," he said. "How you doing?"

"I've been better," I admitted. "You?"

"I have officially been run over by a truck."

"Sounds familiar."

"What!?" He took a seat next to me on the couch. "You? Hungover?"

"Yup."

"I don't even believe it!" He was clearly feeling well enough to tease me. "You must have had some night out!"

"It was fun," I told him. "But this is what happens when I let loose."

I moved to rest my head on his chest and we stayed like that while the ending to *Dirty Dancing* played in the background and we caught up on our special weekends away.

"Our friends did good," he said.

"Yes, they did."

"More people have RSVP'd from your side than mine," Brad told me one day during the last approach to the wedding.

"Aww! But half of the people are our friends together!" I pointed out to him. "Don't feel bad about it!"

"But more of your family is coming than mine."

I couldn't tell if he was sad about that or not. "But we don't have much to do with any of them. Your extended family or mine!"

"True."

"Julie did just tell me that she is going to make it after all," I told him, of my cousin.

"See!"

"I really don't think you should feel bad about that, Brad."

"That's actually really nice that Julie is going to come. You guys used to be so close."

"Yes, I'm really glad she's coming. I'm thinking I might ask her to sign as my witness at the ceremony."

"That'll be really nice, babe."

"Have you given any more thought to who you want to sign for you?"

"Probably my brother. Makes most sense." He shrugged. "Ruffles the least amount of feathers."

"Ya."

"I think we've finally gotten past his being upset at having to come to Mexico for the wedding. At least I hope so."

"That's good, Brad, I'm glad. I didn't know what was going to happen between you guys there for a while."

"Ya. Me neither."

"That brings me to another point that we haven't really discussed lately. Who are we getting to come over to sign the papers with us when Hugo is here?"

Brad and I had been taking marriage counselling with Hugo, the father of one of his childhood best friends, who is a minister.

Hugo married Brad's brother and his wife and since Brad and I wanted to get legally married in Canada before going to Mexico for the wedding, he sought out Hugo, who lived in a nearby town with his wife.

"Well," he sighed. "We talked about having someone over who isn't able to make it to the wedding but has really been there for us."

"Ya..."

"You had mentioned Jenny and Lawrence?" Brad reminded me, referring to some dear friends of ours.

"I think that's a great idea. I'm sure they'd be honoured."

"I talked to my mom about that again the other night." He sighed again.

"Uh oh..." I said. "Why do I feel like you're going to tell me you had the same conversation with her that I had with my mom?"

"Because I probably am."

"She told you she was upset that we were getting legally married here?" I prodded.

"You got it," he said with another big sigh. "I just don't understand why the legalities of it matter so much to them. Well, I get it, I guess, but to make us feel guilty about something that we've already decided is just so awful. Especially this close to the wedding."

"I totally agree." I nodded. "My mom even went as far as to tell me how disappointed my aunt and uncle would be if they found out that we weren't getting legally married at the wedding."

"Huh. No one is stopping to think about what we want, or what's best for us."

"Nope."

"They don't even know that we're signing our papers on Rachael's birthday. To honour her. In a way."

"It wouldn't matter even if we told them, Brad," I said quietly. "They're all making the trip to see us stand up in front of our family and friends and profess our love for each other and exchange our vows. I don't know why it matters when we sign the papers."

"It doesn't matter that it's easier for us either."

"Nah. Part of me feels like we should look into the details of getting legally married there, just to get them off our backs."

"Since when do we do anything just to make other people happy?" He looped his arm around me. He had a point.

Just then, my phone started ringing, surprising me. I had already spoken to my mom earlier in the week before she left for Puerto Vallarta with my aunts. I pulled away from Brad and grabbed my phone.

"Weird," I said to Brad. "I'll just take this in our room. It's my mom's number."

"Hello?" I answered cautiously.

"Hi kid," my dad said.

"Hi."

He had called me. I waited for him to do the talking.

"I know I'm not going to your wedding," he said. "But I want you to know that I love you and support you and Brad. Together."

I was shocked. "Wow. Thanks, Dad."

"Is that okay then?"

"Ya," I told him. I guess it was.

Our friends Barry and Kelsey picked us up on our way to the airport early in the morning on the day that we left for Mexico. There we met our friends Scott and Rebecca, who brought her mom and their only son at the time, Kael. Her mom would watch Kael for them during the wedding. Barry and Kelsey left their son, Matthew, with their family back home, so it was an even more special trip for them to get away together and meant even more to us that they were making the trip.

My mom and aunties Bernie and Laura spent the week before the wedding in Puerto Vallarta on a girls' trip before joining us all at the resort for our wedding week. My cousin Julie came with her parents, Auntie Kelly and Uncle Steven, from Prince George. They were on a direct flight from PG with Brad's parents and brother as well as his cousin Scott and my cousin Kevin. Your parents also came from PG, but they detoured to Mexico City following the wedding so I am not sure if they were on the same fight as everyone else. Brad's cousin Danielle came from Alberta, as did his friend Joe. Brad's high school friend Lylah came from Victoria. It was the first time I met her so it was even more meaningful that she made the trip for our wedding! Our friends Ashley and Richard came from Vancouver; Richard was starting out his wedding photography business so we hired him to take our wedding pictures for us. Rounding out the group was a friend of my parents who lived in Puerto Vallarta and his wife. It was a lovely addition to have them there. I have known Jose for years, ever since he befriended my dad when he first started visiting Puerto Vallarta.

It was a lot of fun to have a group of our closest loved ones together at a lovely all-inclusive resort. On the first night, the drinks flowed, the mouths flowed perhaps a bit too much, and everyone bonded and got to know each other better. I definitely let myself have too much to drink, which I'm beginning to think you're not going to believe that I don't do that often any more.

"Kelseyyyyy," I said as I slung my arm around her. She stood next to me, a drink in her other hand.

"Anya!" she replied, just as drink-happy as me.

"You know…" I leaned in. "I totally love ya, girl. And I'm so glad that you and Barry are here!"

"Me, too!"

"And," I drunkenly went on, "I have to tell you, I always thought that you and I would make out some time!"

She laughed. "Maybe later!"

We were standing there together, laughing and smiling, when Brad's brother walked past. I reached out to bring him into our hug and he backed away, out of my reach.

"Oh well," I said with a roll of my eyes. "You don't love me anyways!" I was joking but obviously felt something along those lines deep down or I wouldn't have said it. Gerry walked away, not saying anything to me in return. Shortly after that interaction Brad took me to our room to put me to bed.

The next day, we all relaxed together in and around the pool.

It was nice having such a big group of friends staying together at the same resort. You never had to go too far to see someone you knew.

By the afternoon, we were all feeling pretty good, some more than others. I was walking back to our pool chairs from the snack bar when Gerry stopped me.

"Anya," he said as he pulled me aside. "Let me talk to you."

"Okay," I said. I was a bit surprised but I could tell that he had been drinking, a lot, so I appeased him.

"You know, it really hurt my feelings what you said last night."

"And what was that?" I asked. My memories of the previous night were a little fuzzy.

"You said that I don't love you," he slurred. "And that's not true."

Right. That.

"Okay," I said. I was kind of at a loss.

"I'm always the one to stand up for you guys, for Brad," he went on. "And it's really unfair that you think I don't love you. I love Brad and that means that I love you."

Does it? I wasn't really following what he was trying to say, but it seemed like he was being…nice?

"Okay," I said again. My go-to word. He didn't seem to notice that that's all I said in response. This conversation wasn't actually about me at all anyways.

"And I'm here, and I came without my family," he kept going. "And I just love Brad so much. I'm always the one to stand up for you guys."

I really had no idea what he was going on about but he had

started to cry. He was even further gone than I initially thought.

"I'm so happy for Brad. He's happy!"

"Yes, he is." I chuckled. "I'm happy for him, too."

"So, we're good?"

Sure, Gerry. "We're good." Not an actual word of an apology, or anything to make me feel like he actually cares about me as a person, but he was happy for Brad. And he was there for Brad, which was what mattered the most.

It's hard not to think he was being sincere, what with the tears and all. But he had a lot of liquid courage before he talked to me, so the conversation wasn't really sitting well with me. That's just the way it is with him, I've learned.

There was only one thing that I would have done differently during our wedding week if I could do it all over again, and that would have been the night before our wedding. Brad and I had planned on spending the night together before going our separate ways early in morning on the day of the wedding when I left with my mom and aunts to spend the day at the beach at Las Caletas.

My future mother-in-law, however, had other ideas.

"You can't spend the night before the wedding together," she said to us when we mentioned going back to our room for the night.

"Well, that's what we were planning on doing, Ma," Brad told her.

"You can't!" She said as if it was final. Turns out it was, but it shouldn't have been.

I just stared at Brad. It was his mom. He should tell her our plan and that should be that. Shouldn't it?

"But..." he tried. I'll give him that. He did try.

"You're staying with us!" she told Brad. I'd like to think there was more to that conversation, but there really wasn't. Brad walked me back to our room when it was time to turn in.

"I can't believe you aren't staying with me tonight," I told him. I was angry, but I was trying really, really hard not to be.

"What did you want me to do?" he said as he gathered a few things to take with him for the night. "You heard her!"

"Ya, I did."

"What's that supposed to mean?"

We've all had those arguments.

"It means that you should have told her no!" I exclaimed.

"Sure. And then what?"

"Then we would spend the night together as planned and wake up next to each other on the day we're getting married."

"It's not that I don't want that, Anya," Brad tried to explain.

"I know," I said and, in an effort to keep the peace with the family I was marrying into, I said good night to my groom-to-be and spent the night that we were supposed to spend excitedly together alone. He and I would be alright and I did get it. Brad didn't want to disrupt the peace. He spent a lot of our first week in Mexico trying to make sure that everyone else was having a good time, so I understood why he gave in and listened to his mom.

On the morning of our wedding, I spent a lonely time getting ready before heading over to my mom's room to catch our cab to the marina, where we would hop on a boat to our destination. I had a hard time getting excited by myself. Brad was supposed to be with me on our special day and his absence made your absence even more obvious.

Before leaving my room, I walked out onto the patio overlooking the resort, still quiet with the sleep of its guests. I watched the calm blue of the water in front of me and I pushed my sad feelings aside in an effort to not be a miserable mess, crying alone on the morning of my wedding. I carried you with me, close to my heart, for the rest of the day.

Typically, the bridal party would join the bride at the beach for the morning of the wedding. There hadn't been anyone else in my life who was special enough to be my bridesmaid, so Brad and I had chosen not to have a wedding party. We also didn't want to put pressure on anyone to come to Mexico just because we asked them to be part of our big day. Instead, I asked my mom and aunts to join me for the day.

The boat ride over to Las Caletas was exciting. The sun was out and there was already a warm breeze coming off of the ocean. We were on a catamaran with a group of people who were spending the day at the same beach. They were there for lunch, swimming and other activities and would be heading home in the afternoon before the beach was prepared for our wedding. The atmosphere was exciting as we departed the marina, all ready for the beauty that the day had in store.

The staff at Las Caletas greeted us, waving in unison from shore as we approached the dock. They sent a parrot out from the beach to the boat to greet us; it glided over the crowd of people on the boat and thankfully avoided flying directly over my head. My love for birds runs deep. And by love I mean whatever word expresses true hatred. And by deep, I mean terrifyingly so.

We disembarked and as we walked across the dock I looked for the sand of the beach where in a few short hours Brad and I would be married. The group of tourists were led one way and Bernie, Laura, my mom, and I were taken up through the trees to a little casita. The earthy walkway leads back and forth up and downhill. You could glimpse the ocean through the trees and hear the waves crash below. When we got to the top, the path split along some buildings. We took the right path. The left one lead to the spa and the area where Brad would get ready when he arrived later on.

The casita was full of character. It was basically one large room with massive windows open to welcome the breeze off the ocean. There was a couch, a bed and an area with a big counter and mirrors where I got my makeup done. Then there was a funky tiled washroom with a shower and out back there was a spot in the shade where a hammock whispered my name, encouraging me to climb in, relax and stay awhile. I did, of course, and was laying there when the team came to do my hair and makeup. But first, we had our choice of things to do to pass the time and enjoy our day. We opened a bottle of sparkling wine and snacked on some fresh fruit before heading back towards the dock for lunch. Celebrations were getting underway with the women in my life who were most important to me. I went back down the trail to take a minute to myself and found a beach chair sitting beside the path. I sat for a minute and welcomed my thoughts. I was going to become Brad's wife in front of our family and friends on the beach just down the hill from that very spot. Happiness was in every crevice of my existence and yet I also felt strangely calm.

When my aunties and I went down to the beach after lunch, my mom didn't join us. She said that she wasn't feeling well and chose to rest. She thought that she must have gotten sick from something she ate or drank, but I honestly have a hard time believing that. She has been to Mexico as well as numerous other countries all over the world countless times and as far as I'm aware, she has never gotten sick. Not to mention I don't remember her looking sick at all and she's usually the type to wear her emotions all over her face. If I had to guess, I'd say that she was worried that my dad's absence would somehow rear its ugly head and dampen my spirits on our special day. Or she was just plain sad that he wasn't there for her on this day either, when their only daughter together was getting married. I'll never know, as I was too busy relaxing and having a good time to ask, but she didn't drink and hardly ate a single bite all day. I don't think she would ever admit it to even herself, but something tells me that she wasn't suffering from any form of food poisoning.

Bernie, Laura and I continued our relaxing adventure and went down to see the wedding beach and take a swim. The water was more beautiful than any I'd ever seen up close, so we all dove in and swam out to a small dock. I stood on the dock, the gentle sway of the ocean comforting me. As I looked out over the clear ocean water at our beach, I realized that my dreams were coming true. I was about to marry my soulmate, my best friend. We had so many of our important people there to support us and have a great time celebrating our union. I was so thankful and felt an insane happiness from deep within.

We went back to the bridal casita where I showered and then went out back to relax in the hammock. I feel like not many brides can say that they napped on their wedding day, and certainly not on a hammock near the beach. I was completely blissed out when it came time to do my hair and makeup. I don't remember ever being so pampered. I brought pictures for inspiration for my look, but the hair/makeup artist didn't speak great English and didn't follow my pictures at all. I must say; I am glad that he didn't! My makeup looked awesome in pictures and stayed put all night. He put even more makeup on my face than I had ever worn in my life. My hair was also very different from the pictures; he put it all up, which I hadn't thought I wanted, but I am grateful that he did it. It was so hot that day and night, I would have suffered even more in the heat if I had had my hair stuck to my neck and back. It was falling out of its style by the end of the night, but that was more because of the dancing than anything else.

"You look beautiful," my mom said to me as the finishing touches were put on my hair.

"Thanks," I said, smiling up at her. "I think it's a good thing that he put my hair up. It's so hot."

"Hello??" Someone called from just outside the casita. It was Richard and Ashley.

"Hi!" I said. "Back here!"

Richard came around the corner, camera in hand already, and started snapping pictures.

It was so good to see them; it meant that Brad was there, too.

"Don't mind me!" Richard said. He did such a great job for us, blending so well into the background.

"Hi," Ashley waved from across the room.

"Hi!" I said with a big smile. My cheeks were already beginning to hurt from all the smiling and we hadn't even started taking pictures yet.

"They took Brad to another spot to get ready," she said. "In case you were wondering."

"Great!" I said. "How was the boat ride?"

"Choppy," she said with a laugh. "It was a small boat. But I'm glad I got to come over with the boys!"

"Me, too! It's really nice to have you here."

We planned to get pictures done before the ceremony to take the pressure off and not have to race the setting sun after we said our I-dos. It was extremely hot that day and there wasn't much of a breeze to relieve us of the humid weather.

"Shall I get into my dress?" I asked Richard once my hair and makeup were complete.

"Yup!" he said with enthusiasm. "I'll go see if Brad's ready."

When just the girls were left, we took my dress down from its hanger. Richard had taken some pictures of it hanging from the rafters and in the windows of the casita.

My mom helped me step into it and carefully laced up the back for me. Her hands were shaking as she said, "I'm not sure how tight to pull it."

"As tight as you can!" I said with a laugh. Laura stepped in to help her.

"All clear for a boy to come in?" Richard called through from the door.

"Everyone is decent!" I replied as I stepped in front of a giant industrial fan and lifted my dress to allow for some breeze on my legs.

He came in and got to work. He took some candid photographs of my mom and aunts as they finished lacing up my dress, and of me alone around the casita before Brad joined us.

"How about you stand in the window?" Richard suggested. "We'll close the shutters and get Brad to come and stand outside. Then he can turn to see you in the window for your first look!"

I did as I was told, pulling the shutters closed in front of me. I heard Richard and Brad talking to each other, Richard giving Brad his instructions for where to stand.

"Alright," Richard said through the window. "All set to open the shutters!"

I pushed the shutters open and saw Brad standing there with his back to me. My smile felt permanent.

"Go ahead and turn around, Brad," Richard instructed.

In that moment when my groom turned to me, I felt a calming happiness radiating through my smile. I could see only him, for all the beauty of the world around us. He looked up at me, smiling back at me, and he started to cry. "You look amazing," he said.

"Don't start crying already!" I said as I reached out to take his face gently between my hands. He leaned in and gave me the most romantic kiss. Richard took some more pictures and then suggested that I come outside.

I walked out of the casita to where Brad was standing. He

gave me a big hug along with another kiss.

"You look so beautiful."

"Thanks. You're looking pretty sharp, yourself."

We took pictures all around the casita and amongst the tropical trees and along the pathway to the lunch area. Then we went to the beach and got some really cool shots in the sand, rocks and waves. By this time, the staff was preparing for the wedding, so they were blasting music while they worked. We danced and laughed and by the end of our session, our cheeks hurt from smiling. I went back up to the casita, where my mom and aunts had finished getting ready. Brad went to greet the remaining guests as they arrived on their boat. Shortly after that I was left on my own for the last few minutes before the ceremony.

The next time I would see Brad, I would be walking down the aisle to him in the minutes before he became my husband. We had known each other for four years, give or take only a couple of days, and we were about to pledge our love and commitment to one another in front of our family and friends. We had been planning this day, these moments, for well over a year and had been looking forward to them for a lifetime. I was always in doubt that I would ever find my soul mate, someone to marry me. I didn't want to hope for my person only to never find him and spend my life alone. But there he was. We were in the country where the stars had aligned for us to meet for the first time, ready to begin our forever.

Our wedding coordinator let me know it was time. I started walking down the hill, following her in the opposite direction from where we had arrived, hours before. When we got to the top of the stone steps that lead down to the beach, she stepped aside for me to continue on my own. I wanted to look at our guests, but like most people in important outfits, on important days, I was more focused on not tripping or falling down the stairs. When I got to the bottom, I glanced up, my eyes finding Brad at the end of the aisle. I could feel the love pouring out from everyone around us, but my eyes only saw his. I looked up as I reached the aisle between our guests and saw Kelsey, crying her eyes out. I saw our parents on either side of the aisle, and I saw the beautiful arch we stood beneath to say our vows.

As I walked forward through the sand while Ben Harper's "Diamonds on the Inside" guided my way, my eyes locked again with Brad's. Just like that night shortly after we first met, I saw my soul reflected back at me deep in his beautiful brown eyes. It felt as if we had come full circle; there was nowhere else I would have chosen for us to stand in front of our loved ones, laugh, cry, pledge our love to each other and finally become husband and wife.

Our ceremony was short and sweet—at least it was supposed to be. It passed in a flash to me; I enjoyed every minute. Julie and Gerry signed as our witnesses and we exchanged vows that we wrote ourselves in front of our family and friends.

After the morning alone and the unexpected ache to start my day, I didn't think of your absence with sadness but instead chose to honour you in special ways. My bouquet was made up of yellow lilies, your favourite colour and my favourite flower. We had a table with a couple of candles and a vase with a sunflower for you. And, of course, your parents were there.

Following the ceremony, we took pictures with everyone in

attendance before we all headed up for dinner.

"Psst," I said to my Auntie Laura before I sat down for dinner.

She looked up at me and said, "What's up sweetie?"

"Can you come here for a second?" I asked as I pulled her to the side near the dinner table. "I don't think I can sit down with my dress done up so tightly!"

She smiled and turned me around to help. "How's that?" she asked after she was able to loosen the back a bit.

I attempted to sit down in a nearby chair. "I think we're good! Thank you!"

How did no one at the bridal shop ask me to sit down in my dress so I would realize it couldn't be too tight if I wanted to comfortably sit? No harm done, I guess!

Since we didn't have a wedding party, no one was designated to give a speech. Brad's dad welcomed me to the family on behalf of his parents, and then my mom said a few words about how excited she was. When I say few, I mean it. She literally said, "Welcome to the family. I'm so happy!" and then giggled before handing off the microphone.

Brad's cousin Scott and our friend Barry each said some lovely words to us as well but I was most surprised when your parents stood together.

They told a story about how when they were at a wedding in Europe, the bride and groom each were presented with a clear shot, one of which was vodka and one was water. They each took a shot and it was said that whomever got the shot of vodka was going to be the boss of the marriage. Your mom and dad arranged for Brad and I to each take a shot, only this time one was tequila and the other was a non-alcoholic mix of something that looked like tequila.

When they presented us with the shots, I inspected them carefully, grabbing the one that I was sure wasn't the tequila.

Who was I kidding? Of course I'm the boss.

I got the shot of tequila!

It was just so lovely to have them there for us and it was even more special that they arranged their speech and the shots. They had always been part of my life growing up with you, and since you couldn't make it to the wedding, I was so grateful that they could be there.

Their speech wrapped up the events at the dinner table and everyone was encouraged to move back to the beach.

They had set up a bonfire next to the dancefloor on the beach where the ceremony had taken place. Chairs lined the dancefloor where we had our first dance (to a combination of two songs—"Thank You" by Led Zeppelin and "Better Together" by Jack Johnson). "Thank You" had been our song since the early days of our relationship when Brad asked me if I had any favourite truly romantic songs. He had this one, which states, "Til mountains crumble to the sea, there will still be you and me." Candles accented all of the stairs and pathways surrounding the beach, giving a gorgeous ambience for dancing and a few more pictures.

They had clearly hosted a wedding or two on this beach before; they were prepared with mini bottles of water and even passed around cold towels for us to cool down with. The waiter approached with a huge tray of white cloths that looked like they were steaming because their cool temperature was so shocking in the humid weather. It was such a relief! By this time, I had accepted that my sweaty dress was going to remain stuck to my legs, but it was nice to have a cold cloth to hold to my neck.

As a final surprise for our guests, we arranged for fire dancers to put on a show for us to end the night. They surrounded Brad and I as we clung to each other in the middle of the dance floor. They moved to the music with ease and managed not to light anyone on fire. They were professionals, but I was still scared for my dress.

On the boat ride home, I remember your mom resting her tired head on your dad's shoulder. It was a sweet moment between two beautiful people. It means the world to me that they travelled all that way to witness our vows; I hope they and you know that.

At the end of the day, Brad and I got the wedding of our dreams. We couldn't have asked for more. We decided to follow our hearts and let people think what they would, and I am so glad that we did. You can never please everyone. Even if we had chosen to get married at home or in PG, someone would have been unhappy with the event or something someone said or did. Myself included. It's just the way the world works.

All things in life are fluid, ever-changing and ever-growing. I feel that our relationship continues to be fluid; it changes the person I am becoming. Same with Brad. If we go forward together with love, we really can't go wrong. There will be bumps in the road, of course, but as long as we choose to find strength and support in each other, I know that we will make it.

Loving and missing you always,

Anya

Chapter Six

December 4, 2017

Dear Rachael,

I'm a mom! There's really no other way to share this news than to just come right out and say it. Brad and I created life... and we're working on the second one as we speak. I am constantly fascinated by the fact that we created this tiny human who makes us laugh and cry and yell and second guess what we're doing all within a five-minute span every day. Welcome to parenthood!

If you could see me now, it would make me even more proud than I already am when I take a step back to appreciate how hard this role is. Mothering is the most difficult thing I have ever done and is even in steep competition with the labour and delivery itself (which we'll get to later). There really isn't a guidebook to being a parent, though there are countless online resources, bloggers and authors who try their best to help you manage a teeny screaming, pooping, sleeping human while they (and you) learn to navigate this world. Based on my experience, you read it all, you listen to it all (whether solicited or unsolicited) and then you take it and run because your baby is nothing like any other baby who has ever lived. Note to self: remember this when number two arrives.

I don't think you and I had ever really talked with each other about having kids. I mean, come on, we were in our early twenties. Babies were FAR in the future for both of us. I had my first baby at 29 (two days before my 30th birthday, to be exact) and the little mister or miss in my belly is set to arrive at the age of 33 for me and 32 for Brad. I'm not entirely sure whether you ever actually wanted to have kids. I know you definitely got excited when we talked about other people having babies, we just didn't talk about it for us. If I had to guess, I'd say you'd be on the baby train eventually, on your own schedule and in your own way.

While the topic of your hypothetical children is up in the air, mine is not. There are set to be two of them. We waited to discover the genders of both, so we have one surprise left. I'd like to share with you this piece of me that was developed long after the last time I saw you. An unknown piece of me to you. Hell, it's a work in progress to me!

When Brad and I got married, I promised that if we ended up having babies in the first year of our marriage it would most definitely be a mistake. I wanted to be married for at least a year before expanding our family. I was even bold enough to say that to our friends when we were still on our wedding trip! But then that pesky little baby fever crept up from somewhere. Maybe I realized that I was turning 30 and clearly not getting any younger.

The day I decided to pee on a stick for the first time was September 12, 2013. Brad and I were living in Coquitlam in a rented two-bedroom basement suite. We had talked about buying a place and were saving for our down payment. Even though we hadn't started looking for our home we scoped out a neighbourhood of townhouses where we eventually bought our home. We got advice from some friends who candidly told us that there really is no "right time" to have a baby. They said if you cannot think of a good reason not to have a baby, there's no time like the present to throw caution to the wind. So we decided to let nature take its course. Voila, I was pregnant within a month of going off of birth control.

Now, I have never really been one to do things the usual way, so I dragged Brad along every step of the way through my pregnancies. We were doing our weekly grocery shop when I dead-stopped the cart in front of the pregnancy tests.

"I think we should get one of these," I said to Brad, pointing at the tests on the top shelf.

"Ya?" he replied. "There's a chance, is there?"

"Well ya. You've been there."

He laughed in response. "Kay."

"I could be late by a day or two," I told him as I grabbed a test and put it in the cart. "Or it could be something."

He stopped my hand before I was able to put the box in the cart.

"Might as well get that one," he said, pointing to a different box on the shelf. "It has two tests for pretty much the same price."

We got home, unpacked the groceries and proceeded to ignore the test for a couple of days.

Thursday rolled around and I finally brought it up to Brad. "I think I'm gonna try one of those tests tonight. I've gotten up the last two nights in a row to go to the bathroom."

"Kay."

"Which is weird."

"Kay."

"I'll do it after dinner," I said from the kitchen. "And don't say 'kay'."

He just laughed and kissed me on the cheek.

After dinner, I went into the washroom with the test. When I came back out, I set a timer on my phone.

"So?" said Brad.

"It's not that fast. It has to sit for a couple of minutes."

"Oh, okay. I didn't know."

"Neither did I!" We both laughed. "Plus, you're going to be with me when I look at the damn thing. I didn't do it all by myself, and this isn't going to be any different!"

"Haha, okay babe," he said as the timer went off. I silenced it and stepped towards the bathroom, where I had left the test.

I turned back and looked at Brad. "You go first."

"Okay," he said obligingly. He leaned over to look. "What does two lines mean?"

I glanced down at the box in my hands. "Holy shit!"

"Woah," Brad replied.

"You knocked me up!" I told him, skipping over to give him

a big hug.

We celebrated but we were both in shock.

Brad almost immediately dove into Papa Provider mode. "We should probably start looking at places to buy. I want to have more space, and our own place to bring a baby home to."

"Okay," I said. "Let's slow down!"

"Well, we could stay renting this place, but think about how nice it would be to already be living in the place where we want to raise our kids."

He was right. "How about we start looking around in the new year? It's only September so I'll be a few months along by then. And we'll be past the safe point to start telling people."

"The safe point?"

"The chance of having a miscarriage goes down after thirteen weeks or something," I explained. "Most people wait until after that to start sharing the news."

"Okay. So, you want to wait to tell anyone?"

"I think so." I wasn't really sure, but seeing that this was our first baby, I wanted to wait to share our news until we were sure that the baby was going to make it.

Some people say that a mom becomes a parent the day she gets the positive pregnancy test and a dad becomes a parent the day his baby is born. I never really felt like that. I was completely absorbed in the process that my body was going through and I knew that I was going to be a mom. But when Mother's Day 2014 came around, I didn't let Brad celebrate with me. I just didn't feel like I deserved it quite yet. I think that's because my first pregnancy was rather straightforward, so to speak. I was naive as to how trying pregnancy and parenthood can actually be and let me tell you, there have been a lot of days that I feel like I am paying for that naiveté through my current pregnancy. But nothing in life worth having is easy. I digress.

Shortly after we found out that I was pregnant, Brad and I watched the movie *The Business of Being Born*. It touched us in a way that I certainly never saw coming. We quite easily decided that we wanted to retain the services of a midwife to help us welcome our baby into this world in the most natural way possible.

We decided very early on that we were not going to share the details of our birth plan with many people. Nor were we going to share our baby names. The name that we used had been chosen before we even planned on trying for a baby! We agreed that we didn't want to open ourselves up to anyone's comments about our chosen name or birth plan. The fact that we were planning to have our baby in the comfort of our own home was bound to bring on a lot of negative, undereducated opinions. It was easier to answer the questions of where the baby would be born by saying which hospital our midwives had privileges at. It seemed to deflect the question effectively.

The first step in planning a home birth was to find a midwife who would support this decision. I do not remember how far along I was when I started calling around to the midwives in the Tri-Cities, but it was late by midwifery standards. I was able to find a local midwife that took me on as a patient and was very enthusiastic about supporting our home birth, and so our journey began.

Being that this was our first baby and my parents' first grandbaby, Brad and I decided to drive up to Prince George when we were ready to tell everyone that we were expecting. We managed the drive all the way into Vanderhoof from Coquitlam in one day. It was dark when we got there and, true to form, Brad decided to completely surprise his parents by walking up to their back deck, banging the door down and peeking into the small window at the top of the door.

I heard Brad's dad from the other side of the door. "It's Brad!" he said loudly.

"My boss?" I heard my mother-in-law say, referring to the employer who shared her youngest son's name.

The door swung open and Brad's dad pulled him into a big hug.

"What are you guys doing here?!" his parents asked.

"Well," Brad looked down at me after we had a chance to hug them hello. "We wanted to tell you in person that Anya is pregnant!"

"Eeeeeee!" Brad's mom shrieked. She threw her arms around Brad again. "That's so great! Congratulations!"

We all exchanged more hugs before settling into the living room to fill the first set of grandparents in on the baby details. Hope and excitement filled the room. Our trip north was worth it already.

The next day we drove into Prince George to continue to share our happy news with family. We managed to surprise my mom with our visit and our news over lunch at Earl's.

She was excited, of course, but I would be lying if I said she seemed overwhelmed in her reaction. Come on, lady! It's your first grandchild from your only child who has always told you she never wanted kids! (I figured that was easier than having to face the "when are you having babies" questions. I am positive that everyone saw through that, but it felt right at the time. Smooth, Anya.)

We bought her lunch and told her all about the baby before we headed to my Auntie Kelly's house to tell her our news as well. We walked into her house behind my mom, surprising her enough with our presence. She jumped up and down when we told her about the baby, and when I moved aside for Brad to give her a hug, I saw that my mom was crying. Not that I wanted her to cry, but that was more like the reaction I was expecting!

"I didn't want to cry in the restaurant!" she said in typical Mom fashion. Sheesh. Who cares what other people think! They're happy tears!

The rest of our trip was a blur. We went over to Brad's brother's place to surprise them, but his brother wasn't home. We pretended we were just in the neighbourhood with my sister-in-law, who I am sure saw right through it. And then when my brother-in-law came home, we shared our news. It was happiness all around! We returned home after a quick weekend trip and carried on, belly and excitement growing.

It was on the heels of this trip that I decided to make amends with my dad. It was too difficult to maintain a regular relationship with my mom if we weren't visiting at their house, or if I was barely even calling there in case he answered.

It was important to both Brad and I that our future baby be protected from what I experienced from my dad and his drinking.

Not only that, but I wanted to protect myself moving forward. I promised that I would no longer let him say rude things to me or Brad, demean me or make me feel guilty or ashamed of my life choices. We would welcome him back into our lives, but would leave at the sight of any unwelcome negativity or treatment. It's gone well so far, though I have had to stop conversations or stand up for myself on some occasions to protect my feelings and demand the respect from my dad that I deserve.

Brad and I stayed close to home for Christmas that year and in the new year we started looking for a place to live. It was easier said than done.

A few weeks into our search, we had increased our budget to our max and were losing hope. Our realtor had taken us to see all of the places in our price range that had come even close to meeting our criteria, when Brad miraculously found our home online. It had only just been posted to the realtor's website and wasn't even on the MLS website yet. We contacted our realtor right away and arranged a viewing for the next day. I left work early, and met Brad at the place, which was situated in the townhouse complex we had previously said we wanted to live in. Before we left the showing we had signed an offer to purchase at list price. We could have offered less, seeing that the home had barely hit the market, but we wanted the owners to know that we were serious.

We had to wait through the entire weekend to hear whether our offer was accepted as there were open houses scheduled for both Saturday and Sunday. We resisted visiting the open houses, but did visit "our place" just to look at it from the outside and dream. When the news came through that our offer had been accepted and that the owner was happy to choose a growing family to raise their child in the same house where he had raised his family, we knew we had found our home.

At one of our routine midwife appointments that spring, we started discussing my labour and birth in more detail.

"Have you thought about having a doula present at your birth?" our midwife asked. "Since you are planning on having a home birth?"

"No," I answered honestly. "I'm not sure what a doula is."

"A doula is a labour support person," she explained, "who is there for Mom during labour and delivery. She can help with breathing techniques, positioning during contractions and be there to help you manage your labour."

"That sounds great," I told her. "Do you have anyone you recommend, that you've worked with before?"

"Yes. I will give you her card so you can call and set up a meeting with her. To see if you get along."

"Thank you so much!" This side of labour and delivery was new to me. It's not exactly something you see in the movies. Brad and I agreed that it could be beneficial to have a doula with us for my labour, given that we were completely new to birth and labour and weren't going to have any other support persons present at the birth. We also didn't plan on taking a prenatal class, so this all made sense for us.

We met with our prospective doula at JJ Bean one rainy afternoon.

"It's so nice to meet you," she told us both as we sat down with a tea for me and a coffee for Brad. "Tell me, when are you due?"

"May 22," I told her.

"Okay," she said. "I am still accepting clients for May, so that's perfect. I'm not sure if your midwife explained to you that I am currently finishing my training as a doula, so I can offer you a lower rate for my doula services."

"That sounds great. Are you still going to school?"

"No, I'm finished school. Now I'm just working on completing certification hours."

"That sounds great," I nodded along.

"Our midwife recommended you; have you worked quite closely with her?" Brad asked.

"That's very nice to hear. I have attended a few births with her, but I didn't think we had worked that closely together," she said, followed by a light laugh.

She was friendly and her approach was warm. I felt very comfortable with her and it seemed to be a great fit.

"What sort of role do you usually have when it comes to labour?" I asked her.

"It really depends on what you're feeling when you are in labour. I can be as present as you need me, as long as I have a couple of hours to get child care together. I have two kids at home. I can come over and then leave again, or stay with you the whole time."

"That's great. What about postpartum?"

"I will stay with you once baby is born to help you breastfeed for the first time and do whatever else you might need. Then I will come to visit you at home once you've settled in with baby, or whenever you need me."

"Okay," I said. The help sounded like something I never knew I might need!

"And I am available for you at all times by email or text starting from when we decide to work together up until the postpartum visit," she added.

"Wow," Brad said. "That's awesome."

"Do you have any questions for me?" she asked.

"Yes," I told her. "I have a couple of things I wanted to say about myself as well."

"Go ahead," she encouraged me.

"I don't usually do very well at hiding my true emotions," I explained. "So I am not sure if I will be unkind at times during my labour. To put it mildly. I don't know how I'll handle it all."

She smiled. "That's okay, Anya. It's expected and happens more than you think. It's my job to be there for you, to support you through your emotions and encourage you to think positively about your labour and birth."

"That's great, thank you," I said. I looked over at Brad, feeling relieved. He smiled his approval at me encouragingly. "Where do we go from here?"

She went on to explain that since we were not attending any prenatal classes, she would come to our house twice prior to the birth to give us private lessons on birth and what to expect. It felt like a natural step for us towards the birth that we wanted for our first-born babe. Preparations were coming together and I was learning things about the birthing experience that I had never been aware of before. The team of women I was building would be there to help me bring our baby into this world. I felt at the time that they were on my side, to help me birth the way I wanted to. Little did I know, I needed more.

Baby number one was scheduled to arrive near the end of May. I worked up until two weeks before my due date, took some holidays and started my maternity leave right around the day baby was estimated to arrive.

Baby missed the memo.

I was told by my midwife that as soon as I hit the 37-week mark, which is considered "full term", baby could come at any time. I tried all of the "labour-inducing" techniques: I drank copious amounts of red raspberry leaf tea, I did all the things with evening primrose oil, ate all of the spicy foods morning, noon and night, "enjoyed" my husband (seriously, who really enjoys that when you're smuggling a massive, immovable beachball under your shirt that you don't want to squish?), got gloriously enticed into relaxation with acupuncture, bounced on a birthing ball, went for extra-long walks and tried to relax as much as pregnantly possible. My due date came and went. I actually had a midwife appointment on my due date and the midwife student told me to do something nice for myself that day, as this baby was not coming any time soon. How did no one tell me this sooner? I, as I am sure all of the other first-time moms believe, really thought that my baby would come at least near my due date. And yet, nine days later, there was still absolutely no sign of this baby making their entrance into the world.

I had an appointment at the nine-day post-due date mark.

"Well, Anya," my midwife told me as I sat beside Brad on the awkward and uncomfortable couch. "It doesn't look like this baby is ready to go anywhere any time soon."

I nodded. Brad took the reins. "What are our options?"

"Well," she said cautiously. "It is protocol to attend the hospital for another non-stress test." We had been to Royal Columbian Hospital in New Westminster for an ultrasound and monitoring a week past my due date to check and make sure the baby wasn't in any stress. "Everything was healthy so in the meantime, we can try to induce you naturally."

"What does that mean?" I asked.

"We can make a labour-inducing cocktail made with apricot nectar, almond butter, castor oil and verbena oil. You drink it twice and then contractions should start naturally following the second dose of the cocktail."

"When would we do that?" Brad asked.

"We could do it when you're comfortable. You could wait a few days, or take it soon. I would advise getting up early in the morning to take the first dose, then going back to bed and taking the second one an hour later."

"Okay," I nodded. This was the first time we had discussed any sort of induction. I needed time to process.

"And what about the day?" Brad asked. "Which day should she take it?"

"We'd like to avoid having to go to the hospital for the birth," she replied. "And it is recommended at 14 days past the due date that birth takes place at the hospital. So, a couple of days before that would be best."

"Okay," I agreed. Fourteen days past my due date also happened to be my 30th birthday and I wanted to avoid giving birth that day if I could help it.

"I am not on call until the day after tomorrow," our midwife explained, "so, you take a couple of days to think about it. I'll give you the oils and then if you decide to take the cocktail on Monday, just let me know when labour starts."

"That sounds reasonable," I told her. It gave Brad and I time to think about it and to see if baby would decide to come before it got to that.

"And I'll see you here Tuesday at 10:00 am if labour hasn't started by then," she told us as she gave me a syringe with the verbena oil.

"Thanks," we said as we left her office. The fact that she did not suggest a trip to the hospital for Pitocin to induce labour was great in my books. We talked it over before deciding whether to go ahead with the cocktail.

"What do you think about all this?" Brad asked me on our way home.

"I don't know," I answered. "I really thought the baby would be here by now. I didn't know that an induction cocktail was even a thing."

"Me neither," he said. "How are you feeling?"

"Okay, I guess. You know I don't want the baby to come on my birthday," I told him honestly, "but I just want baby to get here safe. Obviously."

"It's all going to be alright, babe," Brad assured me.

"How are you feeling?"

"Good. Excited."

"So, you think I should take the cocktail?"

"Yes, I think so. We've tried everything else. And she wouldn't be recommending it if she didn't think that it was for us."

"This baby is just way too comfy in there," I said jokingly as I patted my belly and I rolled my eyes over at Brad. He just smiled back at me.

We had decided to go ahead with the induction on our own on Monday morning. This gave us one more day to ourselves, just the two of us, before we started the final stretch into parenthood. We went for lunch at our favourite local pub and took a drive out to Cypress Mountain. We snapped a pic together, our last as a family of two. The next morning when I first woke to pee (other than the middle of the night!), I mixed and drank the first dose of the labour cocktail and went back to bed. An hour later I got up to take the second dose. Not even an hour after that, my contractions started.

Brad was supposed to be going into work the morning I went into labour so he ended up making a few calls downstairs while I managed early contractions upstairs. I spent a lot of time that day walking around the main floor of our house, out onto the front patio, through the kitchen, dining room, living room and hallway, in an effort to help progress my labour and keep those contractions coming.

I texted our doula to let her know that my contractions were coming consistently, even though they were still far apart. She came over in the early afternoon.

"How are you doing?" she asked as she joined Brad and me in our living room.

"Pretty well, I think," I told her.

"When did your contractions start?"

"Around 10:00 this morning," I explained, "about an hour after I took the second dose of the cocktail. I had already updated her about our decision to take the labour-inducing cocktail.

"And what have you been up to this morning?" she asked gently.

"Pretty much just this." I gestured to the couch. "And I've been walking around when the contractions come. It seems more comfortable for me when I feel them coming to be standing up."

"Okay, that's good. Do you want me to put the TENS machine on you?" She asked, referring to the electrical machine used as pain management in labour.

"Sure." We had discussed using this as an alternative to pain medication. She placed the sticky pads to my lower back and gave me the controls.

"You can increase the intensity here," she said, showing me the remote control, "and here is the button to adjust the frequency and the button for when you're experiencing a contraction."

The machine prickled on and off. I pressed the button to initiate the contraction feature and was hit with high vibrations through the pads on my back and hips. I'm not entirely sure if it did too much for the pain, but it was most definitely distracting, which was helpful.

"Are you okay if I take off for a bit then?" the doula asked.

"Yes, that's fine," I told her. "I will text you when we'd like you to come back."

"Sounds good. Right after I give you a quick foot rub," she said with a smile.

Shortly after, Brad and I were left on our own. We watched movies and I paced around the house. By later in the afternoon I felt as though my contractions were picking up so I texted the doula and asked her to come back to the house. Her presence was helpful, especially since I hadn't been visited by the midwife yet. I hadn't realized that she wouldn't come by the house at all until I was much further along. It made me even more grateful that we had a doula.

Night time fell. I ate and drank as I wanted. I remember grabbing myself, the doula and Brad a granola bar at some point, possibly around midnight. That was the last food I ate until the next day, over 24 hours later.

"Why don't we move upstairs?" the doula suggested. "And then maybe try to take a shower?"

"Okay," I nodded. Brad helped me upstairs and stayed with me through each contraction.

"You're doing a great job, babe," he encouraged me.

I climbed into the shower and let the warm water wash over me. Brad had lit candles and placed them around the bathroom and our room. The environment was soothing; the shower was anything but.

"It feels worse," I told the doula. "I don't know if I can do this."

"You can, Anya," she told me. "Try rocking back and forth

when the contractions come. Shift your weight from side to side. Focus on your movement."

I did what she suggested. The contractions were increasing while I was in the shower, but I didn't stay too long under the water. I moved back to the bedroom, lying in bed for a while, standing as each contraction crested. I felt more equipped to deal with the pain if I was able to stand and sway back and forth.

Sometime in the middle of the night as a contraction started, I sprang from the bed and felt a pop of immense pain along with an increase of pressure in my pelvis. I found myself unable to sway as I had been doing; liquid was making its way down my leg.

"I think my water just broke," I said to the room. "But there's not a lot of it."

"Let's get into the washroom and have a look," the doula said as she walked me into the next room.

"It doesn't look like there was any meconium that leaked out," she said, "so I don't think baby has pooped. But it's hard to tell in the dark. And there wasn't much fluid."

She waited while I breathed deep and rocked through my next contraction before she spoke again.

"How are you feeling, compared to before?"

"About the same," I told her. I would've thought that my contractions would increase following what certainly felt like the rupture of membranes.

"Should we tell the midwife?" Brad asked her.

"Yes," she said. "I think I'll let her know."

The midwife's first visit was uneventful. Other than when I asked her not to lay her hands on me when I was in the middle of a contraction.

"Get your hands off me!" I said as I moved away from her touch.

She threw her palms in the air and once my contraction had passed, she said, "That's the way I know how to help, with my touch."

"Well, I don't like to be touched during a contraction," I explained as I lay down to be examined.

"Okay," she said cautiously. This was the person I feared would come out during my labour. However, no harm done; I just needed to be left alone to manage contractions in my own way.

"Three centimetres," the midwife told us. "Still a ways to go, my dear."

"Her contractions were two minutes apart for quite some time," the doula explained.

"Okay," the midwife said. "Keep it up and let me know as things progress." And with that, she was gone.

To say I was crushed is a gross understatement. I thought that I would have been further along by that point. We were quickly approaching morning and with it the 24-hour mark since my contractions had started.

"Hey Brad," the doula said, "why don't I take Anya into the spare room and you can lay down and have a sleep for a while."

"I'm fine..." he started to say.

The doula interrupted him. "Take the rest, Brad. It's been a long day and it's not over yet. There's no need for you to power through."

"Okay," he reluctantly agreed.

I felt my contractions increase in the quiet of the spare room. The doula was sitting cross-legged on the bed behind me. Fatigue was catching up with me. I sat, perched on the edge of the bed, waiting for the next rush. I actually started nodding off in-between contractions, bursting to a standing position when each one hit, waking me from whatever sleep I managed to get while sitting upright on the bed.

"You're doing a great job, Anya," the doula whispered softly from behind me.

"I don't think I can do this," I said to her.

"Yes, you can," she encouraged me. "You're going to get to meet your baby before you know it."

"I can," I repeated. "I can do this."

"Yes, you can. You're really going to like pushing."

I'm not sure how long we stayed in the spare room, but eventually Brad woke and I returned to our bedroom. I crawled into bed after a contraction and shot Brad an evil look.

"I'm never doing this again," I told him.

"Okay," he said. I don't think he wanted to risk saying anything else to me at that point, in that condition. Every woman says that at some point during their labour, right?

Daybreak passed without attention from me. At some point the midwife returned. Whether the doula asked her to come back or she came on her own, I'm unsure.

Following another vaginal exam, she told me I was in the

same position as I had been overnight.

"Three centimeters," she said. "Four if I'm being generous."

I didn't know what to think. I was exhausted. Looking at Brad was like looking at my own, non-pregnant, male reflection. He looked beat. Neither one of us knew what to say or do.

"You have some options," the midwife explained. "We can change the plan and go to the hospital for an epidural. Then you will be able to rest."

Brad and I looked up at her together, waiting for the other option.

"Or you can get back in the shower," she suggested.

"The shower was so bad," I told her in between contractions. "I don't know what to do."

I was starting to feel myself crack. I had now been in labour for over one full day. I hadn't expected it to be like this. I have friends who have popped out their first babies in eight hours and know of people who had their babies even quicker than that. Here I was, essentially stuck, and confused. I wish that someone had warned me about what a marathon it could be.

It wasn't in the plan, but I broke.

I looked up at Brad and said, "I'd like to go to the hospital for an epidural." He had a tired and worried look on his face.

The midwife said she would meet us at the hospital and told us where to go once we got there. I don't think the doula suggested another option for staying at home. I don't remember feeling supported enough to say that didn't need or want to go to the hospital absent of a medical reason involving the health and well-being of myself or the baby. I needed to hear that birth was a difficult experience and that by focusing my energy on progressing my labour and relaxing as much as I could between contractions, I'd at least be giving myself and baby more of a chance for the birth Brad and I had imagined. I don't need to point fingers, but I do need to say that looking back, I do not believe I had a strong advocate for the birth I wanted, nor did I have an understanding of what would happen once we got to the hospital.

And so, we packed a bag and headed to the closest birthing hospital located in New Westminster. We got there in the early afternoon, were admitted and waited a while for my epidural. Once it was in and began to work, our midwife left to see her other patients and our doula went home for a nap as well.

Brad and I were just starting to drift off to sleep when all of the sudden we were jolted awake.

"Anya," one of the nurses said to me. "I'm going to need you to turn onto your side. Baby doesn't like it when you're on your back."

She was followed by at least three or four other people. Brad sat up in response to the swarm of people in our room and watched as I turned onto my left side.

We waited a moment before the nurse asked me to turn onto my right side.

Another nurse came in and tried to explain what was going on as I turned onto my other side. "The baby's heart rate isn't coming up as quickly as we'd like following each contraction. The OB is on his way and we have paged your midwife."

I waited on my right side, facing away from Brad. I was petrified. All I could think was that I hoped the baby responded to this position. I hoped more than anything that he or she was going to be okay.

"That's not working," I overheard one of the nurses at the bottom of my bed say to her audience. "Dr. B isn't here yet, what should we try next?"

"Okay, Anya, we're going to help you up onto your hands and knees," the first nurse suggested.

I did as I was told and with the help of several people that I had never even met before, I heaved my overly pregnant self onto my hands and knees. The swarm of people in the room were all watching the monitors I was attached to.

One nurse held her hand to my stomach, pressing the disc that was reading the baby's vitals. "There we go, baby, there we go. We'll stay like this and make sure baby calms down a bit, okay?"

I nodded. My eyes searched the room to find Brad, who was standing next to my bed. He reached for my hand and gave it a squeeze. It was too much for either of us to speak at this point.

The OB finally arrived, followed closely by our midwife.

"Hi Anya," Dr. B said as he came up to the end of my bed before turning to consult with one of the nurses. Our midwife stood by him, listening carefully.

A couple of the other nurses helped me onto my back before the doctor addressed me again.

"It seems as though baby is not too happy right now," Dr. B started to explain. "And following each contraction, the heart rate isn't recovering quite as quickly as we would like to see."

"Okay," I said. "What does that mean?"

"Well. My recommendation is that we should prepare you for

a cesarean. You've already been in labour for so long and baby has still not dropped into your pelvis. I don't think you will progress sufficiently before labour becomes too hard on the baby."

I nodded.

"It's not an emergency at this point," he went on, "but your midwife agrees that this is the best course of action for your well-being and the safe delivery of your baby." She stood beside him, saying nothing.

"The nurses will continue to watch the monitors and we will step out and give you some time to think."

And with that, Brad and I were left alone.

"What do you think?" he asked me.

"They're telling us we need to do the c-section, then I guess we need to do the c-section."

"This is exactly what I was afraid of in coming to the hospital," he replied.

"I know. Maybe we can wait it out a bit and see if the epidural helps to move things along?"

"For sure." Brad squeezed my hand and kissed me on the forehead. "He did say that it's not an emergency at this point."

I texted our doula to let her know what had happened and to tell her that they were recommending a c-section. She replied to say she was on her way back to the hospital.

It took a while for the OB to come back into the room. Our midwife followed behind him.

"So," he said. "What are you thinking?"

"We'd like to wait a bit," I told them, "to see if things progress at all before we go for the surgery."

"As long as the baby is okay," Brad added.

"That's certainly fine," Dr. B said. "We'll check back soon and continue to monitor you both."

When the OB left the room, our midwife finally came over to my bedside.

"You're in great hands with Dr. B," she told me. "We have to do what's best to make sure baby gets here safely."

I just lay there, scared. I didn't feel as if there was anything for us to do in the situation other than just go along with whatever we were told. We had not been educated in this department and while I cannot say for sure, I doubt that things were as urgent as we were made to believe.

How long we waited, I don't know, but by the time the OB and midwife came back to our room, our doula had returned and was present for the final discussion.

"Your cervix has not progressed," my midwife told me following another exam.

"What would you like to do?" Dr. B asked.

"We'll go forward with the c-section," I told them.

"Isn't there another position or something we could try to help the baby drop?" the doula asked the midwife. She just shook her head.

"Okay folks," Dr. B responded. "There's still no rush, baby is doing fine. We'll see you in a couple of hours in the operating room."

By this point, I truly believe that we had passed the point of no return. I had gotten the epidural, I was more than halfway to the operating room in everyone's eyes and I sadly wouldn't be able to avoid having a c-section.

To be clear, there is no part of me that is sad that we delivered a happy and healthy baby. I would repeat the process over an infinite amount of times to make sure that baby arrived safely. However, I cannot help but think if several small things had happened differently, even in the slightest, I wouldn't have had to have a c-section.

Brad and I have always been very private about our lives and had chosen not to let many people know that I was in labour; only his work and our care providers were aware. I don't think that either of us were handling the situation very well as we waited for our trip to the operating room. I think I had already entered protective mama-bear mode and just wanted to make sure that my baby was okay. Brad's worry showed clearly on his face.

"You should call your parents," I told him. "And mine."

"Ya? But none of them even know you're in labour."

"You shouldn't have to go through this alone. They should know."

"Okay. I'll call my parents and then your mom and I'll be right back," he said as he stepped out of the room.

"How are you doing, Anya?" The doula asked as she stepped over beside me. "I know this wasn't in the plan."

"I'm okay," I answered as honestly as I could. "As long as the baby gets here safely. At this point, that's all that matters."

It felt good to have her there. She knew us and she knew how unsettled we were at having to go down this road. In a hospital full of strangers, someone was on our side.

Brad came back into the room. "Okay, I told my parents to

hang tight and that I would let them know when the baby is here. And I talked to Gerry and your mom to let them know what was going on."

"Okay," I said. "So your parents aren't going to show up here unannounced?"

Brad's parents happened to be in town from Vanderhoof. I had asked my mom to stay in PG until the baby was born as we wanted the privacy.

"Nope," he said confidently. "I told them to wait to hear from me."

"They better."

The nurses returned to the room with our midwife.

"Brad, you can stay here and I will show you where you can get into some scrubs," the midwife explained. "You can join Anya once she's transferred over to the bed in the operating room."

"Can I bring the camera?" Brad asked.

"Yes," she responded. "I can take it for you. I promise to take lots of pictures so you can focus on your wife and baby!"

In the last moments before we officially became parents, we paused for one last picture. The overwhelming truth was that we were going to meet our baby very soon. I looked up at Brad before they wheeled me out of the room.

"I'll see you soon, Dad," I said as I tried my best to smile up at him.

"I love you," he said.

"I love you, too."

They wheeled my bed out of the room as I fought back tears. My midwife walked beside me.

"I will go change and see you in there," she said as she rubbed my shoulder.

One of the nurses walking with us gently took my hand in hers.

"You're doing great," she told me. "You're going to meet your baby so soon!" Her kind words helped settle my nerves. I could tell she was smiling behind the mask that covered her face.

I looked up at the bright lights of the hospital's hallways, my eyes scanning the other pregnant patients and visitors who wandered the halls. We passed countless people in scrubs and turned several hallways that all presented the same dull walls. We could have been passing in circles for all I knew. I was lost.

We entered the operating room through a set of double doors. Everyone inside wore near identical scrubs. I felt so alone.

The anesthesiologist introduced himself while the other people in the room moved me from my hospital bed to the operating table. The cold metal of the table seeped through my hospital gown and the thin blankets.

I couldn't stop shaking.

"I'll get you a couple of warm blankets when the doctor is done here," the kind nurse assured me. She hadn't stopped holding my hand. I never got to see her full face and I am sure I wouldn't recognize her if I saw her again, but I am eternally grateful for her kindness.

"The shaking is a side-effect of the medicine," the anesthesiologist told me. "It'll be over soon."

It will be over soon.

I repeated the phrase in my head but quickly turned it around.

Sure, the procedure would be over soon, but really, it was only a short time before it would all begin.

A few minutes passed but the bustle of scrubbed persons around me never stopped. One of the masked faces was all of the sudden very close to my own.

"Hi sweetie."

I looked up at the unrecognizable one-third of a face, then glanced down at her identification tag. It was the midwife. "We're here," she said kindly.

She stepped to the side and my eyes locked with the only two eyes in the world that I would recognize in a heartbeat. "Brad," I said softly. "I am so glad you're here."

I had felt so cold and helpless but with Brad by my side, holding my hand, I knew that we would get through what was coming together.

Dr. B came into the operating room, joining the nurses and our midwife in the sea of unidentifiable people.

"Alright folks," he said. "Let's have a baby. And remember, Mom and Dad don't know what the gender of the baby is and dad would like to be the one to announce it to everyone."

Brad sat next to me, both of us sheltered behind a curtain of material so that we couldn't see the surgery taking place.

"Okay, Mom," Dr. B said to me. "You're going to feel a bit of tugging."

My eyes watched Brad. They couldn't go anywhere else. I

didn't allow myself to notice what was being done to the lower half of my body. I focused on my husband while we waited to meet our babe.

"Just a reminder," Dr. B said, "that Dad is going to be the one to tell everyone what the gender of the baby is."

Moments later, we heard our first-born cry out.

My maternal instinct took over and I turned to look in the direction of my baby's cries; all I could see was the blue of the curtain in front of us.

"Okay, Dad," Dr. B finally announced, "stand up and meet your baby."

Brad stood, still holding my hand. He peeked over the curtain and immediately started to choke up.

"It's," he tried before he brokenly announced, "it's...a, it's a boy!"

Tears began to fall from both of our eyes as Brad looked down at me.

"Archer Bruce," he said as he choked back tears.

"Our Archer Bruce," I replied.

Brad leaned down to kiss me as we listened to Archer cry.

Someone, whether it was our midwife or the OB, brought Archer around the curtain and laid him on my chest.

"Oh, hi there," I said through my tears. There is no sufficient way to describe the moment when you hold your first child in your arms, moments after they entered this world for the first time.

"It's so nice to finally meet you," I said as I continued to cry softly to myself. Brad leaned over and kissed me on the forehead.

Brad and I managed to compose ourselves and he kissed me

again as I held our son. Our little monster started rooting around for food right away, revealing himself to be the bottomless pit he is on most days now. We snuggled as our midwife snapped pictures for us, capturing the gift of Archer's birth, whether planned this way or not.

"Okay, Mom," one of the nurses said. "We're going to take baby over to be weighed while Dr. B finishes up."

And for the first time since his conception, Archer existed without touching my body.

"Dad," the nurse called to Brad. "Do you want to come and cut the cord from baby's belly?"

"Sure," Brad said as he turned to me. "You okay?"

"Yes, go! I'll be here."

He let out a chuckle and went over to help cut the cord and see them weigh our new baby.

Dr. B finished up and the curtain was removed from in front of me. "Congratulations!" He said as he patted my leg and left the room. His benevolence has stayed with me to this day. While he didn't necessarily point out the fact that we were scared and out of our element, his words and kind gestures reassured me that everything was going to be okay.

"You'll be going up to recovery for a while," a nurse said to me. "And Dad can go with baby up to your room."

"Okay," I said as I tried to sneak a look at Brad and Archer. I didn't realize we would be separated. And I didn't have a choice. I didn't know what to say, other than to tell them I loved them as I was wheeled away. I closed my eyes, fighting back tears.

I thought I would at least be given the opportunity to catch some sleep while I was alone in recovery. I was sadly mistaken.

"We're going to have you hooked up to this automatic blood pressure cuff," one of the nurses in recovery told me. Also known as the automatic wake-you-up every two minutes machine. "Your blood pressure has been a bit low since the delivery, so we need to keep an eye on it."

Again, I just went along with it all and was woken every two minutes to the whirr of the blood pressure cuff. The nurses were also checking my incision and chatting beside me as they worked. Sigh. Welcome to life as a new mom. I thought it was supposed to be the baby's fault for the lack of sleep?

The nurses were kind enough, but their interactions felt cold to me. They didn't seem to understand that I had just been abruptly separated from my baby so soon after he was born. They just wanted to make sure my blood pressure didn't drop too low and that I was in good shape postpartum. They didn't seem to have any regard for me, other than for the well-being of my physical self. I'm grateful for their care, of course, but I felt lost. Unsure. And so tired. I still don't think that what had happened had really sunk in for me. When I started to feel numbness and tingling in my lower extremities it was completely unnatural. I felt like I couldn't even make my toes wiggle when requested, even though they clearly moved eventually as I was wheeled up to my room to more officially meet my son.

Being confined to a hospital bed was so foreign to me. I whole-heartedly embraced the independence that comes with moving away from your family. I had been living out of the care of my parents for over ten years at this point. Ever since I left home, I have done things on my own, come hell or high water, and even since being with Brad I have had a difficult time letting other people do things for me. Yet in the hospital I had no choice. I had to let my independence go and accept other people's help, my body on display and my dignity far out of reach. This lesson was well timed, what with becoming a new parent. Being a mom has taught me that there isn't really anything that is in my control any more. Just try to get a three-year old to leave the house on time. On time? What is that anymore!

As I was wheeled into the room where Brad waited with Archer, I felt so unsure of what was waiting for me. I was confused, having spent just over two hours alone in recovery. Being tired certainly didn't help.

"Hi, Mom," Brad said softly as they locked my bed into place in our semi-private room.

"Hi, Dad," I replied with a smile. Brad was holding Archer to his bare chest; Archer was sucking on Brad's pinky finger.

"They suggested I let him suckle on my clean finger while we wait for you," he told me. "How are you doing?"

"I'm okay. It was really weird to be separated from you guys."

"You're telling me. I didn't expect that at all."

"Looks to me like you're doing a great job."

He smiled a sort of half-smile. "I have to tell you something."

By this time, it was almost 11:00 pm.

"Okay," I said. Nothing good ever happens when someone starts a conversation with those words.

"My parents are here."

What the actual fuck?

I just stared at him. He had to be kidding.

"They went to move the car for me so they're not here, here. They showed up shortly after I got up here with Archer."

"What do you mean they showed up?" I asked. I wasted energy I didn't have on trying to pretend I wasn't immediately pissed off.

"They just walked in. I hadn't had a chance to call them so they took it upon themselves to come to the hospital."

Tears started to fall. I already felt like I had missed out on the first couple of hours of my baby's life. I was so relieved to just be back with my family and here I was being told that my in-laws had showed up, completely unannounced and uninvited. To the hospital. While I was in recovery after being sliced open to deliver my baby.

"I didn't let them hold him, babe," Brad answered the question I hadn't yet been able to ask.

"Good," I told him honestly. "I haven't even had a chance to properly hold him."

"I know. Believe me, I was just as shocked as you are right now when they walked around that curtain."

I didn't know what else to say. This was not only a very late visit, but was completely unwarranted given the fact that Brad had told them that he would let them know when we were settled and baby was here.

"They came in and said hi. I told them his name and then asked them to leave until you were back in the room," Brad explained. "I got them to move the car to the long-term parking lot from emergency. I thought that it was only fair for you to have a chance to meet our son officially, first. Outside of the operating room."

"Thank you."

Brad stood and brought our little bundle over to me. I had never held such a new, small baby before. He was sleeping.

"Wow, hey?" I said, staring down at our tiny babe.

"I know. It's totally surreal," Brad said, stroking my hair. "That we're here, and that he's here. What are we supposed to do with him now?"

"Haha," I laughed. "No clue."

Brad stood by my bed, resting one hand on my shoulder and one on the blankets wrapped tightly around Archer.

I wanted to explain to Brad how I was feeling, but I also wanted to choose my words carefully. "You know, Brad. It's bad enough that I had to have that difficult conversation with my mom. To tell her that we wanted the birth of our baby to be private and that we would let her know when she could come and stay with us after the baby was born."

"I know, Anya," Brad responded. "I know."

"But I don't think you do, Brad. They took it upon themselves to show up here unannounced. After you asked them to wait."

"I know, I really do. It's not what we wanted, but I couldn't exactly tell them to leave."

"So, what? They're coming back?"

"Yes. They want to see you, too."

For some people, having their families at the hospital when they give birth is what they want. For us, it wasn't. This was a moment when we were bringing another life into this world and we wanted that to be an experience for just us. We were the only ones there when the baby was made; surely it wasn't too unreasonable to want to be the only ones there when we met the baby for the first time? Just for one evening? Evidently, it was too much to ask.

Brad's parents came back to the room briefly. I do not remember anything about the conversation. I don't think they stayed long. And I did not let either of them hold Archer. In the back of my mind all I could think was that I didn't want my mom to know that they had met Archer on his first day of life. She would be so upset that she didn't get to meet him that day too. She had respected our wishes, even though she didn't want to. I didn't want her to hurt any more than she probably already did. It wasn't my intention to hurt her feelings, just as I am sure it wasn't Brad's parents' intention to hurt mine or to invade our space. But just like the birth and everything surrounding having children is not entirely in our control, neither is what our families do or how they react. This I have most certainly learned.

Life lessons are at their finest in difficult times, aren't they? We can be vulnerable, in a hospital gown, hooked up to an IV, just wanting to get out, and people who are simply supposed to provide love and support can be overheard saying that they shouldn't see us like this. We can do what we think is right for ourselves, and still end up hurting the ones we love. That's what makes the world go around, I suppose. It's not about the destination; it's the journey. But sometimes the destination needs to take priority.

The vision of a beautiful, un-medicated and amazingly empowering birth in the comfort of my own home had not materialized. Quite the opposite occurred, actually. I've accepted it. After all, Archer had arrived as a healthy 8 pounds 1 ounce snuggly little being.

And still, I felt like so much had been taken from me. It had been, technically. While I know that I shouldn't focus on what I missed out on as my son is here and that is so much more than what a lot of would-be parents can ask for, I wouldn't be being honest with myself if I didn't admit how I felt after my c-section. I felt awful. Guilty. Like I did something wrong. That I was broken, inefficient somehow. Even worse, I didn't feel that immediate bond of unconditional love towards my son. This is a heady confession that I have not spoken a lot about out loud. But since my first birth experience I have had time to accept what happened and learn that I didn't do anything wrong, whatsoever, during or after the birth of my first born. I accepted that there was nothing I could have done differently in that situation to change the birth that we had.

Sure, of course I did things wrong when he was a tiny infant whom neither Brad nor I had any idea how to care for. But I know that I didn't fail to physically or emotional prepare for birth. There isn't anything that I can change about the situation as I obviously cannot go back in time. There is no need to focus on the things I feel other people could have done to help things along in a different way, as, again, Brad still hasn't perfected his time travel machine.

What I *can* do is move forward with my next birth when that time comes. Prepare. Educate. And rise above the feelings of guilt from the last time and fear for this time, fear that the same thing might happen again. I will let myself go into labour and allow my body to do what it knows how to do naturally to bring our second baby into this world. If that doesn't work out, I will make the informed choice, along with our new midwives, new doula and my husband, to ensure that our baby arrives safe and sound. I owe that to myself, my baby and my growing family.

Love,

Anya

Chapter Seven

January 31, 2017

Dear Rachael,

Life as parents has treated us pretty well. We stumble, sure, but we have learned to trust our instincts and not take other people's opinions personally when they differ from ours. I was perfectly content being a family of three, but Brad and I had always agreed to have two kids. After my birth experience with Archer, I told Brad that I didn't even want to talk about getting pregnant again until Archer was at least a year old. And then, and only then, would I even begin to think about it. Brad left it to me to bring the subject of more kids up when I was ready.

"So," I said to him one day. "Three years apart will be a pretty good age difference for our kids, hey?"

"You're finally ready to talk about it!" he replied teasingly.

"Haha, very funny."

"So, you don't want Archer to be an only child?" Brad said with a wink.

"Noooooo. I've always said that you can't know what a sibling is like unless you have one. And I want that for Archer."

"Three years sounds great. By then Archer will be older and able to help more. I think that's a great idea."

"Me, too. I think he's going to be a great big brother," I said as we watched Archer crawl into the dog's bed, stick his fingers into his own mouth and snuggle into Eddie like he was ready for a nap.

"We're certainly in no hurry," Brad laughed.

Near the end of 2016, Brad and I decided there was no time like the present to stop trying to avoid getting pregnant. This would put my due date after Archer's third birthday, which was the minimum age gap we wanted for our kids. We threw caution to the wind shortly before Christmas 2016, when we were set to go up to PG for the holidays.

I had just started a new job the previous October but was lucky enough to get a few days off to allow for our trip. We started the near 9-hour drive a few days before Christmas and I spent almost the entire time holding my seatbelt away from my chest. My breasts were super tender, which is not a symptom that I typically have. Even during that time of the month. This was my first clue that we might have been a foursome travelling the snowy roads.

We spent a relatively quiet Christmas with both of our families in Prince George. Come Boxing Day, we left my parent's place for Vanderhoof, to visit Brad's parents. On the way there, Brad and I were discussing what our plans for the rest of the year would be.

"We still haven't decided when we're going home, hey?" I asked Brad as we started the hour-long trek to his parents' place.

"No," he answered.

"Well, what do you want to do?" I asked the silence.

"I don't know. We could stay until the weekend. Do you want to stay until New Year's?"

"Not really," I answered. "It's Monday today, so that would give us a couple of days with your parents and then a couple of days to spend at Gerry and Tanya's."

"That sounds fair. Are you okay driving home on New Year's Eve, or do you want to go home New Year's Day?"

"If we go New Year's Eve, that'll give us more time at home before we go back to work," I reasoned.

"Let's do that, then," Brad agreed. "It's not like we usually do anything on New Year's Eve anyways."

"Sounds like we have a plan."

It was strange; the entire time we had been discussing our plans, I couldn't help but feel like I was on the verge of tears.

"What's the matter, babe?"

"I don't know."

"Are you sure? You look like you're about to cry!"

"I don't know, Brad! I've felt like I'm going to cry the whole drive so far!"

"Uh oh," he said with a smile. "I think maybe we should go and get you a pregnancy test."

I couldn't think of much to say in response. "Oh. You have a point. It's hard being back up north, but it's not that hard!"

And so, we unloaded our things at Brad's parents' house, left the dog and our napping first born with them and went down to the drug store for a pregnancy test. The thing is, Vanderhoof is a very small town. So small that their main grocery store didn't have any pregnancy tests! None that we could find on display anyways. And, of course, the pharmacy was closed for Boxing Day. Over to the drug store we went.

When we got back to my in-laws' place, I went into the bathroom and took the test. Minutes later a little pink plus sign told me I was expecting. I left the washroom and glanced down the hallway towards where Brad was sitting on the couch. I caught Brad's eye and nodded. He took a deep breath and smiled. We were going to be parents of two!

The first time I got pregnant, we had waited the typical 13 weeks before we told any of our family members or friends that we were having a baby. But since we do not see our families often and we just happened to be staying with them, we shared our happy news right away. They were very happy for us and it was really nice to be able to tell them in person. We returned home and started our 2017 with great hope for what the year had in store for us.

We returned to work and all continued as normal. I contacted the midwife that we had for my pregnancy with Archer and all seemed to be well. I wasn't feeling too many symptoms other than the tender breasts and that feeling of being pregnant that I cannot really explain. We arranged for our dating ultrasound at eight weeks pregnant and we were able to go after work one day while Archer was still in day care.

I went into the exam room by myself while Brad sat in the waiting room. "I'll come out and get you shortly," the technician told him. She took quite a bit more time taking the measurements than I remembered from my pregnancy with Archer.

"Have you ever had a transvaginal ultrasound?" she asked.

"No," I answered.

"Okay. I'll just get you to go to the washroom to empty your bladder completely. Then we'll do the transvaginal ultrasound to get a better look."

I went to the washroom as instructed but something wasn't sitting well with me. I was still having all of my pregnancy symptoms and that "feeling" of being pregnant was still there. Surely everything was fine.

I was nervous as she got me to put the ultrasound wand inside myself. She took some more pictures and then told me I could get dressed.

"I'll go get your husband and be right back," she said before leaving the room.

A couple of minutes later, Brad came in alone. "Is everything okay? Where'd she go?"

"I don't know," I told him. "I don't think it's good."

He stood beside me and took my hand in his.

The technician returned to our room after what seemed like hours later. She was joined by someone who looked like one of the Sedin twins.

"Anya," she said. "This is the onsite doctor."

"Hi Anya," he addressed me. He was kind. He maintained good eye contact with me while he delivered the sad news. "There's no easy way for me to tell you this, but the baby didn't make it."

Brad and I looked at him, waiting for an explanation.

"These things happen more often than you think," the doctor went on. "There's nothing that you could have done differently. Your body knew that the fetus was not viable. A miscarriage is your body's way of doing what was necessary to make sure the pregnancy would not continue. Your baby looks like it stopped growing around six weeks."

"Okay," I said out loud. I was numb. "What do we do next?"

"Well, your body could start to process the miscarriage and you will bleed out," he explained. "Or you might have to go to the hospital for a procedure or some medication to help move the miscarriage along."

I was in shock. I felt as though the doctor and technician were looking at me like I was supposed to burst into tears on the spot. I didn't.

"I will send the results to your midwife. You should call her to discuss the next steps."

"We'll just leave you two for a minute. You can stay as long as you like," the technician told us.

Once they left, I turned to Brad. I still didn't have any tears.

"You okay?" he asked me.

"I will be."

"That wasn't our baby Mav, you know?" he told me, referring to the baby using our nickname for him/her. We had already decided baby number two's name before I was pregnant, just like with Archer.

"I know."

He hugged me closer as we stood together in the small, dark room.

I pulled away from him slightly and looked up at him. "Maybe we could go get Archer together? I'll meet you there?"

"Okay," he said. "Are you sure you're ready to go?"

"Yes, I'm ready."

We followed each other in separate vehicles, up the hill towards Archer's day care. I started to feel the tears when I thought about going home to where my cousin was staying with us from Bosnia. I called Brad using hands free while I drove.

He answered quickly. "Hi, Babe."

And then the tears started. I sobbed as I followed Brad's car in our van.

"Oh, Babe," he said to me.

"I'm okay," I said through the tears. "It's okay. I just don't think I can stand to face Semir when we get home."

"Okay," he said.

"Do you think you could call him and ask him to make himself scarce for the evening?" I didn't want to see anyone. I didn't want to have to explain my sadness just yet.

"I can absolutely do that. I'll call him before we get to day care."

I have the best husband in the world.

"Thank you," I said. I had calmed down, having gotten that off of my chest. I didn't want to still be crying when we went to pick Archer up.

We ordered dinner in that night and talked and cried and hugged some more. I felt hurt, shocked and sort of hollow. And I wanted to get the process to remove the baby from my body underway as soon as possible. It was all I could think about.

I remember feeling so damn lucky to have Archer. We were so blessed to have our little munchkin to distract us; I couldn't imagine having to suffer that sort of loss on our own. For that I am grateful and my heart goes out to those who suffer with infertility and loss. It is something that I wish society didn't made women feel so ashamed of. We as women do not have anything to be ashamed of. The suffering is bad enough on its own. We should be encouraged to share our stories without judgment.

I went into work the next morning and waited to hear from my midwife. She called to discuss my options. I could wait until my body processed the miscarriage itself naturally, or I could contact a clinic on Commercial Drive to have a D&C done to remove the embryo. I had a forceful urge to have my body back. I just wanted to not be pregnant any more as physically I still felt like I was carrying a growing baby. I hadn't had any cramping or bleeding or any sign of no longer being a healthy pregnant woman. If I could have forgotten about our visit to the ultrasound clinic and continued on, my body would have still felt pregnant. I wanted to run from it as fast as possible in the opposite direction. I wanted to erase it and move on. I know it's not the choice everyone would make, but it was all that I wanted. For it to be over so that I could properly grieve and move forward. The desire to get my body back outweighed any of the other options.

I contacted the recommended clinic and answered what seemed like an excessive list of questions only to be told that I was too overweight to be seen in their clinic. They said I would have to go to the hospital to be seen by an anesthesiologist before being put under for the procedure. They were going to call me back with an appointment to see the anesthesiologist the following week, after which it could take up to two weeks for me to have the procedure done.

I was crushed. I felt like I was exploding in infinite ways. I was told that it was my choice whether I wanted to allow my body to naturally miscarry, or if I wanted a D&C. But I was now being told that I had to possibly wait three weeks to have the procedure. It angered and upset me. I felt like my rights were being denied and there was nothing I could do about it. Not only that, but Brad was set to be out of town for work in the following weeks and the last thing I wanted was to have to go through the procedure alone.

I spoke to my midwife again and she said if I truly wanted the procedure to be done as soon as possible, I should visit the hospital and tell them I was experiencing cramping. I left work and met Brad at home. I changed into comfy clothes and grabbed a book and we headed to the hospital. We waited for hours and were not seen by a doctor until after 6:00 pm. Thankfully, one of the day care workers had taken Archer home for us after day care.

"I'm very sorry for your loss," the OB resident said to us when we were finally able to see her. "Can you tell me what happened?"

"We went for a dating ultrasound yesterday," I explained, "and were told that the baby stopped growing at around six weeks. I should have been eight weeks along."

"Okay," she said as she took some notes. "It's our practice to check with our own ultrasound. Is that okay?"

"Yes," I told her.

"Does Dad want to stay in the room?"

"Yes," I said quickly. "He's not going anywhere."

The resident continued with the ultrasound. It took some time before she said, "Did anyone mention an ectopic pregnancy to you?"

"No."

"Okay," the resident said. "I'm just going to go get the OB and I'll be right back."

"She's not trying to suggest that the baby is still alive," I asked Brad. "Is she?"

"No," Brad said. "I don't think so. Even if she was, we know what the doctor yesterday said. They don't make those kinds of mistakes."

The resident returned to our room with the OB, who introduced herself.

"I'm just going to have a look at your ultrasound and we will discuss the options," she said to us.

She looked at what the resident was doing on the small monitor of the portable ultrasound machine. "What makes you think there may be an ectopic pregnancy?" the OB asked the resident.

"The black around here," the resident said as she pointed at the screen. "I really don't think it's conclusive that the pregnancy is in utero."

"I disagree," the OB said. She turned to us. "The pregnancy is definitely no longer viable, but it's too late for us to do the procedure today."

With that, I burst into angry tears. "So, we've waited here all afternoon for nothing?"

"I'm really sorry," the resident told me, "but it's out of our hands."

"I was told by my midwife that I could have a D&C if I wanted one and you're just telling me that's not possible. This may not be an emergency, but I am here for treatment that I am essentially being turned away for," I said through angry tears.

"We'll be right back," the OB said as she gestured to the resident to leave the room with her.

"Fine," I said as politely as I could while the anger boiled over inside me. "This is ridiculous," I said as I turned to Brad and reached for my phone.

"What are you doing?" He asked.

"I'm calling the midwife," I said to him as I dialed.

"Hello?" she answered almost right away.

"We're at the hospital and they're telling me that they won't do the procedure tonight."

"Okay," the midwife responded. "It is a little late. Ask if you can come back tomorrow. They should give you a note so you don't have to wait in emergency."

I wasn't clearly listening. I was angry and hurt. "They said they won't do it and it makes me mad that I have no rights. I need this baby out of me so that I can move on!"

"Leave it with me," the midwife told me. "And call me back after you leave."

I hung up the phone and Brad moved in to hug me tight. "It's going to be okay, Babe," he told me.

"It's not fair!" I screamed at him. "I'm being told that I have rights but no one is helping me get what I want!"

I cried into Brad's arms. He tightened his grip around me and let me cry.

"I just want this baby gone!"

He held me for several minutes before I started to calm down. It was taking the doctors a while to get back to us. I hoped this meant good things.

When they finally returned, the resident had a piece of paper in her hands.

"We just spoke to your midwife," the OB explained.

"I know," I said. "I called her."

"Well, she's very persuasive. She advocated for you to have the procedure at the hospital," the OB said. I don't think she was very impressed.

"Bring this to the admissions desk first thing tomorrow morning," the resident told me.

"It's a note for the OB who will be on call. You shouldn't have to wait in emergency," the OB said as she turned and left the room.

We returned first thing the following morning with our note. I hadn't eaten anything and was only permitted sips of water. Even though we had been told we wouldn't have to wait, wait we did, with all of the sick patients in emergency. They took samples of my blood every few hours and when we finally saw the new OB resident for the day, we weren't told what we wanted to hear.

"We've been monitoring the levels of the pregnancy hormone, HCG, in your blood all morning and comparing them with the blood taken yesterday," the resident said. She was much kinder and more confident than the resident we saw the day before. "The levels aren't dropping as quickly as they typically do with a miscarriage, so I'm going to recommend that you go for an ultrasound before we go forward with the procedure."

"Okay," I said as I nodded slowly. "When can we get in for an ultrasound?"

"The next appointment is at 2:30 pm," she responded. It was 10:30 am at the time.

"No," I said perhaps a bit too sharply as I started to fight the tears. I felt Brad tense up at my immediate reaction. "We waited here for six hours yesterday and were told that it was too late for the procedure by the time we actually saw the doctor. We've already been here for almost three hours; I'm not waiting for four more hours for the ultrasound and then longer to see the doctor only to be told it's too late to do the procedure again."

"That's fair," the resident told us after a pause. "I will go speak to the OB and see what he says."

All of the rigmarole that we were going through seemed to imply that I wasn't actually having a miscarriage but I didn't allow any of it to give me hope. I trusted what the doctor at the clinic had told me. I wanted to get the tissues removed from my body so that I could start to heal.

We were left, once again, alone in the emergency room. This

time, however, it didn't take long for the resident to return with the new OB on call.

"Anya," a very tall doctor said as he sat down on the chairs beside me. "I am Dr. U. My resident here says that you're quite upset at the idea of having to wait for an ultrasound."

"Yes, doctor," I said. "We waited a long time yesterday and came first thing this morning. We were told that we wouldn't have to wait and that the D&C would be done some time today."

"That's true," Dr. U said. "I compared your blood work from today to blood drawn yesterday and I can see that your hormone levels have dropped significantly."

"Okay," I said, listening intently, trying my hardest not to cry.

"We will send a nurse by to draw your blood one more time," he explained, "and as long as the HCG levels drop again, we will schedule you in for the procedure this afternoon. How does that sound?"

"That sounds good. Thank you." A nurse returned to draw my blood for at least the third time that day. Before noon, the resident returned to speak with us.

"Your HCG levels have dropped again," she said. "We will get you hooked up to an IV and admitted soon."

I thanked her and let out a big sigh of relief. I looked up at Brad.

"The squeaky wheel gets the grease," I said as I rested my head on his shoulder. I was exhausted. Was the worst even over yet?

I was given an IV of fluids in the early afternoon, but it took another several hours before I was taken upstairs to a room. I had just gotten settled when Brad realized the time.

"I guess I should be going to get Archer from day care," he said.

"Ya," I agreed. "I don't want you to leave, but no one is getting back to us to pick Archer up."

"I'll go get him and we'll come right back," Brad said as he kissed me on the forehead. "I'm sure we'll be back before the procedure. I love you."

"I love you, too." I was in a room in the general surgery ward with three other people. The guy next to me spent the majority of the time I was in there on his phone, trying to convince his wife to come and visit him. His bed was across from a lady who had visitors who brought takeout and played games together, laughing loudly. I hadn't had anything to eat since the previous night's late dinner, so needless to say I would have taken the loud neighbours over the smell of food any day.

Speaking of food, Brad returned with Archer right around dinnertime. Archer approached me in the big hospital bed cautiously.

"It's okay, buddy," I told him. "Come and give me a big hug!"

He came close to the bed and I picked him up. He threw his arms around my neck and I instantly felt a calm wash over me. Everything was going to be okay.

"Do you want to have a picnic?" I asked Archer. Brad had brought them dinner.

"Sorry," Brad apologized.

"No worries," I told him. "I'll be able to eat soon enough. I just want to get this over with."

Archer snuggled into me while he ate his dinner. Soon after they were done eating the nurse came in to tell me it was time to go to the operating room. Brad lifted Archer onto his lap and I put on my brave face as I was wheeled from the room by a pregnant orderly who looked like she was ready to pop. How's that for irony? It distracted me in a terrible way from the fact I was leaving my baby and my husband behind.

"See you soon, Mama!" Archer and Brad called behind me.

The orderlies left me alone in my bed in the pre-op room. It was slightly dark and eerily quiet. A doctor in scrubs approached my bed and told me that he was going to be my anesthesiologist. "I'm very sorry that you're going through this, Anya," he said. "But I'm going to take very good care of you."

Instantly tears fell down my face. It was the first moment all day that I felt like I was being treated as a human being with justified feelings of despair. That I wasn't just there for these doctors and nurses to do their jobs, that I was there because I was experiencing something that no woman should ever have to go through. And having someone recognize that brought me back to earth. It allowed me to feel. Sad. Confused. And not just like I was another patient. I was a human being in a terrible situation.

"Thank you," I said as I tried to smile. He went on to explain what was going to happen.

"You'll be awake again before you know it," he told me with a small smile.

I was at peace. When I awoke I felt a little crampy, slightly lethargic and different somehow, though I couldn't put my finger on it.

It was only after I was discharged, when Brad was wheeling me out of the hospital with Archer at his side, that I realized that I felt empty. The sadness that I had carried over the last two days had relocated itself. I felt hollow, listless. I was empty. Emotionally and literally. But as I watched my two-and-a-half-year-old beautiful boy skip alongside his dad, I knew that everything was going to be okay.

Following the ordeal in the hospital, I dealt with the loss quite well. I felt sad, of course. And fragile and sore. But I was able to check myself mentally and move forward one day at a time. I was extremely lucky to have Brad and Archer by my side. They were so good to me; they always are. Our family was okay and I knew deep down that it just wasn't meant to be at that time. That it would happen for us one day and we would become a completed family of four.

Brad called his mom and told his brother about the loss, and I called my own mom. She seemed supportive on the phone; she said she was sorry and asked all about how I was doing and what had happened. I opened up to her and when she arranged to come and visit near the end of February, I was really looking forward to having a comforting ear to turn to that didn't belong to Brad.

Somehow, I had misread her support over the phone because when I casually brought up how I was feeling about my miscarriage in person, she barely responded.

I mentioned to her that my period had returned. I was excited because Brad and I had been given the okay to start trying for another baby after that happened. I had already told Brad, and in typical dude fashion, he nodded in support. But, like the wonderful husband he is, he also gave me the biggest hug and said that he was excited that my body was getting back on track. My mom just stared back at me as if I had said nothing at all.

Why had I expected more from my own mother? What I had gone through was a difficult situation that you can never even begin to understand if you haven't experienced it yourself. And as far as I knew, my mother had never had a miscarriage. I had assumed that because she had spoken to me in the past about an aunt's miscarriage, she would be open to talking to me, especially when I was the one who brought it up. Sadly, she was just not emotionally prepared to talk about my sadness or my loss.

I tried to talk to Brad about it, but, as usual, it was difficult to put into words.

"I don't really know what I expected of her," I told him as we got ready for bed that night. "I just know that I put my feelings out there and she ignored me. And that hurt."

"I don't think she was ignoring you…"

"She didn't say anything at all after I told her I got my period back!"

"Well…"

He was trying, I'll give him that.

"I know you think that listening means that you're not ignoring someone," I said, exasperated. "But the textbook definition of ignoring someone is not saying anything in response to something they've said."

"I know, babe."

"And it would be one thing if she had ignored me once, but when I tried to talk about it again when we were alone at lunch, she changed the subject! Straight up just shifted what I was saying and asked me about Archer instead! Who does that!?"

"Your mom does."

"She just thinks we have this wonderful relationship, but she can never talk about anything that's difficult! It's really frustrating!"

I threw a pillow across the bed and just stood there, staring at Brad. I don't think either of us knew what to say, but it felt good to have let it all out.

Brad took a deep breath and proceeded gently. "We can't blame her for not saying the 'right thing' when you tried to bring it up. She's doing her best to be there for us in her own way."

"I know. There is no right thing to say, really."

"Exactly. And she did come down here specifically to stay with Archer while we go to Seattle. Let's just take advantage. Have some fun!"

"Okay."

I was feeling so many different emotions, most that I never could have predicted. Other people's reactions, my mother's included, were not in my control. Sure, I expected that my mother would be a safe shoulder for me to cry on and would say all the right things to make me feel like everything was going to be okay. But I couldn't blame her for doing her best to be there for us in her own way.

Brad and I were able to get away from it all for a couple of days. One of his favourite bands was playing at a small venue in Seattle, and since my mom was watching Archer for us we made a mid-week trip out of it. We left our worries, our babe and my mom behind and shared a few days together, just us.

We came back from our trip refreshed, and ready to move forward with our attempts to expand our family. We took the same approach we had in the past and kind of just forgot about it, which took a lot of the pressure off. After we had started trying again, I thought about the miscarriage less and less and it wasn't until Brad's parents came for a visit that I spoke out loud about it again.

Brad's mom shared with me that between having Brad's brother and Brad, she, too, had miscarried. The fact that she sat in front of me, crying and opening herself up to the vulnerability that comes along with losing a child—however long it had been since the loss occurred—reminded me that I wasn't alone.

A change occurred inside of me. I recognized that the person my mom knew, the one who would bring stuff up to her in hopes of hearing what I needed from her, wasn't there anymore. I needed my relationships to be a two-way street. I had no desire to be the one who would talk about herself all of the time. I wanted to know that the person I was talking to cared, too. Enough to ask.

There are a lot of emotions following a miscarriage, especially because of the way that other people react to or treat you. I have relationships that I believe have changed following the events of that year. But the change is for the better because I've learned the limitations that certain relationships have and have embraced the ones that have grown. My past has made me into the woman, mom, friend and wife that I am (in no particular order!) and for that I am so appreciative.

I miss you, dear friend, and I hope you know how much.

Anya xoxo

December 21, 2017

Dear Rachael,

Our midwife gave us the go-ahead to try to get pregnant after waiting for one cycle. Brad and I are very lucky not to have had difficulty in getting pregnant and I will never take that for granted. I think that for us, our relaxed approach and perhaps a few too many green beers on St. Patrick's Day helped us conceive quickly.

As the days passed, I found that familiar feeling of pregnancy seemed to be upon me again. Even though I hadn't yet missed a period, I decided to have one last glass of wine before taking a pregnancy test. After all, I wouldn't be able to indulge after seeing that second line.

I got home following an outing with some friends and said hi to Brad before heading upstairs. I stood in the washroom and waited for the three longest minutes to pass before checking the little plastic pregnancy test. I took a deep breath and flipped it over. Positive. I closed my eyes and let my emotions wash over me. Barely a month had passed since we had been given the okay to try, and here I was, pregnant. I was feeling so grateful, but I was also apprehensive. The last time I found myself in this position, it was followed by one of the saddest events in my life. Still, I was excited to share our happy news and went downstairs to tell Brad.

"So, I told you I was feeling a bit funny," I told him as I entered our home office.

"Ya," he said, turning in his office chair to face me.

"Well, I'm pregnant!" I said with a big smile.

"Babe!" He scooped me into a big hug.

We stood there with our arms wrapped around one another, the swell of expecting the worst pressing in on us from all sides.

He pulled away from me slightly to give me a kiss.

"I'm scared," I said first.

"Me, too. But we just have to believe that it's going to be okay. We can't do this to ourselves: thinking the worst is going to happen again."

I was already in a vulnerable state. It had only been two months since my ordeal at the hospital. This opened the floodgates even more.

"You're right," I told him as I started to cry. "And I know that we are going to have the family we want. It's just hard."

"I know."

It was like there was an air bubble caught in my throat for a time. I wanted to be outwardly positive about our second baby but inside I was nervous and I didn't want to express my concerns out loud in case they were heard and came to fruition. I think there's always that spot in the back of your mind when you get pregnant that can blacken your excitement. It can take over and become a problem if you let it.

Other than admitting that we were nervous after I told him about the positive test, Brad and I didn't talk about being scared. But when a few weeks passed by and all I could think about was what had happened, I brought it up again.

"I've still been thinking about what happened last time I was pregnant," I told him one night at dinner. "Have you thought about it anymore?"

"Yes," he said after a pause. "But I haven't wanted to bring it up. I don't want to say it out loud and have it come true."

It's like he read my mind.

"I feel the same way, Brad! But I'd rather talk about it with you than have neither of us say anything!"

"Okay. It's just that there isn't anything that we can do either way. It's really hard having it be out of our control."

"Totally. So, I think we should go forward as if we'll be meeting our baby in nine months. It's the only way to manage it."

"Yes," he agreed. "Nine or ten months."

"Ha," I laughed. "With my luck I'll be super late delivering this baby, too!"

There wasn't anything that we could have done to avoid having a miscarriage. But I could very well choose not to let the past put a damper on the excitement of expanding our family.

Almost every aspect of my pregnancy with baby number two was different from my pregnancy with Archer. One weekend early on, I felt like I had a minor case of the flu. It took me a few days to realize that the nauseous feeling in my tummy went away when I ate and then it clicked. This was morning sickness! (You know I am normally a "swift" individual. I completely blame pregnancy hormones for the deterioration of my mind.) Anyone who has experienced morning sickness will tell you that it's very unfortunately named. I would have taken it if it was only in the morning, but, alas, it's an all-day, all-the-time, slap you in the face kind of sickness. At least it was for me.

Heading into my pregnancy with baby number two I was a very, very naive woman. I didn't think that morning sickness could really be *that bad.* I wasn't aware that your hormones could take your discomfort to the next level, making you feel sick all day long. That unless you had some emergency snacks on hand at all times, you could start to feel sick to your stomach to the point of vomiting. I ate breakfast as usual at home before work and had to have my first morning snack—or second of several breakfasts—shortly after getting to work. This lasted into June, after which I had a few weeks of reprieve when I could almost even say that I enjoyed my pregnancy. And then the next symptoms found me.

Looking back on my second pregnancy, I feel like the universe was playing a big joke on me. Because I was so naive, I was served up every pregnancy-related symptom there was. There was, of course, the all-day sickness (as it should be named). I also had bloating, heartburn, fatigue, the most uncomfortable rib pain, back pain, changes in my skin pigmentation and headaches. Oh, the headaches. They started conveniently a couple of weeks after the morning sickness had finally subsided and lasted until close to 40 weeks. Thanks, Mother Nature!

Brad and I had pawned Archer off on some friends in late June to go to Vancouver Island for a friend's wedding. We took the Friday off of work and took a mid-afternoon ferry to Victoria. Since we were kid-free, we took in a movie, *Wonder Woman*, on our way to the resort where the wedding was to be held. During the movie, the baby was so active, kicking and wiggling, I was convinced that I was going to have a girl and that she was channeling Gal Gadot kicking ass as Wonder Woman through the big screen.

We enjoyed the "baby moon" that we found ourselves on before the wedding on Saturday afternoon. We had no other plans except for the wedding, so it was truly relaxing. Nevertheless, even though I had turned in early Friday night and slept in on Saturday morning, I got up feeling like I had been run over by a truck. Or worse, like I was suffering from a massive hangover. I really wasn't sure where these feelings were coming from, especially the insane, pounding headache, but I decided that it must have been the different pillow at the hotel.

We had a wonderful time at the wedding and thoroughly enjoyed our weekend away. But when the following weekend arrived and I was still having daily non-hangover headaches, I figured something was not quite right. And, sure enough, both my doctor and midwives explained that hormones can do crazy things and assured me that the headaches were related to my pregnancy. My GP encouraged me to increase my caffeine intake, which helped to decrease the severity of the headaches, but I had not been able to find something to help get rid of them entirely.

It was also around this time that I started looking for a new doula for my second birthing experience. My first one had moved out of town, so she wouldn't be able to be at our second birth. I actually found out about our second doula through someone I used to play softball with; the world being as small as it is, she was also a close neighbour.

Our new doula came over to our house to meet us for the first time. We sat on our patio while Archer finished his dinner one lovely summer evening.

"So," she said to Brad and me, "tell me about your first birth experience."

"Well," I told her, "we had planned a home birth, but following over 24 hours of labour at home, I had only dilated to about three centimetres. We decided to go to the hospital for an epidural, which ended in a c-section that evening."

"We're really hoping to avoid having a c-section this time around," Brad added.

"I see," she said after listening intently. "Can I ask who your midwife was?"

I told her.

"Can I be honest with you?" she asked.

"Of course," I said. "We would appreciate it."

"I'm not surprised that you had a c-section with her as your midwife," she said rather bluntly. "And if you're wanting a vaginal birth after cesarean, I think you should find another midwife."

"Oh," I said, taken aback.

"What makes you say that?" Brad said.

"Well, her history with VBACs, for one," she said, using the shorthand term for Vaginal Birth After Cesarean Section. "She doesn't really have one. Her patients tend to have repeat c-sections."

I was not okay with this.

"You know," Brad said, "that doesn't really surprise me, now that I think about it. As soon as Anya told her she wanted to try for a VBAC, she told us that we would be going to the hospital and would get hooked up to an IV and monitors right away."

"Right?" the doula said. "It is always a mother's decision what happens during labour and delivery. I just don't have good experience with her. I don't respect her style."

"She also told us that home birth was completely off the table," I added.

"That's not true!" the doula responded. "As long as you're informed and a healthy candidate, you can labour at home for as long as you're comfortable. And have a home birth!"

"Wow," Brad said in awe. We were both floored.

"I mean," I said, "it's one thing if she had said she, personally, isn't comfortable with a VBAC home birth, but she just outright said it's not an option."

"Which is just not true," the doula said confidently.

"I'm so glad that we got a hold of you," I told her. "I'm relieved, actually."

"I have to tell you, if you're going to stay in her care, I can't take you on as a client."

"I understand," I said, looking across the table at Brad. His eyes met mine and we both agreed without speaking that we wanted to find another care provider who would be more supportive of our choices and forthcoming with our options.

"Do you have anyone that you would recommend for us?" Brad asked.

"Absolutely." The doula gave us the name of a midwifery collective. "The only thing is that they're located in Vancouver. It shouldn't be a problem for them to take you into their care, but I'm not sure which hospital you'll be able to register the birth at. It will likely have to be in Vancouver."

"That's fine," Brad said. "As long as we're going to have options and not just be told what we can and can't do."

"Thank you so much for your honesty," I told the doula. "I will contact the midwives tomorrow, as well as the others in Burnaby that you mentioned as a backup to see about switching our care providers. And we would love to have you as our doula, too."

"Sounds great, Anya!"

I contacted the midwifery collective the next day and also sent emails to the other midwives the doula had recommended. My heart was set on the collective after reading their reviews online, but I really just wanted to have someone on my side, with my true best interests at heart.

I left my first appointment with our potential new midwives feeling more empowered than I had ever felt in my life. Our team would consist of two midwives who had been working together for years, as well as a new addition to the team. Brad came with me to the initial meeting, where we met with one of them to discuss my possible transfer of care.

"Welcome," the midwife said as she brought us into her office. "Have a seat."

"Thank you," I said as Brad and I took a seat together on the couch.

"So, you're here to talk about transferring your care?"

"Yes," I answered. "We are currently in the care of a midwife in Coquitlam who delivered our first son. I had a c-section with him and I'd like to avoid that at all costs this time around."

"And we've been informed that it's not likely, given our current midwife," Brad added, "and, ummm, her history."

"I see," the midwife replied. "Can you tell me a little more about why you had a c-section with your son?"

"I ended up having the surgery at 41 weeks and 5 days as he wasn't dropping after I had been in labour for about 27 hours. And then his heart rate wasn't coming up as quickly as they wanted to see following each contraction. It wasn't an emergency, but we didn't feel like we had any choice and, of course, we wanted to do what was best for Archer."

"Archer?" she said. "What an awesome name!"

"Thanks. Archer Bruce," I said.

"And do you know what the gender of this baby is?"

"No," Brad said very quickly. "We're having a surprise, which is what we did with Archer as well."

"That's great!" the midwife said. "I would have to look at your records, but it sounds like there's no reason you shouldn't be able to have a VBAC with this birth. Can you tell me why it is that you don't feel like your current midwife will support that?"

"We have retained a doula near home." I gave her our doula's name. "She said that in her history with our midwife, having a repeat c-section is more likely than having a VBAC."

Brad just couldn't help himself with this one. "And looking back on Archer's birth we don't think that everything was done for us to avoid a c-section. Anya really doesn't want another c-section."

"Okay," the midwife nodded.

"And when we discussed having a VBAC this time around, we were told that as soon as I go into labour, I will have to go to the hospital to be hooked up to monitors and given an IV. It didn't seem like I have any choices," I said bluntly.

"I see," the midwife continued. "What is your ideal birth this time around?"

"I want a VBAC. That is number one for me," I told her. "And with Archer, we had been planning a home birth, so if we're able to do that, I'd like to try to give birth at home."

"Ok. Well, it's my position to inform you of the recommendations for someone in your situation, and to help you make the decision that is best for you and your baby," she explained.

"We understand the risks of a VBAC," Brad explained, "and we'd like to try to have the baby at home."

"That's great," the midwife said. "We will, of course, go over all of that with you when the time comes. You're a little ways along and you've done this before, so I don't see any problems."

"Thank you," I told her. "It makes me feel so relieved to know that I have the power to make decisions for myself and my baby. Instead of being told how everything will go down instead."

"And which hospital did you give birth at previously?"

"Royal Columbian in New Westminster," I replied.

"We do not have privileges at that hospital," the midwife told us. “So the hospital that we would register you at would be one of two hospitals in Vancouver—St. Paul’s or BC Women’s.”

“That sounds good,” I told her, looking over at Brad while he gently squeezed my hand. I think that he liked what he was hearing as much as I did.

“And you would be cared for by myself and two other midwives, one of whom is joining our practice later in the summer. We rotate appointments so that you get to know us all, and then whomever is on call when you go into labour will be the one to deliver your baby!”

“So, you’ll take us on as patients?” I asked her excitedly. I was so hopeful that she would say yes, that the worry I carried deep down about having a repeat c-section would be dissolved when my baby was in the care of these wonderful women.

“Yes,” she said. “I will have a consent form prepared for you to sign so that we can request your records from this pregnancy and your birth with Archer. We should be able to get those transferred over to us immediately. Do you have any more questions for me?”

“Do you see this often?” Brad asked. “That patients are switching so far along, because of the care they’re receiving?”

“I don’t see this specific situation much,” she replied. “But people switch care providers all the time. You’re still not quite halfway; there’s plenty of time.”

“Thank you. I think that’s all for now,” I told her.

“Alright, well let’s get your first appointment scheduled and the consent form signed. Then we’ll be good to go!”

On the drive home from the clinic, I almost started to cry.

"Brad," I began saying, "I can't even tell you how relieved I am that we got such a great new doula and now we have new midwives!"

"I know. You and me both."

"So, you think that we're doing the right thing?"

"Absolutely, babe. No doubt."

"Me, too," I said.

I was ready to be in charge this time. To be given the options and make decisions for myself and my baby. I had honestly never felt more alive. Not once in my pregnancy with Archer had I felt so empowered in the choices I would have to make in order to bring my baby into this world. I felt lightened in my chest; I knew that it was all going to be alright having these midwives beside us along the way. It was always in the back of my mind that I could end up having to have another c-section and I had a difficult time preparing myself mentally for another surgery, but through many conversations with Brad, our doula, the midwives and even my counsellor, I had put myself in the right frame of mind to get the VBAC that I so dearly wanted. Now I just had to get through the remainder of my already difficult pregnancy.

We hadn't planned too much for our summer, but we had reserved a spot at Golden Ears Provincial Park for camping on the August long weekend, which always falls close to Brad's birthday. Brad took the Friday before the long weekend off to get us ready to go camping while I was working and Archer was at day care.

Sometime in the mid-afternoon I got up from my desk and went to talk to one of the lawyers in her office. As I was standing in her doorway talking to her, facing her straight on, something went wrong with my vision and I suddenly couldn't see her sitting at her desk. I recognized this as a symptom I have had in the past prior to getting a migraine. When I got back to my desk the symptoms worsened. I couldn't see any of the words on my computer screen and as I texted Brad to tell him I thought I was getting a migraine, the sight of my fingers eluded me. I asked him to come and pick me up as there was no way I would have been able to drive in that condition. I was scared, but I had had migraines before, so I knew that I would be okay as long as I could get to bed as soon as possible.

"Hey," I said to our office manager as she walked past my desk, "I think I have to go home."

Let me rephrase. I should call her the biased office un-manager. She has worked for my boss, the BFL (bitch-face lawyer; we'll get to her in due time), for over twenty years and nothing I said to her or anyone in the office was ever confidential. She would be nice as pie to my face, but I never bought it, not for a minute. It was obvious where her allegiances lay, and I knew that they weren't with myself or any of the staff in the office. All that aside, she was kind to my face, which I was extremely grateful for at this time.

"Are you okay?" she asked me. "You don't look so good."

"I don't think so," I told her. I was scared. I was looking up at her, wanting to tell her that I was just asking Brad to come and pick me up but I needed him to bring my parking pass so I could leave my car in the parking lot safely, but my thoughts were not turning into words. I sat there, staring at her blankly, my mind racing, worried that I couldn't speak.

"Can I do anything to help?"

"Brad is going to come and pick me up," I finally managed to say.

"Okay," she responded. "Why don't you shut your computer down and then when he gets here, I'll walk you out."

See, biased doesn't mean unkind.

My cheek and tongue were quickly becoming numb. I was so afraid. As I shut down my computer and got myself ready for Brad to pick me up, I started to lose feeling in my left hand. My fingers were tingling. I was so confused.

Brad texted me when he arrived and the biased office un-manager walked me outside.

"Thanks," I said to her as I climbed into the van beside Brad.

"Have a great long weekend!" the biased office un-manager said to me. Thanks, I am definitely on track to have a spectacular weekend, you insensitive...

If you don't have anything nice to say, don't say anything at all. Back to the story.

"Are you okay?" Brad asked me, a look of concern on his face.

"I think so," I said to him. "My face and hand are no longer tingling and I seem to have gotten my sight back completely."

"Wait, what?" he responded in alarm.

"My hand and arm went all numb," I told him. "And my face."

"Aren't those the signs of a stroke?"

"Ya."

"We should go to the hospital," he said.

"Why don't we go check my blood pressure first," I suggested. "All of those symptoms went away, so let's see how my blood pressure is doing before we head to the hospital."

"Okay," he said, driving over to the closest pharmacy with a blood pressure machine.

It was completely normal. Near perfect, as usual. We went back out to the van to discuss what to do next.

"Camping is out of the question; we'll just have to eat the reservation cost."

"Are you sure?" I asked. It was really hard to give the spot up, even though I knew deep down that we had to.

"Yes, babe," Brad told me, "and I think that we should go to the hospital. There are still a couple of hours before we have to pick Archer up from day care, so it's best to go sooner than later."

I knew he was right.

"Better safe than sorry," I said as we headed over to Eagle Ridge Hospital, the closest to our house.

Time passed in a flash, and before we knew it, it was again time for Brad to leave me at the hospital to go and pick Archer up from day care.

"I'll be back soon and I'll stop and get dinner on the way," he said as he leaned to kiss me on the forehead, leaving me alone in a hospital bed for the second time that year. I don't hold it against him, of course, but it was a scary time to be left alone. I couldn't help but flash back to the last time he left me in the hospital to pick up our son. I tried to ignore the fear and sadness that tried to overcome my thoughts.

"Anya?" A young female doctor parted the curtain with her hands as she asked my identity.

"Yes."

"I'm your doctor," she said as she came to stand in front of me. "I understand you have had some migraine symptoms this afternoon?"

"Yes."

"Can you explain to me what happened?"

"I was at work today," I explained, "and I started to get a headache around lunch time."

"Do you get headaches often?"

"Yes," I answered her.

"Is that just in your pregnancy, or did you frequently get headaches before?"

"Just since I've been pregnant. They started at around 16 weeks or so," I said.

"What happened next?"

"Around 3:00 pm, I started to get disturbances to my vision. When I've had that happen in the past, I have gotten migraines."

"Any other symptoms?"

I was beginning to feel like a number. Get this pregnant chick out of here ASAP so they can fill the bed with someone else.

"Yes," I responded. "I had numbness and tingling in my left hand, fingers and arm, and in my right cheek and tongue. And I wasn't able to speak properly. I could think of what I wanted to say, but the words wouldn't come to me."

"Okay," the doctor paused, reviewing her notes before going on. "I think that your pregnancy is causing these headaches and the related symptoms, but to be on the safe side, I would recommend that you undergo an MRI, which we do not offer at this hospital. Let me check on a referral for you and I'll be right back."

As she was leaving, Brad and Archer returned. Archer was older now and less fearful seeing me in a big hospital bed.

"Hi, Mom," he said, crawling up into the bed with me.

"So," Brad said, "was that the doctor? What did she say?"

I filled him in and then said, "If it's pregnancy symptoms, I really just want to go home."

"What about the MRI?"

"I guess we can go for it," I said, "but I feel like we're wasting our time."

"It's never a waste of time, babe," Brad started to say when the doctor returned.

"Okay," she said, handing me a piece of paper. "Here is a requisition for you to go for an MRI at Royal Columbian tomorrow morning at 10:00 am."

"Okay," I said, taking the paper from her.

"I am recommending that you stay here overnight, just in case your symptoms return. But you said you live close, correct?"

"Yes, we're in Port Moody," I responded. "I'd like to go home."

There was no way I was staying overnight in the hospital. Not when my gut was telling me that the doctor was right. This was all related to my pregnancy.

"I will see that you're discharged," the doctor said as she left us alone for the final time.

"When are we going camping?" Archer asked excitedly.

"Aww, buddy," Brad said to him. "Mom is sick, that's why we're at the hospital. We're not going to be able to go camping."

"Okay!" he said. "Maybe tomorrow?"

"Another time, monkey," I said as I reached over and gave him a hug.

We went home and put Archer to bed.

"How are you feeling?" Brad asked.

"Fine, actually," I told him. "I don't even have a headache."

"So weird," he said as he picked up his phone. "Looks like severe, stroke-like headaches and symptoms can be side-effects of pregnancy. Do you want to go see your GP about it?"

"Yes," I answered. "I think so. And I'm torn about the MRI. I don't want to waste any more time."

"It's worth it, babe," Brad responded. "Stop saying that it's not."

We arranged for our friend Gina to come and stay with Archer at our house while we went to New West the next morning.

"Why didn't you call me yesterday?" she asked as soon as she came in the door.

We were sitting on the front patio. "I don't know, Gina. We didn't want to bother you."

"It's no bother! Now you go and take care of yourself. We'll be fine here."

Archer was thrilled to hang out with Gina, so Brad and I took off to the hospital.

We followed the instructions the nurse had given us the night before and arrived early to the appointment. There was no one else there.

We were taken in right away and a nurse came in to give me instructions. I had to remove all clothes and jewelry as well as anything whatsoever that had metal in it. I gave Brad a hug and a kiss and the nurse took me around the corner to the machine.

He explained everything to me, but all I could focus on was the large machine in front of me. My hearing was fogged and I was losing sense of what was happening. The large machine in front of us whirred. I noticed how tiny the cavity where my head and body would sit was.

I didn't think I'd be able to do it, but I climbed up onto the bed. As the nurse placed the plastic cover over me, pinning my arms to my sides and covering my body down to my waist, my heart rate jumped.

I can't do this.

The bed slid up and backwards and I closed my eyes, grasping the emergency bobble he gave me to squeeze if I needed anything.

"Yes?" a voice came through to my ears.

"I can't do this. I need to get out," I said over and over and over.

"Okay," he said back to me, "try and stay calm. It will take a minute to get you back out."

It seemed to take forever for the bed to slide back out of the machine and down to a position where he could lift the piece that was holding me down. I sat up right away and slid off the bed.

"Careful," he said.

"I need to get out of here," I said. I was panicking. The tears were coming. There was no way I would be able to do that for 30 minutes.

The doors opened and Brad came around the corner from the waiting room.

"What's going on?" he asked, concerned.

"I couldn't do it," I said, falling into his embrace, crying. "Don't make me go back in there."

"Shhhh," he said, rubbing my head. "It's okay."

"Don't make me go back in there," I said, crying.

I don't recall ever being claustrophobic before. When you were a part of my life, I never had this problem.

"Don't make me go back in there," I said softly into Brad's chest.

"Babe," he said when my breathing had settled and I was starting to clearly calm down, "you can do it. Can you try for me, one more time?"

I looked up at him like he was crazy. I stayed silent. I thought about why I was putting myself through this; to make sure that I was okay and the baby was okay. At the recommendation of the doctors, we wanted to make sure there was no other reason for my aggressive symptoms.

"Okay," I said, taking a drink of water and straightening my stance. "I'll try again."

He walked me up to the door, holding my hand. "You're so brave," he said as I walked into the MRI room, the doors closing behind me one more time. I walked up to the monstrous machine and climbed onto it again. I summoned every ounce of strength that Brad believed I had and sat down on the plastic bed. I turned, laying my feet straight ahead, and slowly tried to lay down.

I couldn't do it.

"I'm really sorry," I said to the nurse as I swung my legs back off of the bed, "but I can't do this."

I didn't cry this time. There was just no way that I could do it. The fear encompassed me as the magnets and plastic had tried to and I got up and left the room faster than I can remember leaving any room ever.

"I'm sorry," I said to Brad when I saw him. "I just can't do it."

"Okay, babe," he said. "At least you tried."

We left the hospital, unsure of what to do next.

"Why don't you call your GP and see if we can get in to see him?" Brad suggested.

I tried, but given his shortened hours on weekends there were no appointments available. We went in person to see what the wait time for the walk-in clinic would be, and were told there weren't any more appointments for that day. I explained to the lady at the front desk what had happened and she thankfully told me to come back on Monday morning.

All we had to do next was wait. I was surprisingly feeling quite well overall, but I went home and had a nap. When I got up, I found that Brad and set up our propane fire pit in the carport and he and Archer were ready to roast hot dogs and marshmallows to make s'mores.

"If we can't go camping," Brad said, "we'll bring the camping to us!"

Archer, of course, was thrilled to be "camping" in the driveway. We were robbed of a weekend of creating memories at the lake, but we did our best to create memories at home.

The next morning, I suffered an event very similar to the one

I had experienced on the Friday. I lay down on the couch in hopes that it would quickly pass, and it did. When I finally got to see the doctor on Monday he confirmed that I had my pregnancy to thank.

"Sometimes," he explained, "the blood flow in the brain can be restricted due to pregnancy hormones. It's really quite common to get headaches and migraines and everything in between."

"So, what would you recommend to help?"

"Caffeine," he said. "Lots and lots of caffeine. It will help to open your blood vessels."

"And it won't harm the baby?" Brad asked.

"No," my GP said. "Contrary to popular belief, caffeine is not the devil in pregnancy. It will be your friend."

I was lucky enough not to have any more stroke-like symptoms for the rest of my pregnancy after that weekend, though I did have numerous days where I was overcome by migraines and all I could do was sleep them off. I was still getting daily headaches, which made it incredibly hard to sit in front of a computer screen at work all day. Then I had to go home at the end of the day and provide for my family. Keeping a three-year-old alive was no easy task on a good day, but I did what I had to.

On top of the headaches and migraines, I had an increasing pain in my right side that made sitting up very uncomfortable. I adjusted to having to lean back every time I sat for an extended period of time, whether at my desk, in the car or at home (sorry, not sorry, to Brad for commandeering his beloved recliner). I also made the extra effort to get up and walk around or stand to do my desk job when I could. It quite rapidly got to a point where I was completely spent every day. I was exhausted by noon, unable to come home and give my best self to my family or even play with my son unless I was sitting down (laid back in the recliner, of course). By the time September came, I found that I wasn't enjoying any part of my days. I wasn't doing anyone any favours by pushing myself to my limit at work. I was suffering every day of the week, including on weekends, and eventually decided that I couldn't go on like that anymore.

I brought it up with the biased office un-manager one afternoon in mid-September when we were alone together in the office.

"I think I need to give you my two weeks' notice," I told her. "I can't do this much longer, I'm too uncomfortable."

"Yeah," she said. "I can tell you're not doing too well."

"Thanks."

"But do you think you could wait until we find a replacement to leave? We've been having trouble finding someone to fill other spots, so the longer you could stay, the better."

I wasn't surprised that she asked me to stay longer, but my body was telling me to get out as soon as possible.

"I can try," I said honestly. "Actually, my next midwife appointment is at the beginning of October, so as long as everything is okay at that appointment, I'll stay as long as you need."

"Sounds fair. Thanks, Anya."

And that was the end of the conversation. I have no idea whether she talked to the BFL about it, although if I had to guess I'd say she did; they all talked about everything together in that office.

It shouldn't have come as a surprise to them when, following my next midwife appointment, I showed up at work with notes saying that I was no longer able to continue working. I had wanted to give them my two weeks' notice and exit gracefully, but my body had enough by that point and my care providers agreed.

Leaving work was not a decision that I took lightly. Back in the summer, when I had started to feel the stresses of my job impacting me in a way that they hadn't before, I talked to my counsellor about work. I tried to find ways to deal with the stress of my job and, more specifically, my boss. Brad was behind my decisions one hundred percent. In fact, he seemed to think I should have given myself a break from work long before I actually did, though he never would have told me what to do.

No one had ever prepared me for this situation. I was walking into work to tell them that I was unable to continue, knowing that they would be holding my job for my return after baby, but leaving them abruptly high and dry in the interim. I knew that what I was doing was best for my family and me, but upsetting other people is not exactly enjoyable. Nor is it something I would ever set out to do.

The first person I saw when I walked into the office to give them my notes was the biased office un-manager, who also worked as the receptionist.

"Hey," she said, "BFL wants to see you."

I stared back at her, unsure of exactly what to say. She picked up on something before I could explain.

"Is everything okay?" she asked.

"No," I replied. "I have two notes saying I can't work any longer."

"Okay."

"I just can't do it."

Surprisingly she came right over and gave me a hug before asking, "When are you leaving? Right now?"

"Ya, the notes are effective immediately," I said as I handed her two notes from my GP and midwife, respectively. "I tried to give you notice, and I did say I'd stay until my next midwife appointment at the very least. I'm sorry."

I don't think she knew what to say. I don't blame her.

"I'll just pack up my stuff," I told her as I turned to walk towards my desk.

"I'll copy these for you," she said as she turned her back on me. At least she was still being nice to my face.

I went over to my desk to collect my things as I didn't think there was any reason why I would open myself up to another afternoon of my boss' stress and bullshit. Effective immediately meant effective immediately.

I had been working at the firm for less than a year when I got pregnant. I liked my work. It was close to home and it was in a new area of law, so it provided a lot of challenges. My boss was a strong and very busy female lawyer who appeared to respect me and wasn't in the office much. It wasn't a position that I saw myself in forever, but I was content. I felt appreciated. I was learning new things on a daily basis. When I first got pregnant, I absolutely saw myself returning to the position following my maternity leave.

I'm sure there are people out there who don't agree with me on this one, but I never wanted to put the possibility of expanding my family on hold for a job. Getting pregnant, and keeping a pregnancy, was never going to be in my control. Infertility was a struggle that I didn't know whether I would have, and while I never ultimately had to face that particular challenge, the road to baby number two nevertheless wasn't easy for me. I missed some work when I had my miscarriage, but the timing didn't seem too horrible as my boss had also been taking a good chunk of time off following her husband's sudden passing. I went into work every morning in the week following my D&C to make sure everything was under control, and returned home to rest. I was thankful for what I assumed was their understanding and flexibility.

When I first started at my job, I honestly thought that my boss would be retiring soon. But when her husband passed away my opinion did a complete 180. It seemed clear she was going to be working forever. Then a few months into the new year, a switch flipped. I had been warned that she wasn't as nice as she seemed, and boy did I learn just how true that was.

She didn't care how hard I worked, or how tenaciously I pushed through the unfamiliarity of a new type of law or the pain of the loss of my second pregnancy. She was wicked, constantly focused on whatever it was that had been missed or done incorrectly. It was fine; I put up with it. She was a lawyer, after all.

Then I got pregnant again. I knew there was an end in sight. Towards the end of the year I wouldn't have to deal with her any more. Things were looking up.

When I told her I was pregnant, she couldn't even muster a "congratulations." Instead, I got "Well, that's good for you, not for me." I should have known right away that it would only go downhill from there. She asked numerous times whether I was sure that there was only one baby in my stomach. She called me out in front of a client for looking too big to still have two months left in my pregnancy, only to have the client agree that I looked huge, and add that she had carried twins. There was really nothing that I could say or do as it was in my best interest to keep my job before going on maternity leave. It was not a good feeling.

The twins comment came only a few days before I took my leave. I went to see my midwife on the morning that I left my job. I was told that baby was healthy and I was measuring right on track. Twins that, boss lady.

Given my physical and emotional struggles, I was happy to have decided together with my care providers that it was time to be done with work. It was in my best interest to rest and help my body de-stress in the hope that the headaches would subside at least a little. I felt good about the situation. I felt bad about the fact that I would be leaving my work in a tough spot, knowing that they didn't yet have anyone to replace me. But I honestly thought that I would have the support I deserved to do what was best for myself and my unborn child.

I was, sadly, very wrong.

"Hey Anya," the biased office un-manager said to me as she walked over to my desk. I placed some belongings from my desk in a bag and turned to face her. "BFL would like to see you."

"Okay," I said. I set down my things and went into her office.

"Close the door," BFL said as I walked in.

I did as I was instructed and took a seat across the desk from her. I was in the same seat I had taken the night I came in for an interview only a year ago, when she complimented me on my resume and hired me on the spot.

"So," she said through pursed lips, her posture stiff. "You're leaving?"

No question about how I was feeling or doing.

"Yes," I said.

"Well, don't you just get to do whatever you want to do," the crossfire began, "and leave me to deal with the aftermath."

I just looked at her. I wasn't expecting this.

"But," she said as she smugly shuffled some papers on her desk, avoiding eye contact with me, "you are the employee and you get to do whatever you want, don't you?"

She said it like it was a question, but it really wasn't.

"And I am the self-employed woman," she said as she sat up even straighter, as if she wasn't talking to a fellow woman, let alone one in a difficult situation of her own. "I have to just deal with whatever you choose to do."

As if this was my choice.

She wasn't even close to being done. "First, you take an appointment on a morning when I needed you. The least you could have done was go to your doctor on a Friday when I am not here." She didn't even bother to pretend to understand that maybe my midwives only see prenatal patients on certain days of the week.

I couldn't speak. I would later learn through working with my counsellor that my lack of defensive behaviour was actually a subconscious choice to protect myself. And my baby.

"And now you are leaving me, high and dry, only weeks before a five-week trial."

She sat there, finally silent, staring at me. I don't actually think she expected me to say anything.

"I didn't do any of this on purpose," I finally said.

"But you did get pregnant only a few months after starting here," she said viciously, "only to have that pregnancy end, causing you to miss work because of it."

I was shocked. I was completely unable to speak a single word in response. I sat there in front of this old, bitter, unhappy lady and took every unkind word that she threw my way. She was visibly upset and I am surprised that I didn't join her in that, to be honest. I guess I was simply numb. I listened to every horrible word that she spat at me. I couldn't fathom that she would have any further unkind words to share, but it seemed like she was just getting started.

"Then you go and get pregnant again right away," she said, affirming her BFL nickname with ease. Believe you me, the other nickname I had for her started with the next letter in the alphabet. The word it stands for is one that my own husband has only ever heard me say out loud once, in reference to her.

"I've been unhappy. And I can tell that you've been unhappy, haven't you? You're leaving me at the worst time. It's like you planned it," she accused me.

"I didn't plan any of this," I said, raising my chin, finally having had enough of the attack. "And I have a doctor's note that is effective immediately so I'll be going now."

And with that, I stood and returned to my desk to finish packing my things. I said a quick goodbye to my coworkers and went out to the car where my wonderful husband was waiting for me. I never looked back.

Brad and I went for lunch and we talked and tried to get my mind off of the situation. He was angry for me and wanted to go back into the office to give the BFL a piece of his mind. I assured him that I could've done that, too, but that it wasn't worth it to stoop to the level of the bully. We had a lovely lunch after which I came home to relax and he returned to work for the afternoon. For the rest of the day, I continued to feel off. I couldn't quite put my finger on it, though I knew that I felt wronged. I knew I was doing what was best for my family and me, but it didn't feel good to have sat through a personal attack like that.

It wasn't until we were ready to go to bed that night that I was finally able to piece together my feelings. I felt embarrassed and ashamed. Embarrassed that the good work I had done for this woman, errors and omissions aside, was likely to be overshadowed by her blatant hatred for me. I was especially ashamed that I had let her berate me like that, to my face, without saying anything in my own defense.

In my personal life, I am one to stand up for what I believe in and to encourage others around me to do the same. I am always one to give my opinions, no matter how strong or offline they may seem, while keeping others' feelings in mind as much as I can. But in that moment, I had allowed myself to be a punching bag. I had resolved myself to being whatever she told me I was and I was better than that. I knew that I was. I know that not everyone we meet will like or appreciate us. But incidents such as these should never happen. People, especially women, should never make each other feel as shitty as my boss made me feel.

Had my boss not projected her stress and unhappiness onto me so cruelly over the months before I left, maybe my body would have been able to handle working, even part-time, until I was ready to start my maternity leave. I'm not one to live in "maybe" land, but maybe if we all loved just a little more and dropped the selfish instincts that so many of us seem to have there would be fewer unkind words spoken, fewer heartbroken tears shed. There are no circumstances in which I should have felt embarrassed or ashamed for taking the appropriate steps to take care of myself and my family. Plain and simple. If the BFL didn't want one of her employees to potentially take a maternity leave, then she shouldn't have hired a woman of childbearing age. Whether it's discriminatory or not.

When I started my leave from work, Brad and I chose to leave Archer in full-time day care until the end of the year, making me the resident housewife. I handled being at home by myself a lot better than I had when I was first on maternity leave when Archer was a baby. I had a lot of time to prepare myself for my labour and ready our house for our family's expansion. The time passed methodically and I was happy. It took about a month before I started seeing a difference in my headaches. They never resolved completely, but they weren't happening every day or occurring with the same level of pain. When I did get them, I was able to focus on relaxing and rest them away. There was never any doubt that I had made the right decision for my health and well-being in taking a sick leave from work.

At around 38 weeks, I had a routine appointment with my midwives. By this time, we had met all three of them and felt like they were truly a part of our team, with our best interests at heart.

"So," one of the midwives started, "how are you feeling?"

"I'm having a good day," I told her. "I have the usual rib pain, but I'm feeling good today."

"Okay, that's great," she said, making some notes in her computer. "And how are you feeling about the upcoming delivery?"

"Pretty good," I answered honestly. "We are preparing for the home birth, like we talked about. But I also have it in the back of my mind that we might have to go to the hospital. I still want to do everything possible to avoid having another c-section."

"That's actually what I'd like to talk to you about today. Given that you are attempting a VBAC, it's around this time that we would recommend that you go see an OB to discuss your previous birth and this pregnancy. Because if we end up at the hospital and a c-section is recommended, we obviously will not be able to perform that for you."

"Okay."

"We have an OB whom we work quite closely with at the hospital you are registered at, so if you'd like I can send a requisition over to their office and they can contact you with an appointment."

"That sounds good," I said. "The doctor who delivered Archer was very positive about any future births I might have. At my discharge appointment he said that just because I had a c-section, it didn't mean I would have to for future deliveries. He said that every pregnancy is different and nothing from my first delivery should prevent a future vaginal birth."

"That's great!"

"I think it would be a good idea for me to hear that again from an OB, now that we're getting so close to delivery," I told her.

"Alright," she said. "I will get that taken care of and their office will call you with an appointment."

The following day I found myself in East Van, at the OB's office. I was sitting in the exam room, waiting for the OB to get there. I was his first appointment of the day and he was late.

"Hello, Anya," he said as he entered the exam room. "Congratulations."

"Thanks," I replied.

"So, I see here that you're almost to full term with your second child. That you had a c-section with your first," he said as he reviewed my chart. "And your midwife tells me that you'd like to attempt a VBAC."

He was telling me all of this as if they were facts I was not privy to. "Yes."

"And you are planning on delivering at BC Women's Hospital?"

"I am registered there," I said, "but we are planning to try a home birth."

"Well," he said immediately, "given that you have had a c-section previously it is not recommended to birth at home. Your care providers should have told you that."

"They did," I answered. "We are aware of the risks."

My cheeks were reddening at this point, but I kept it short and sweet. He left it at that.

"Let's have a look at how you're measuring and I'll do a quick ultrasound, if that's okay with you."

"Yes, that's fine," I told him as I lay back on the table.

He measured the fundal height of my bulging stomach. As the measuring tape snapped out of his hands he said, "You're measuring three centimetres ahead of where you should be at this point."

Funny, I had been at the midwife's the day before and was told I was measuring right on track. And they had been consistently measuring my stomach over the last few months; not once was I measuring so far ahead.

He squeezed some cold ultrasound gel onto my stomach before reaching for the ultrasound machine. He tilted his head back and forth, moving the wand over my belly.

"We don't know the baby's gender," I told him. Brad always told everyone that when he could, so since he wasn't there, I did it for him. Better safe than sorry.

"That's nice," the OB said. "You have a very big baby here. He or she is bound to be nine or ten pounds, easily."

I nodded.

"I give you a 65% chance of delivering such a big baby vaginally. And that's only if you go into labour on your own before the 41 week and two-day mark. After that, you will have a repeat c-section."

I sat there, not saying anything. I knew that there was a tendency in care providers in this line of work to encourage repeat c-sections. I, myself, had been cared for by one earlier in my pregnancy. I had expected that an OB would not be supportive of a home birth, but to not support my desire to have a VBAC? I hadn't seen this coming. It sounded to me like he was telling me that I couldn't do it.

"If there are no signs of labour by the time your due date comes," he went on, "I would recommend scheduling a c-section."

He washed his hands and as he was leaving the room he glanced down at my feet and said, "I would also watch for signs of pre-eclampsia. Your feet are swollen."

I have never had high blood pressure a day in my life.

I left the office in a huff. I wandered into the Whole Foods that shared the same parking lot as the doctor's office and pushed a buggy around, trying to calm down before driving home. When I had loaded my buggy with snacks and finally felt calm enough, I texted Brad, still upset, to update him on how the appointment went.

Dr. Youcantdothis was a fucking asshole that wants me to schedule a fucking c-section if I don't go into labour before my fucking due date.

He called me almost immediately.

"Babe," he said to me after I answered. "What happened?"

I paid for the small amount of groceries—most of them involving chocolate—that I had gathered, and headed outside. "This stupid short surgeon wants to cut me open! He basically told me the baby is going to be massive and that I can't deliver vaginally."

"What?"

"He gave me a 65% chance of delivering vaginally. And only if I go into labour on my own," I said angrily.

"How did he even come up with that number?" Brad said, working himself up as well. "Who does this guy think he is!?"

"I don't know," I said, starting to cry, "but I wish I never would have agreed to go to this stupid appointment."

"He doesn't even actually know anything about you or the baby and was likely just regurgitating the recommendations that he is told to give based on the guidelines for women giving birth in BC," Brad said. "This makes me so mad!"

"I know!"

"You know that he doesn't know what he's talking about, right?" Brad said, trying to comfort me. "The midwives haven't said anything about scheduling a c-section. And they've been caring for you almost the whole time!"

"I know."

"He's not even making sense, Anya. There's no reason why you can't do this."

His reassuring words were starting to resonate.

"You're right," I said with a sigh as I started to drive away. "Thank you for calling me."

"Do you feel better?"

"Yes."

"Do me a favour and do something nice for yourself this afternoon, okay?"

"Okay. I was planning on going to Ikea."

"Frozen yogurt?"

"You got it," I said with a smile.

"Don't let what this dickhead said bother you any more, okay?"

"Okay."

I hung up, feeling marginally better. Brad was right, this guy had reviewed my file for two seconds as he talked to me. And he was a surgeon. Hell, he probably would have scheduled my c-section right then and there if I had agreed.

I went to Ikea, as planned, and bought and framed an inspirational saying by Nelson Mandela: "It always seems impossible until it is done." By the time I finished my frozen yogurt cone, I had dusted off my resolution that I was going to have this baby naturally and decided that I was going to prove this guy wrong!

When I was back home for the afternoon, I got a call from our doula. Strange that she was calling, mid-afternoon on a Tuesday. Not so strange when I found out that Brad had texted her.

"Who the fuck does that guy think he fucking is?" came through the line when I answered it.

"Did Brad text you?" I asked, laughing to myself slightly.

"Yes. And I'm glad he did. You don't believe this guy, right?"

"No, but he certainly made me feel like crap."

"This makes me so mad!" she almost shouted. "These doctors just want to do surgeries. It's what they know. Don't let what he said bother you; he has no idea what he's talking about."

"Okay," I agreed.

"What was this about him only giving you a certain chance of delivering naturally?"

"He said he gives me a 65% chance of a VBAC."

"WHAT?"

"And that's only if I go into labour naturally before 41 weeks, two days," I told her.

"This just makes me so mad! Who does this guy think he is?"

By this time, I was the calm one. I appreciated her support and what was clearly her honest opinion so much.

"Don't listen to what he said, Anya," the doula said to comfort me. "He doesn't know what he's talking about."

"I know," I replied.

"You're going to have this baby naturally and show him that he has no idea what he's talking about!"

"Sounds like a plan," I agreed whole-heartedly.

"Are you okay?"

"Yes. I am. Thank you for the call."

"Any time," she said and hung up.

It was a bit of a speed bump, but I wasn't going to let it set me back. I resolved to make Dr. Youcantdothis eat his words. There was no doubt in my mind. Thanks to our lovely doula and my thoughtful husband, I was ready to get back on track with the right frame of mind before delivery.

My due date arrived, as scheduled, with no signs of labour coming any time soon. We were again trying everything we could to help induce labour, with no luck. I was drinking red raspberry leaf tea, eating spicy foods, walking, getting acupuncture, having sex, using clary sage oil—everything short of jumping up and down until my water broke. Nothing helped. Looking back, the ends of my pregnancies and subsequent labours were very similar. I am someone who simply gestates for longer, which is a very irritating trait to have. Anyone want to trade? Kidding, we're done having babies.

The Tuesday after my 41st week of pregnancy, Brad came to

my midwife appointment with me.

"Anya," the midwife said, "your doula told me what happened at your appointment with Dr. Youcantdothis. I'm so sorry that happened."

"That's okay. It's not your fault. There's no way you could have known he would be so unsupportive."

"Still, I really thought it was going to be a positive experience for you."

"It's okay, really."

"Alright," she moved on. "We're just past week 41, correct?"

"Yes," I said, looking over at Brad. Why hadn't I been one of those lucky girls who delivers a week early? Or had a due date baby, even? At the very least?

"We should talk about where you want to go from here," she said. "We can do a vaginal exam today, if you'd like, or we can wait and schedule an appointment for later in the week to check."

"I think an exam today would be fine," I told her. We had already discussed my history with internal exams at previous appointments. As a result, we decided that during labour, if an exam was deemed necessary, I was not to be told the number of centimetres I had progressed to. Knowing that I was only at three centimetres the first time around with Archer had most definitely been a discouragement that informed my decision to go to the hospital. I wanted to avoid that this time. I only wanted to know when my body had progressed past the point it had been at with Archer.

"The good news is that your cervix is softening," my midwife told me after the exam. "But there isn't any dilation yet."

"Okay."

"Our options from here are to have you come back later in the week to check you again," she explained. "Or wait until next week, when you are at 42 weeks. Which isn't ideal."

"We can come back later in the week," I said. "But what are the options then?"

I was desperate not to repeat Archer's birth.

"Has anyone talked to you about the labour cocktail?"

"Yes. That's how I went into labour with Archer."

"If you still haven't progressed in a few days, we could discuss taking the cocktail, to move things along."

"Okay."

"We could possibly take it that day, though we usually take it early in the morning so that you've had a good rest before contractions start."

I nodded.

"Are you comfortable with that plan?"

"Yes," I said. "That also gives me and Brad a couple of days to talk about it before we come back for another exam."

"Okay," she said, "we'll see you Friday then."

We left the office, Brad holding my hand in support. On the drive home, we got to talking.

"So," I said, taking a deep breath. "What do you think?"

"I think that it's good we're going to wait a couple of days to see if things start on their own."

"Ya," I said, staring out the window.

"You?"

"I'm hopeful," I said, "that I'm going to get my VBAC. I believe it, deep down."

"That's great, babe," he replied. Always my number one supporter.

"But it's getting so late again. I think it's a good idea to try the cocktail if I still haven't dilated by Friday."

"I think that the doula would disagree," he said with a smirk.

"Ya. But we're on track to do what we want all around. Never mind anyone else's opinions!"

"True. Now what should we do with Archer?"

We decided to have our friend Gina pick up Archer from day care that Friday afternoon. If I hadn't gone into labour on my own already, Brad and I would head into the appointment Friday morning, prepared to take the cocktail. In the meantime, I continued trying to walk the baby out and jumpstart contractions in any other way possible. None of them worked, so when Friday came, we dropped Archer at day care for the last time before he became a big brother.

Brad and I stopped for a nice brunch before heading to the appointment. What a luxury before becoming parents of two!

"How are you feeling?" the midwife asked as she welcomed us into the clinic.

"Honestly?" As if anyone could count on me for anything but my honest opinion. "The same?"

"Okay," she said as we all took a seat. "I see that you discussed taking the verbena oil mixture if nothing had progressed by today."

"Yes," I nodded.

"Well, let's take a look," she said. When she returned to the room with Brad after the exam, she explained that things had not progressed much, if at all. “It’s hard for me to say since I was not the one that did the exam on Tuesday, but I think that we should talk about the plan to take the cocktail.”

“Okay,” I replied. I was sad to hear that I hadn’t progressed, but I wasn’t surprised. I was trying so hard to induce labour; I think I may have wanted it too much.

“I’ll give you the verbena oil along with directions,” the midwife explained, “and you can get the rest of the ingredients yourselves and take the mixture starting tomorrow morning.”

“Tomorrow?” I asked.

“Yes,” she replied. “We normally recommend taking the first dose early in the morning, with two further doses every two hours. You take the third regardless of whether contractions have started to really get things going.”

“We were ready today!” I told her. “But we will wait until tomorrow, that’s fine.”

Selfishly, I wanted my baby to have his or her own birthday, and if I didn’t go into labour until Saturday, I had a feeling that baby was going to share a birthday with another family member on Sunday. What I wanted most was for baby to arrive with no outside encouragement, but I also didn’t want to make it to 42 weeks with no signs of labour whatsoever.

We left the midwife’s office prepared to try and induce labour ourselves naturally the next morning.

“So,” Brad asked, “how do you feel about this plan?”

“It’s not ideal,” I told him, “but it’s what we decided if we got to this point again.”

"And the bigger question is what do we do with Archer?"

I called Gina to discuss it with her. She would pick up Archer as planned and that she would keep him for the weekend. She had a flight to visit family for Christmas the following week, so she would only be able to keep him through Monday. I wished more than anything that this baby would make an appearance before then.

Brad and I did some shopping together and went home to take a glorious afternoon nap. We went for dinner at our favourite local Italian restaurant, one of the first places that we had visited when we moved to the neighbourhood. The weather was turning slightly cold, but I was committed to walking the baby out of me so after filling up on amazing food we went down to Rocky Point. We video chatted with Archer to say good night while we were there and continued our walk. We went home and watched *Top Gun* before turning in early.

I hadn't felt any different after our big walk that evening, but something clicked. I awoke around 3:30 am that night with contractions.

Contractions following a c-section can be irregular, which mine definitely were. Our doula told me not to stop what I was doing to "do labour" and so I went back to bed and tried to sleep, with little luck. We got up that day and I made Brad vacuum the house while I tried to ignore my contractions, which were coming anywhere between four minutes and fifteen minutes apart. They were strong, but manageable, as we continued with our day. I was able to take some Gravol and Tylenol in the afternoon and had a two-hour nap, which was much needed. When I tried to do the same thing that evening, I was unable to sleep. The intensity of the contractions was increasing.

I was in our bedroom, trying different positions to help cope with the pain. I honestly think that I have a rather high tolerance for pain, but by this time I was not coping with the contractions well. I tried. I really did. And I was able to get on top of some of the contractions, but I felt myself being slowly overtaken by others. It was around 11:00 pm when I asked our doula to come over.

"Let's try leaning over the pillows," she suggested as she helped me rearrange the copious amounts of pillows on our bed so that my belly was resting on them with my chest sort of propped up.

The next contraction came. They were closer together and more consistent at this point.

"I can't do this," I voiced as I felt the wave start. "No, no, no, no."

"Yes, you can," the doula encouraged. "You can do this, Anya. It's okay."

I finished breathing heavily into myself and looked up at her. "I just don't know what to do."

"Have you tried the shower?"

"No. But we can. It made the contractions so much worse last time, but I will try."

Brad helped me get undressed and into the shower. Warm water rushed over me as the next contraction started.

"I can't do it, Brad," I said, panicking. "Help me out!"

"Okay, babe," he said as he grabbed my hand to help me out of the tub. "It's okay."

The doula came back upstairs as I was drying off.

"Done already? That was fast."

We went back into the bedroom. She gave me some water, rearranged the bed more, and then suggested that I try the exercise ball.

"Sit like this and lean over the edge of the bed," she suggested. I followed her directions and breathed deep and heavy into the ground as I hung my head low off the side of the bed.

"It's just not working," I said after the contraction passed. "I'm not able to get into it. I'm too close to the wall."

"Do you want to try the tub?" She knew that we had a birthing tub at the house as I thought I would like to try to birth in the tub. It was something I never got to try with Archer that I thought might be my saving grace this time around.

"Sure," I said as I crawled back into bed, snuggling against the headboard and clutching a pillow. Anything to get me through.

"I'll go down and get it out," Brad said. They tag-teamed setting up the birthing tub in our living room, which took quite some time to fill with warm water.

In the meantime, I continued to labour in our room. Every time, just before a contraction crested, I felt myself saying "No, no, no, no." I didn't mean to be negative. I didn't think I couldn't do it. I wasn't able to get underneath the pain, to accept it and use it to my advantage. I was trying. I was determined to get the baby out naturally if it was the last thing I did. The thought of going to the hospital hadn't yet crossed my mind but I was clearly not managing the labour pains well at all. At some point, Brad called the midwife.

"She wants to talk to you," he said as he passed his phone to the doula.

After she spoke to the midwife the doula came back and told us, "It's all good. We will call her when the contractions get closer together in a bit."

"Okay," Brad said.

"The tub is getting there," the doula added. "I'll be downstairs."

She left the room and we were alone again.

I was standing in the washroom and felt as if the contractions were intensifying. The doula had shown Brad how to apply counter pressure to my hips during each contraction, which helped tremendously. I called out for him to come and apply pressure every time a contraction started. We went back and forth like that in the washroom upstairs while the tub filled downstairs.

"I don't think I can do this," I said, exhausted, looking at myself in the mirror. I shook my head back and forth, knowing that another contraction was coming. And quickly. "No, no, no, no."

"Yes, Anya, you can." I heard the voices behind and beside me and felt the pressure on my hips of someone helping me with the contraction. I don't know who it was; it was either my doula or my loving husband, but I couldn't tell. I couldn't focus; I didn't care. I just wanted it to pass.

"I think we should call the midwife back," the doula suggested to Brad. They spoke a few more words quietly to each other and then Brad left the room to call her.

"You're doing so great," she encouraged me. "The tub is almost ready for you. It's going to feel so good when you're in there."

She did her best to help me through the next contraction.

"I'd like to go back to the bed," I suggested. "I'm tired."

"You've got this, Anya," she said as she escorted me back to my room. "You're doing great."

Brad was there as I climbed back into the pillows. "She's on her way."

I rested as best I could; I may have even fallen asleep a little in between contractions. There wasn't much difference.

"The tub is almost ready."

"No, no, no, no."

"Yes."

"I can't."

"Yes, you can."

More time passed. I remember standing in the washroom again when the midwife arrived. She crouched in the hall, watching me deal with each contraction, Brad helping. They all spoke in quiet tones. Finally, my midwife asked me how I was doing. I was so happy it was her.

"I can't do this," I told her. I wasn't making sense at this point. I couldn't think. I had almost been up for 24 hours, minus the small nap.

"Yes, you can, Anya," she said gently. I believed her. I believed all three of them but still the words were coming out of my mouth, saying that I couldn't.

The midwife checked the baby with her stethoscope and took my blood pressure. "You're doing great, Anya. I think the tub is ready; why don't we go give that a try?"

I walked slowly down the stairs. Someone helped me. I don't remember who.

It was a surprisingly beautiful scene. The Christmas tree stood by the front window, sparkling. At its feet, the tub magically reflected its colourful lights. Brad took my hand and helped me step over the side of the tub and. I gently lowered myself to a seat in the warm water. The lights in the living room were off; everything was lit by the colours of our Christmas tree. I felt a calm wash over me with the welcome of the water but I still felt like I was fighting an uphill battle and that I was at risk of tumbling over backwards at any moment.

When the next contraction came, I felt a little more prepared. I closed my eyes, trying to remain relaxed. I let the water guide my body slowly upwards. Floating was like a drug that allowed me to forget what a hard time I had been having, even if it only lasted a second.

It was in these moments, as I floated by the lights of the Christmas tree, that I voiced to my team that I didn't feel like they were listening. My support team was nearby, and my husband was holding my hand, watching with concern, but the feeling that something wasn't right sat deep within me.

"I don't think I can do this," I said, almost whispering. I remember looking up at my midwife and doula, their kind eyes looking back at me. They believed in me. And it's not that I didn't believe in myself; I did. I was set on having this baby naturally but I needed these people to understand that I wanted to go to the hospital. I needed reprieve from the pain. I needed direction. I was feeling so lost.

I pressed on.

I continued to float.

No one said anything.

"I want to go to the hospital," I said with conviction.

They all looked back at me. I know they wanted for me to experience what was in my plan, but in the moment, I felt ignored.

I think the reason they were reluctant to take me to the hospital was that I had so desperately wanted to give birth at home. I had wanted to be able to labour, manage my contractions and give birth without having to go anywhere. But there I was, 24 hours into my labour, surviving on only two hours of sleep, give or take a minute here and there. I felt like nothing was changing; there was no difference between the labour I experienced when I tried to go to bed the night before and what I was currently feeling. I didn't think that something was wrong, exactly, but I didn't feel like what was happening was right and I knew that there was relief out there for me.

"Why don't we check you?" the midwife suggested. "See how far along you are?"

I was hopeful that I had progressed further than I had with Archer and that she would tell me I was close to transition, gaining ground to start pushing. I knew that if I didn't hear a number, I couldn't let it hijack my resilience. I also knew that if she suggested we go to the hospital, I wasn't anywhere close yet.

"Okay," I said. With Brad's help I climbed out of the tub and dried off. We went upstairs and the midwife did her exam. Then she said, "I think we should go to the hospital. If you want to."

I knew then that I had not even reached 3 centimetres and that I was making the right decision to leave home and go to the hospital.

I selfishly paid no attention to Brad while he helped me gather my things. He was scared. He was remembering what happened last time when we headed to the hospital like this. What happened with Archer. I had prepared a hospital bag this time; I just had a few last-minute things to pack. I got dressed and grabbed my pillow. We were going to meet our midwife and doula at the hospital.

Before we left the comfort of our room, where I had spent so many hours labouring, I pulled Brad into a hug, crying.

"I don't want to disappoint you."

"Babe," he said, bringing me in closer. "There's no way you could disappoint me. I don't know how you're doing it. You're so strong."

"Are you sure?" I looked up into his eyes.

"Of course," he said as he felt my body tighten. I hugged his neck and bent into the incoming contraction. It was going to be one long ride to the hospital and when we got there, I had no idea what to expect. In order to get through my labour, I was not allowing myself to think about surgery. I had blocked out the possibility that what might be best for my baby could be to go under the knife again. All I thought about was pushing and delivering this baby, naturally. It didn't matter where. It didn't matter how. All that mattered was that I was going to do it. I believed in myself and I happily threw the plan out the window in order to get there.

Was I being too naive? Was I setting myself up for disappointment again? Would I be crushed when what I so desperately wanted was taken away?

Like the way it was with you?

All of the questions that crossed my mind on that trip to the hospital reminded me of what it felt like to lose you. Of what I felt when I learned that I would never see you again.

What I felt when I learned that you had disappeared without a trace in the mountains that you loved.

Missing you desperately.

With love,

Anya

Chapter Eight

NOVEMBER 15, 2010

Dear Rachael,

In my darkest nightmares, I could have never imagined this. This is the single thing that I would have never wished upon even my worst enemy.

Receiving the news that a loved one, someone so close to my soul, at the prime of their life, is reported missing. Receiving the news that *you* are missing.

With death, there is closure. When someone is ill, they could recover. Or they could die. Either way, there is typically time. But when someone disappears, essentially without a trace, that's it. There are hours spent searching, days spent wondering and countless sleepless nights spent hoping. I am not able to quantify the amount of time I have spent wondering what happened to you and Jonathan, or hoping that there has been some grand mistake and you are actually completely fine, living a happy life in the mountains where you belong.

The hope that I carry with me now is strange. It has only come after accepting that you are no longer with us in this world. That no one will ever know what exactly happened to you. But still, the hope is there. I hope that we will meet again. That you are at peace. That you know how much I love and miss you, mostly when I turn around and you're not there.

All I know is that you are my first and only true broken heart. Here's to hoping you will be my last.

It was the first and only summer that Brad and I had lived in Prince George together. We had already decided we were going to move back to the Lower Mainland. We were preparing to move at the end of September, giving ourselves plenty of time to get settled and for me to look for work before Brad started at his old job. The first weekend in September was the Labour Day long weekend. With that extra day off work we would likely spend the time visiting our families, who would undoubtedly miss us once we left. Also, packing. We were moving from a three-bedroom, three story townhouse to a small one-bedroom place in our friends' basement. It's a good thing I love to organize!

On the Thursday following our rather uneventful long weekend, I received a completely random message via Facebook from Jonathan's sister-in-law, asking whether I had heard from you since your last trip with Jonathan. I wasn't aware that you had been planning a trip with Jonathan before you were set to leave for South America. I told his sister-in-law that I hadn't heard from you since some time at the end of August. I then wrote a message to your sister, to let her know about this message and to ask if she had spoken to you or not. I really didn't think there was any way that Jonathan's sister-in-law knew what she was talking about. How could she? So, I went about my Friday as usual while I waited for your sister to get back to me.

I was the first one to get home from work that Friday afternoon, which wasn't unusual. One of the reasons that we hadn't stayed very long in Prince George was that Brad worked out of town almost every week from Monday to Friday. He was home on weekends, but it really wasn't a lifestyle either of us wanted.

I logged onto my computer as soon as I got home and saw that your sister had responded to my message:

> *No, we haven't heard from Rachael or Jonathan and currently there is an extensive search going on in the Pemberton area for the two of them. They have been missing for 4 days now. Please send all your prayers this way as we are very worried right now.*

I responded right away to let her know that they were all in our prayers and to let me know if they heard anything.

She responded again:

> *Yes, I will be sure to let you know as soon as we hear news. The search and rescue are doubling their efforts tomorrow. Teams*

from the island and three helicopters are joining the search.

The date was September 10, 2010. The day my world changed forever. I was in shock, my heart racing abnormally. I didn't cry right away, I think because I was in disbelief, numb to the truth. I didn't know what to believe even though I had basically heard it right from the source that you were missing. I turned to the Internet but all I could find was an RCMP report confirming that you were a missing person and that there was an open search for you.

When Brad got home from work, I ran straight to him before he had a chance to get through the door.

"Hi, babe," he said as he hugged me hello. "Babe?" he asked when I gave him no response.

The tears had finally found their way onto my cheeks. "Rachael. She's missing." It was all I could get out before dissolving into his chest, one of my favourite places in this world.

"What? What do you mean? Come here," he said, pulling me into the living room to sit down. He was as shocked as I was.

Once I had settled down, I filled him in on the very small details I knew about your situation. "I got a message from her sister when I was at work. I only read it just now."

"Okay."

"She confirmed that Rachael and Jonathan are missing together, that they have been missing for the last four days."

"Oh my god."

"She said there is currently an extensive search going on for them in the Pemberton area, north of Whistler."

By this point, my brain was operating separately from the rest of me. I was speaking the words but I wasn't feeling any of it. The tears chose to fall as if on their own; my ability to process what I was saying had dissolved. What was my world without you in it?

Brad held me while I cried. While I wondered and speculated and hoped and wished for your safe return. He was my rock when I hadn't expected to need one and I will be forever grateful for his love and support through this most difficult time. My need for him to continue to be my rock comes and goes, but he is always there for me, no questions asked.

Most importantly, he has been my number one supporter since I told him that I wanted to write to you. After all, if I can't talk to you, I can still write letters. Brad understands. There are no words to describe how lucky I am to have him.

I can't specifically remember how I moved forward while I worried about you. I know that Brad and I stopped by my auntie's place the night that we found out. After we told her what had happened she just kept asking why. And how. The same questions that I have asked myself so many times, in countless different situations. We all have.

When the search for you and Jonathan was called off, I was invited to Whistler to be with the family and friends who had gathered to be together in the wake of your disappearance.

Brad and I left for Whistler from Prince George on Saturday morning in mid-September, arriving in the late afternoon after many people from up north and the Lower Mainland had already arrived. I remember getting to the house where everyone was staying, where I had never been before. We opened the door to see so many pairs of shoes. We could hear all of the voices coming from the rooms beyond the entryway. I was starting to feel overwhelmed when a friendly face came around the corner.

"Anya!" My friend Matt said as he picked his way through some shoes to come and give me a hug. "You made it!"

"Hi," I said as I hugged him back. It wasn't time for tears yet.

"And you must be Brad," Matt said as he turned to Brad. "Come on in, guys!"

We took off our shoes and made our way into the kitchen behind Matt.

"Hi Jane," I said to Matt's girlfriend, whom I already knew.

She came over to give me a hug. "We're so glad you made it," she said kindly.

I didn't expect there to be so many people; there were so many of them gathered in the kitchen whom I didn't recognize. I was beginning to wonder if I even belonged when I heard your dad behind me.

"Anya," he said as I turned to him. He embraced me in the most gentle, meaningful hug. Then it was your mom's turn.

"Hi," I said to her as I gave her a hug as well.

"Welcome," she said. "We're so glad you made it safely."

"This is Brad," I said as I introduced him to your parents.

"It's so nice to meet you," your mom said. "Rae spoke very highly of you."

Brad smiled. I don't think either of us were quite prepared for the seemingly casual mention of your name, but we smiled and allowed ourselves to be welcomed into the home.

"Your room is just through there," your mom told us. "We're so lucky that our friends opened their home to us. There are plenty of rooms!"

"Thank you," I said with a small smile. I was unsettled and still in disbelief as to how we had found ourselves in Whistler with so many people who loved you.

"You two come on in," she continued, "and make yourselves at home. Dinner should be ready in an hour or so."

We went back out to the car to get our bag. We had packed lightly for just one night as we both had to return to work on Monday and would be driving home the next day.

"You okay?" Brad asked me.

"I think so," I said. "It's weird. I almost feel like I shouldn't be here. There are so many people in there that I don't even know."

"She had so many people that loved her," Brad replied, "of course you wouldn't know them all."

"Ya."

"And of course you belong here," he said as he turned to face me. "Don't ever question that."

"Okay," I said as I leaned in for a hug. "You're right. I've just never really been in a situation like this. You know?"

"It would be awful if you had," he said as he draped an arm around me and we walked back to the house together. Once we dropped our stuff in our room, we joined everyone in the dining room.

"Bananagrams!" Matt said. "Grab some tiles and we'll show

you how it's done."

I sat down at the table to learn how to play. There were a few more people I recognized by now, even a couple whom I could pick out just based on the stories you'd told me about them. Your sister, brother and his future wife were there, as well as some of your med student friends and other friends from PG. I found that I was able to relax a bit and have a little unexpected fun.

It felt good to be distracted and before I knew it, dinner was ready. Sharing a meal was such an intimate thing; the work that went into feeding everyone and the hands pitching in to help serve and then clean up. This felt more like what I had expected. Everyone gathered together to break bread and reminisce. Especially when the conversation turned to what you would want to do, if you were there with us.

"Have you guys been down to the lake at all?" one of the med students I didn't recognize asked.

"Ya," Matt replied, "we walked down when we first got here. It's really nice; would be even better in the summer. Though we're going to go for a swim later, right guys?"

"Only if you join me," your brother said to Matt in response.

"I think we all know Rae would be down," Matt replied. "So why not? Who's in?"

"Clothing optional?" another friend chipped in. They knew you well; a chuckle rippled through the group, along with a few head nods.

"You in?" Brad asked me quietly.

"I don't think so..." I said. I was hesitant.

"Awwww, come on!" he teased, nudging into me with his shoulder.

"It's too dark," I said honestly. "And I'll never warm up."

"True," he replied. "I'll represent."

"You will?"

"Of course," he said with a smile. "It's been a while since I had a nice night time swim."

And so, a group of people stripped down and went for a night-time swim in Alta Lake, in your honour. I'm not sure who was wearing what, but it felt great to be there while so many people who loved you did something that you would've been a part of in a heartbeat.

I was so proud that Brad had joined in, especially while I stood back. Someone counted down before I heard everyone running and yelling, splashing into the water together.

Brad came back up, dripping wet, and grabbed a towel. He was rubbing his face dry when he paused and looked up at me. "Uh oh."

"What?" I asked.

"Did I give you my glasses before I ran down?"

"No," I answered, sure I would still have them in my hands if that were the case.

"I'm pretty sure they were on my face when I jumped in."

"Brad!"

"That's not the first time I've done that," he admitted, laughing. "I lost my glasses in Mexico, too."

"I love you to pieces," I laughed along with him, "but you really shouldn't make that a habit!"

"I'll try to go back in the morning to look for them," he said with a shrug.

"You know," I said as we went back inside to warm up, "that is totally something I could see Rachael doing."

"Whoopsies," he smiled at me. I sense a commonality in the people I love.

I didn't sleep too well that night; I hadn't been sleeping much since I first heard that you were missing. In the morning Brad and I were the first people up besides your parents. I sat down at the kitchen table while your mom handed Brad a cup of coffee.

Your dad walked up behind me and said one of the kindest things anyone has ever said to me. "I know how sad I feel," he said as he placed his hand on my shoulder, "but I couldn't imagine how sad it must be for you to have lost your best friend. I'm so sorry for your loss."

This from the man who had just lost his eldest daughter to unknown circumstances, who had been told that the authorities wouldn't be searching for you anymore. That they had done what they could to find you, but they couldn't continue to send crews out to look because the unsafe weather conditions could cause something horrific to happen to the rescuers as well.

It was the most beautiful thing anyone has ever said to me and has been engraved permanently on my heart ever since.

"Thank you," I muttered as I stood and embraced your dad, our tears falling together in our love for you, in recognition of the loss that hung in the air around us all.

For a father to acknowledge another person's pain after experiencing his own unfathomable loss was inconceivable to me. Your dad has to be the most selfless and caring person I have ever met. I was inspired to start writing based on these words he said to me. They are and were so meaningful; they confirmed that I did belong in that gathering of people who were there to support each other in the wake of your disappearance. I was worthy of being there and of being recognized as someone who was important to you. The quality of the people present showed how much you were loved and why you had been such a wonderful person at your core, starting with your parents.

They were having a mass at the local church for you the next morning, but given that neither Brad nor I are very religious, we chose to take off early to start our long trek back to PG. We said a quick goodbye after breakfast when Jonathan's family arrived. The plan was for them to come and meet your family. Your mom invited us to say hello before we departed.

"Meilleire amie," your mom tried to explain to Jonathan's parents in broken French as she introduced us. Jonathan's mom nodded in acknowledgement that she understood who I was and why I was there. His family seemed to be just as lost and confused as yours.

I would have rather not beaten you to the punch in "meeting the parents," but I am sure they would have loved you. We waved hello and then left the two families to get to know one another and share space in their sadness.

"So," Brad said as we drove out of Whistler, "do you still want to try and go up there?"

"Yes," I replied after thinking about it for a moment. "I think I would regret it if we didn't."

We had talked about going up the Spetch Creek Service Road where they found Jonathan's car before going home, but neither of us had mentioned it since we had been at the house with your parents.

"Do you think we could find somewhere to get some flowers?" I asked Brad.

"Absolutely," he said. "I think that's a great idea."

We stopped at a small flower shop along the road through Pemberton. I chose some vibrant gerbera daisies in your favourite colour, yellow. We continued our drive out towards Pemberton and found the service road where the police had found Jonathan's car. I don't think we had a plan for when we got there, but I wanted to see what it was like. What I would feel. We weren't entirely sure that we were in the right place, but based on the description we read online for where they found Jonathan's car, we thought we had found it.

I could picture Jonathan's car, which is bizarre given the fact that I have never known what he drove. It was just the car I pictured you two leaving Vancouver in at the crack of dawn the day you left, stopping at Timmy's for coffee and breakfast. You left the receipt on the floor of the car where it was later found by police. I'm sure Jonathan treated; we all know how much free coffee means to you. I could see you walking away from the car, planning to return to it a few days later when you would make your way back to Vancouver, shortly before boarding your flight to South America.

We got out of Brad's car and walked around a bit, exploring the area.

"That's probably where they went," I said to Brad, pointing towards a path that led uphill. I stood, staring through the trees, imagining you and your beloved happily embarking on your next adventure together.

I walked around, my feet crunching on the ground. There were signs of a light rain that had stopped before we arrived. The ground was wet beneath our feet; we could hear water nearby, dripping from branch to branch with each rustle of the wind between the trees. There was also a heavier sound of a moving body of water. We walked towards a couple of picnic tables and found a river rushing with force through the woods.

We stood along the riverbank for a while, tears leaking onto our faces.

"They were here," I said to Brad, clutching the flowers we bought for you. "It's so weird to think that they were here last."

He nodded quietly and reached his arms out to hold me. I started to sob while he held me. Through my tears I reached out and threw my flower into the river. I couldn't find any words. I was capable only of releasing my heartbreak in tears.

Brad gently threw his flower into the river shortly after mine. He uttered a broken goodbye before turning back to me and releasing his cries into my shoulder. We remained together in our pain for what seemed like hours before calming enough to leave. We walked back to the car, hand in hand. I couldn't help but picture you and Jonathan returning to his car in the same way Brad and I returned to ours. You would have been weary from your hike, but radiating happiness from the inside out. Instead, you were never seen again.

We drove the winding roads towards PG in a blur of silent tears. The weather was sharing in our grief, rain pounding on the windshield as we drove north. Given that Brad didn't have any glasses, I was the seemingly logical choice to be driving, but I was in no state emotionally to be behind the wheel of a car. I was having trouble saying anything without crying so we drove along in silence, crying together for some time.

Eventually, I broke the silence. "I'm really glad we went," I said to Brad. "And it was really nice that you said good bye. I just don't want to have to say goodbye. I couldn't."

He responded in silence, concentrating on the road ahead. "Grab my phone and open up the contacts," he told me when he finally spoke. I did as he suggested.

"Look up the Bs," he said.

"Okay," I replied when I had found the Bs in his phone's contacts.

"Do you see an entry for Bruce?"

"Yes," I said through tears.

"Bruce was a close friend from my childhood," he explained as we drove on. "There was an accident during my first year at BCIT. He was shot and killed in Vanderhoof when he was just 18 years old."

"Oh my god, Brad," I said, in shock. "I'm so sorry."

"I still have an entry for him in my phone because I've never been able to say good bye to him, either," he said quietly. I could tell he was again on the verge of tears. "So it's okay if you don't want to say good bye to Rae."

Brad and I bonded more than I think I even know now during that trip. He has officially seen me at my lowest, my heart broken into a million pieces. I have seen him at his most vulnerable, watching me be shattered by an unfair life event and finding it in himself to open up about his most devastating loss. Both of us having lost someone that holds such a dear place in our hearts, who was taken before they were able to recognize their full potential in life. We had each other, and while we hadn't experienced losing the same person in the same way, we were in it together.

With so much love,

Anya

January 8, 2011

Dear Rachael,

The strangest thing about moving on following the events of your disappearance was simply going forward with life knowing that you were not there and never would be again. Brad and I settled into life in the Lower Mainland with no plans to move any time soon. The new year came and along with it, ups and downs of missing you and dealing with the loss. Brad eventually suggested what I had already been considering and I decided to talk to someone about you, your disappearance and my grief. It was time to see my old counsellor again.

When I finally sat down in my counsellor's familiar office, I felt my worries relax.

"Hi Anya," she greeted me. "How have you been keeping?"

"I've been okay, but I've been dealing with the loss of my best friend."

She told me how sorry she was to hear that and encouraged me to start at the beginning and tell her all about you.

"We met at school when we were in grade eight. I just remember her being my best friend since then. We've lived apart, even with an ocean between us, for most of our adult life but she has always been my closest and most treasured friend."

"And how do you feel without her?"

"I can't begin to describe the hole that it has left, not having her around anymore," I answered as honestly as I could. "I keep turning around and expecting her to be there, or for the phone to ring and have her cheerful voice greet me on the other end."

"It sounds like you miss her very much," she encouraged me.

I nodded. " I have a really hard time thinking about my future without her."

"Do you have a way that you can keep her active in your life? Such as talking to her, writing to her or even just talking about her with your significant other?"

"I actually started writing to her shortly after her disappearance."

"That's great! Tell me more about that."

"I've always kept journals. And it was so abrupt, not having her around anymore. I chose a special journal that I use to write to her. As if she's listening to me."

"That sounds wonderful, Anya. Writing is a great way to deal with emotions, especially grief."

"Thank you."

"Tell me a bit more about how you met Rachael."

"It was at school. I went to Catholic school because my parents were no longer happy with the public school near where we lived."

She nodded kindly.

"We met in our first year of high school. I don't really remember how; I kind of remember that she was just always my friend."

"You said you met at Catholic school? Tell me about your religious beliefs."

"I don't follow a religion at all since leaving high school."

"Okay."

"I believe that there is some sort of other worldly power out there, but I'm not sure that it's God. It could be but I am not a follower of any specific religion."

"Was Rachael religious?"

"Yes, she and her family were. Very much."

Encouraging silence followed.

"It gives me comfort that she had her faith to get her through whatever she had to deal with," I continued. "In the end."

Tears began to flow down my cheeks as I thought about how you had moved onto a better place, how your family's beliefs had given them the solace of life after death.

"You know, I think it would be helpful for you to continue your friendship with Rachael. Write to her, as you're doing. Talk to her. Ask her to let you know, in a way that will make you undoubtedly know it's her, that she is out there and that she hears you and that she is still, in essence, walking with you."

"Okay."

"It may feel silly. Actually, I know that it will. But I promise you, it will be worth it."

I nodded.

"I'm leaving you with three pieces of homework then," she said cheerily. "First, talk to her! Tell her about what you're thinking out loud and ask her for a sign to show that she's listening. Second, continue to write to her when you feel so inclined and third, get creative."

"Creative?"

"Turn to your crafty side and create a picture or a painting, something that shows how you see her now. Encourage your connection with her."

"Alright," I agreed. I could do those things. I had hope that they would help.

The end of my session was near. "Now, we ground our feet," she said as she slid forward in her seat and firmly planted both feet on the ground, gently folding her hands in her lap and closing her eyes. I did the same. "And we ask Rachael to hear Anya when she talks to her, to welcome her into our universe with the love that will always exist between these two friends."

I sat there, listening, with my eyes closed as well. This was a routine at the end of each session with my counsellor that I looked forward to. She would put positivity out into the world based on what we had discussed. Then I would choose a card with a word on it from a box and we would relate that to what we had worked on. Finally, I would blow out the candle she had in the middle of the coffee table that rested between us.

I reached forward for a card, shuffling them around a bit with my hands before choosing one.

"Presence," I read out loud.

"Presence," she repeated back to me. "Beautiful. Feel your own presence in your friendship with Rachael, and be open to receiving hers in return, Anya."

I smiled as I gathered my belongings and left. Leaving my counselling session on a positive note was a priceless gift this counsellor gave to me each time we met. I needed someone to remind me that it was okay to think of the light in the darkness, and to put it out there was to bring it into my life. And by being able to put one foot in front of the other without being reminded of the brokenness around me, I began to heal and learn who I was in a world without you.

Later in the week following my appointment as I was driving home from work, I started to think of you.

"Hey, Rae?" I said out loud. My counsellor had been right. I felt silly. But I went on.

"If you're out there, can you let me know? Somehow?"

I drove on, both hands solidly on the wheel, trying to ground myself. I felt very silly, indeed. The second I gave into my skepticism, Madonna's "Like a Prayer" started playing on my stereo. You listened! I felt you in that moment as the tears came. The song brought back the memories of you and me, Cass and Stef dancing around to that song like the crazy teenage girls we were, with glow-sticks and vodka watermelon. I laughed out loud while I cried and embraced the feeling of your presence. I felt that you were with me there in my car. I know that it was my iPod playing the song and I had chosen the playlist but I honestly had no idea that song was on there. It felt great to embrace you once I gave in.

"Thank you!" I said out loud, releasing the breath I hadn't realized I had been holding. "I miss you and it's hard and I don't think it'll just get easier overnight, but I feel better about missing you."

I think I was starting to be able to tolerate your absence.

Love you always,

Anya

May 16, 2011

Dear Rachael,

This year has moved on faster than I knew was going to be possible without you in it. I have not been doing so well. I am so sad for you and I miss you so very much! It's probably a very selfish thing for me to say but it's true. It's now been over a year since we last saw you. This time last year Brad and I were in Ireland and I knew I would still have you when we got home. I had no idea that the last time I would see you would be on the street when we parted ways after spending the night at your place. I would give anything to give you one more hug and tell you how much I love you and remind you of how much you mean to me. I would have made note of where you were going because I know that it's important to me now. I vaguely remember you saying something about meeting someone at the climbing gym—was it Jonathan? It makes me sad that I can't remember where it was you were going at that moment when we last said goodbye. I wish I could.

It's still so surreal to me at times that you're gone. Lately I've really been feeling like I want to know what happened to you guys. More than ever before. I'm not really sure why that is, but I can't stop thinking about it. We were out for lunch with Brad's Grandma the other day. It's so hard to be around people who just don't understand what I've gone through.

I got up from the table to go to the washroom before our lunch arrived. I sat back down at the table, listening to the middle of the conversation I had rejoined.

"I don't know if you heard," Grandma said to Brad and I, "a woman from Alberta was missing for seven weeks and they found her alive."

Brad and I both just nodded. I consciously pushed down the lump that was forming at the base of my throat.

"They're still searching for her husband, who had wandered off to find help. They don't know which way he went and there hasn't been any sign of him."

I know she didn't mean anything by it; why would she? But I couldn't help but feel that familiar tickle of tears deep down.

"I'll be right back," I said as I excused myself from the table again.

As I left, I heard Grandma say to Brad, "What, does she have a bladder problem or something?"

I stood in the bathroom, alone, trying to compose myself. Dealing with my emotions internally when I'm reminded of my sadness is one thing. But having people speak casually about situations that dredge up my sensitive feelings unexpectedly was something new that I had to learn how to deal with.

I stepped out of the bathroom stall and stood in front of the mirror. I watched myself take a deep breath, looking intently into my own eyes. I composed myself and felt silly as I returned to the table.

"The food's here," Brad said, looking up at me as I came back to the table. "You okay?"

"Yes, thanks," I said briefly. I didn't want to talk about it.

"This looks delicious!" Brad's Grandma said as we all started to eat. No one said anything about anyone disappearing or my supposed bladder problem for the rest of our meal.

It was only when Brad and I were alone in the car on the way home from lunch that he brought it up again. "She didn't mean to upset you, you know."

"I know that," I said as I gazed out the window. "How could she have known?"

"Well, she knows about Rachael. I reminded her about it when you went back to the washroom."

"It's okay, Brad. I can't expect people to walk on eggshells around me."

"But still. She didn't mean it."

"I know. I've just been thinking a lot lately about what happened. To them. And it doesn't help to hear that it happens to other people, too."

"I had heard about that couple. And it made me think of her, too."

"Why are other people found, but they aren't? It makes me wonder if Jonathan left to find help, or maybe she left him if he was hurt. Or what if something happened to both of them and they couldn't search for help?"

"Don't do that to yourself, Anya. It's not fair."

I stared silently out the window, thinking over Brad's words.

In the long run, I didn't follow his advice. When do I? I've never liked being told what to do. I thought to myself that regardless of what really happened, I hope that you felt loved. And that you had some sort of idea how much you would be missed, especially by me. To this day, I think of you every time I see a blonde woman with curly hair from behind. Especially if she is riding a bicycle. I don't think that will ever change.

The emotions I felt following that conversation stayed with me for a few days. I was sad today at work and ended up emailing with Brad. He said some really beautiful things that I wanted to share with you. After I told him I was sad you wouldn't be there for my birthday, he said:

> *I know it's unfair and hard to think about your b-day without her, but you know that she would want you to have a good time in her honour. She always loved life and all it offers so I think that you should, as hard as it is, try not to dwell on the fact that she is no longer with us but rather try to approach the future in a way that she would. With hope that better days await, belief that you can do anything, knowledge that you are loved and aspiration to make a better you than you were before.*

Then he said he loves me, called me sweetheart and encouraged me to take time to write to you in my journal. He even offered to make dinner, which is rare! I tell ya, I don't know what I would do without him. We promised each other that we'd never have to find that out.

I love you so very much and I think about you and miss you every day. All my love to you and Jonathan.

Anya xoxo

May 31, 2017

Dear Rachael,

It took me quite some time before I would agree to return to Whistler.

I felt as if I was wearing a barrier that prevented me from going as far north as Pemberton. The area we had visited shortly after you disappeared was beautiful, as most of our province is, but I associate it with a time when I allowed myself to feel more sadness than I ever had before. I had no desire to return there, in case the sadness returned, or worse, you haunted my dreams.

Brad and I have been invited by some friends on more than one occasion to go camping at Birkenhead Provincial Park, which is right near where you went missing. I have always declined the invitation. People have pointed out to me that it might bring closure to go there again and that I would be going with my friends to create new memories, but there is just no part of me that wants to go there again. Call me crazy. I just can't. I have kept myself removed from that place where I would breathe the air that we once shared on this planet, near where you took your last breaths.

I think that you would understand that it was not like I was trying to avoid you. I carry you with me, so I don't need to go anywhere in order to see you or remember you. Paying tribute to those we have lost doesn't come with a manual. It should be up to me how I grieve this loss. Telling my story is my way of eternalizing my love and respect for you.

In the fall of 2012 Brad and I received an invitation to return to Whistler for Matt and Jane's wedding. There was never any question that I would go back to celebrate the union of two such wonderful friends who were also close to you. They got married at a lovely chapel just outside of the village. Following the ceremony, I shared a meaningful hug with Matt; no words were exchanged, but after we parted from our embrace, I saw the tears in his eyes that I also felt in my own. There was an understanding between us about how much we missed you, a bond that I will always share with him and the others that love you.

Brad and I were having a few drinks between the ceremony and the reception (which unfortunately took place at the same pub where I got sick at my stagette…shhhhh) when the subject of baby names came up. When I asked Brad what he thought about the name Asher he asked me almost reflexively what I thought of the name Archer. We fell in love with the name and I left it to Brad to choose the middle name of our first born, Archer Bruce.

The times that I let grief overcome me pop up when I least expect them. But I am able to approach my grief from a place where I recognize how proud of me you would be, instead of just focusing on your absence. I can even be proud of my*self* sometimes. I've come such a long way.

I have taken Brad's advice and allowed myself to not say goodbye. It's too final. And while I choose not to label my beliefs using standard religious terms, there's a piece of my heart that believes we will meet again in the afterlife.

I used to let my mind wander. I'd think about what exactly would have had to happen to make two grown people disappear without a trace. You would think that one of you would have been carrying something that would have slipped from your hand in the event of an accident. You would think that something from your backpacks or your pockets would be left behind. You would think there would be some sort of clue.

I don't think about the possibilities any more. And I no longer ask myself why. At this point, I am not sure that I want to know what happened. It might be too difficult to dredge up my grief again. To mourn again after learning what horrendous thing stole you from this world. I am at peace with not knowing what happened to you or where your earthly body is. Your beautiful soul is in heaven. And you left our world in the way that you yourself had said was how you would have wanted to. Your mom gave me a piece of your writing dated July 8, 2000, that reads as follows:

> *I just finished Into Thin Air, and that book really made me start thinking. So I decided to write down some of my thoughts. Reading it made me realize how much I want to climb (particularly Everest). It didn't help me understand why, just strengthened my desire. But the problem is the risks–death. 1/4 of the people above base camp on Everest die and I don't want to be one of them. That was my immediate reaction. Then I started wondering why and it's because there's other things I want before Everest. But if I do those things first, then I was considering the most preferable way to die (only because one day everyone will)*

and the best place to die would be in the mountains. Hopefully an old woman. So whatever is meant to happen will be.

For someone so young (you were 15 at the time), this is a remarkably mature and wise statement. I said so to your mom when I first read it.

It's been 19 years since you wrote that—man, I feel old saying that—and I still haven't even come close to finding my purpose. I'm so proud of you for finding yours. For putting words onto paper that would find my eyes and give others and me comfort. How could you have known? I hope you remembered those words in the end.

Now that I think about it, I should take a few steps back. I *have* found a way to add beautiful meaning to my life: my family. Unexpectedly, through them, I have learned endlessly about myself, about patience, tolerance and most importantly, love. Like you, I am capable of so much more than I ever thought possible, and I have finally started to believe it. Thanks to your love, I grew into the woman I am. Thanks to your loss, I became strong enough to overcome any challenge in my path.

Love,

Anya

Chapter Nine

December 31, 2017

Dear Rachael,

As Brad and I stood together in our bedroom holding each other, having decided to go to the hospital, which was not in the plan, I knew deep inside that I could do it. I had been through too much in my short life to let the past get in the way of what I wanted. My body was meant for this, just as Brad and I were meant to be parents. I had set myself up for success; our team would be waiting at the hospital to help us through this next chapter. Just as I knew you would be looking over us as well.

I was going to the hospital and I was going to deliver this baby naturally. I just was.

As I packed my hospital bag and gathered the strength that I knew I had deep down, a story that your mom told me when I was pregnant with Archer came back to me. She had sent me a beautiful message one day, reminding me that you were out there somewhere, looking down on us.

She told me how one of her close friends had had a dream about you. Her niece had been expecting a baby and she had a dream that you were in a beautiful cabin in heaven, holding a precious baby boy.

"Rae," the friend said. "That is a beautiful baby. Let me hold him."

You looked up at her. "Not right now; it's my turn. You'll have lots of time to hold him when he's born."

Your mom told me how she often thought about your brother's first baby, her first grandchild, being held by you before she was born. At the time, she told me she thought you were cuddling another very special baby: Archer.

As I climbed into our van on the way to the hospital for my second birth, I thought about how your precious hands were holding our baby in the last moments before reaching our arms on earth. I knew that the ride to the hospital wasn't going to be easy, but I drew strength from you and my belief that you were with us.

I focused all of my energy on managing my contractions on the thirty-minute drive into Vancouver and while we checked in and waited for the epidural. This was the first time during my labour that I felt aware of just how ridiculous I may have sounded as I battled my contractions. I stood in the hospital in the middle of the night making guttural sounds that helped me endure the pain as each contraction passed. I didn't feel ashamed, I was just hyperaware. Of my sounds echoing off of the walls. That Brad was concerned. That this was not in the plan. That, nevertheless, I felt like I was right where I needed to be and I was closer than ever to getting relief from the pain.

When we chose to switch midwives and settled on the collective, we also switched hospitals, should we end up needing to go to one. That was why the car ride was a bit longer than it otherwise would have been. Looking back, I am so happy that we ended up at BC Women's Hospital. The care was excellent, our midwives had privileges there and the labour and delivery ward was in a brand-new wing of the hospital. The room that I was admitted to was huge, with more than enough room for my entourage. Which makes me happy since it was probably the only time in my life I will have that many people surrounding and supporting me.

Shortly after we were brought to the labour and delivery room, I was prepped for the epidural.

"Do you remember the drill from last time?" the midwife asked me as she helped me onto the hospital bed.

"Vaguely," I told her.

"You're going to hug onto this pillow," she said as she handed me a pillow from the bed, "and lean forward. You have to stay as still as possible while they put it in."

Another contraction forced its way through my body. I clutched the pillow and rocked back and forth through the pain.

"I don't know if I can," I said once it had passed.

"Yes," she assured me, "you can. I know you can, Anya. You are so strong."

I nodded and leaned forward, holding her hand while they administered the epidural. I will be forever grateful for her kind approach and sensitive bedside manner.

"This is what is called a walking epidural," the doctor explained. "So you should still have feeling in your legs and be able to walk around a little bit."

"Go ahead and lay back while it starts to work," the midwife told me as the nurse arranged the tubes that were now affixed to my wrist and back.

"You did such a good job, babe," Brad said as he came over to my bed to hold my hand. "I'm so proud of you."

I have learned so much about myself in this whole process of becoming a mom but one thing that stands out to me is that I respond most positively to empathy. Having people recognize my feelings while I was experiencing them made me feel more at peace and less alone. Sometimes I just need a little recognition that things are difficult and that it's reasonable that I'm reacting the way that I am. I may not always realize what I'm feeling in the moment, but I feel so much better to hear that I am not alone. It empowers me to hear that I am doing a good job even though what I am experiencing may be difficult.

I spent the first few hours after the epidural resting and trying to sleep, as it was still the middle of the night. A couple of hours had passed when the first nurse stationed in our room went off shift. The second nurse spent the entire day with us and, sadly, went off shift before baby was born. One of the luxuries of this hospital was that we were assigned a nurse who stayed with us the entire time I was in labour, in 12-hour shifts. Having a familiar face constantly by my side, keeping an eye on baby, was comforting.

After a couple of hours of rest, the midwife suggested another exam. "I think we should check your progress."

"Okay."

"Are you hungry at all?" the doula asked. "I can go grab you some toast?"

"That would be great, thank you."

"Do you want anything?" she asked Brad.

"Sure," he said. "I'll come and help."

They left the room and the midwife proceeded with the exam. "There hasn't been any change," she told the nurse.

The OB resident had come in a moment earlier to introduce herself, and, not knowing that I had asked not to know what my progress was in numbers, said out loud, "So she's still at 3 cm dilation?"

I had not progressed past the point where I had been with Archer. Even during all of this time in labour and in the hospital.

But I was in a very different place than I had been with Archer and my mind was set on having a VBAC. It hadn't even crossed my mind that I could possibly end up with another c-section. I was that sure that I would be delivering this baby vaginally.

"The OB will be in soon to speak with you," the resident told me. "Hang in there, you're doing great."

"The OB is really pro-VBAC," the midwife said after the resident left. "I am confident that he will be supportive of a natural delivery."

I was just glad that Dr. Youcantdothis wasn't on shift.

"I think at this point, we're going to break your waters,"

the midwife continued. "The membranes haven't ruptured and there's a better chance that your labour will progress once we do that."

"Okay," I said. "That sounds good to me."

I hadn't yet tried to get out of bed. I was trying to rest, occasionally turning from my right side to my left and back again.

The midwife broke my water and then told me they would wait to see what happened. "I think we'll check again in another two hours. I'll leave you to rest for now."

Brad and the doula had returned with food. I had never been so grateful for peanut butter on toast.

Another two hours passed before I was checked again.

"Still no further progress," the midwife said. "We can go ahead with oxytocin to help progress your dilation."

"Is that safe, with the VBAC?" I asked.

"Yes, absolutely."

"Okay." I was agreeable as long as we were still moving towards a VBAC.

The only thing I would've changed about the situation would be knowing that, once they started the oxytocin, I wouldn't be able to eat anything. Too little, too late. And so, over the course of the day I "filled up" on popsicles and broth, juice and water. I didn't feel hungry at any point until much later in the night, but I did start to feel that weakness you get when you've been up for over thirty hours and haven't properly fueled your body.

The oxytocin started to work. Baby's head was dropping even more and I dilated a couple more centimetres within a few hours. The OB finally visited and was very positive about a forthcoming delivery.

"I'd say you're about 5 cm," he said after performing an exam. "And there's no reason why we can't have this baby naturally."

I was ecstatic to hear that news. "Thank you so much!"

Dr. VBAC turned to the midwife. "I'll leave it in your capable hands."

What a tremendous improvement over my last visit with an OB, Dr. Youcantdothis.

I had reached the point when someone who had been prepared to come to the hospital would have brought out something to do. I hadn't, but I honestly enjoyed passing the time by getting to know my nurse, midwife and doula, and just chatting with them and Brad while dozing off and on and resting.

At some point in the afternoon, the midwife suggested that I try to get up. "It might help baby drop more if you get up and move around a bit."

"That sounds good to me," I told her.

"We'll change the monitors to the wireless ones so that you can move around the room while we still keep an eye on baby," she told me as she helped the nurse change the monitors that were strapped to my belly.

"Easy now," the midwife said as she helped me to my feet once they were done. "We don't want you to fall, so go very slowly as you're getting up."

I slowly made my way to my feet, Brad at one side, the midwife at the other. It felt odd to not entirely be able to feel my legs, but I had no trouble standing or walking.

I was enjoying standing and felt proud that I was doing okay when the alarms monitoring the baby started to go off. My heart jumped into my throat. I looked up at the nurse and then quickly over to the midwife.

"It's okay," she assured me, "I think we just have to hold the monitors. They're not sitting as close to your belly as they were when you were lying down so they're having trouble picking up baby's movements.

"Thank you," I told her. "It's nice to be out of that bed for a bit."

"Let's go and have a seat on the toilet," she suggested, "and I'll just hold the monitors for you."

"That's certainly a sentence I never thought anyone would ever say to me," I said with a laugh. "Why the toilet?"

"It can put your body in an encouraging position to help move baby down," she replied.

"Would you like anything?" the doula asked. "A popsicle or some broth?"

"A popsicle would be nice," I told her, setting the scene for one of my favourite labour memories. "Thanks."

And so, my midwife, who was such a lovely human, sat on the bathroom floor while I sat on the toilet, eating a popsicle. It's a lasting memory that I have of cultivating a bond with the beautiful woman who was going to help me bring my baby into this world. I asked her how she met her boyfriend and we talked about how I met Brad.

When they checked me again a couple of hours later, I had progressed even further.

"Not long now, Anya," the midwife assured me. "You're doing

so great."

We had spent a couple of hours with the lights dimmed, resting again. Our nurse said good-bye before her shift change; it was bittersweet.

"Good luck," she said. "You're going to do great!"

Shortly after our new nurse joined us, my body was ready to push.

Ready to push.

I was ready to push; I was getting my chance. I was going to do it.

Pushing was an all-new experience for me. Our new nurse and midwife did a great job explaining to me how to do it. The nurse would give me a heads up before each contraction started based on the indications on the monitors. I could still feel tightness and a dull contraction each time as I readied myself to push, and for that I was really grateful. I may not have been able to get on top of the pain of the contractions, but I was happy to still feel them. To feel the pressure of my body getting ready to bring my baby into this world.

Brad remained up by my head and helped our doula when she was taking breaks to take pictures. I had glanced at my midwife's watch when they told me that I was ready to push and saw that it was 7:15 pm.

We tried a few different positions, first on my back with the nurse and my doula each holding a leg in assistance. Then they added a bar across the foot of the bed and got me to use a bedsheet tied to the bar for bearing down and pulling while pushing. They also brought out a birthing stool. Neither of those options were really working for me and I agreed with my midwife when she suggested we go back to the first position on my back.

All three of the women I had supporting me were so encouraging and positive. The nurse and midwife reassured me that I was doing a great job pushing and I could tell that they were impressed when I got really good pushes in. I was so proud of myself and I hadn't even come close to accomplishing what we were there for. But I *was* doing it. I was in the moment, tackling this birth with all that I had. It might not have been what I had envisioned, but in those moments, with my wonderful husband and support team by my side, I was conquering my biggest fear of not delivering naturally. I was bringing my baby to meet us. I couldn't have done it without the people surrounding me but I was also aware of my strength in doing it all myself.

Brad held my hand almost constantly while I was pushing. He had been such a great father from the very beginning of my first pregnancy, attending appointments and listening to my hormonal rants. I never doubted that he would be there for me through it all. I made sure to take a moment to see him, feel his love and appreciate his presence for not only me but also our family. He was my biggest cheerleader throughout it all.

"One more push, Anya," the midwife said. "After the next contraction, you're going to meet your baby."

I bared down and gave it my all. There was a pop and I looked down to see my midwife pull my babe up onto my chest.

I was so overcome with emotions that I didn't even look to see the gender right away. I clutched my baby to my chest while they cleared the airways and made sure baby could breathe. Brad and I cried together in joy and love for the newest member of our family.

I simply lay there with my second born in my arms, knowing that there was no rush for me to go anywhere or do anything. I hugged my baby to my chest with an abundance of love no person will ever be able to put into words. I felt Brad's relief and saw tears running down his face. Our eyes met and I could tell that he was getting impatient as we had agreed that I would announce the gender this time. As I finally lifted baby off of my chest and announced to the room that he was a boy, I saw Brad turn his head and see our son at the same moment.

I was overcome with happiness to finally meet our Maverick Everest and know that our family was complete.

Sadly, I was unable to avoid the operating room. The unfortunate placement of Maverick's shoulder when he came out resulted in a third-degree tear that required a trip to the OR for repair. And so, even though I had naturally delivered my son, we had to be separated shortly after his birth.

"Do you think you could wait until I'm back to weigh him?" I asked the nurse as she lifted him off of my chest.

"Absolutely," she said, smiling.

"Are you coming with me?" I asked the midwife. I was scared to be leaving my family and wanted to know there would be a familiar face nearby.

"Of course," she said, "I'll just go change and meet you in there."

The procedure was going to be overseen by a new OB, who had since replaced Dr. VBAC, and performed by the same resident we had met earlier.

It was overwhelming to be in an operating room. I had immediate flashbacks to my cesarean birth with Archer as soon as we entered the OR. Every person on the medical staff was dressed in identical scrubs with their heads covered. It's very difficult to tell who you know and who you don't and I couldn't help but feel scared.

"Hi Anya," the anesthesiologist said to me as he introduced himself. "I'll be taking good care of you to make sure you don't feel any pain during the procedure."

I had started to shake uncontrollably.

"It's a side effect of the meds," he told me. "We'll get you a warm blanket once we're all set here."

I repeatedly told myself it was going to be okay and was trying my best not to panic. I searched for my midwife's kind eyes in the sea of unidentified green people, which helped me find my calm.

"You're doing great," she told me as she squeezed my hand. "I'm right here for you."

"Thank you," I told her as I felt my eyes droop. I was so tired, and I was feeling so vulnerable as they moved me around on the operating table, lifting my legs into these giant stirrups that supported me from the knees down. Thankfully, having been up for so long and having been through as much as I had, I was able to fall asleep. I felt a bit guilty that I had asked my midwife to stay with me during the procedure only to fall asleep, but she remained with me and was there when I awoke.

The procedure actually took a couple of hours, though it didn't seem that long to me since I slept through most of it. In the meantime, Brad and Maverick were moved from the labour and delivery suite and were able to meet me in the recovery room. It was really nice, actually, that I didn't have to be alone in recovery. That's the way it should always be, if you ask me.

When our midwife, doula, Brad and Maverick joined me in recovery, my breath came easily once again. There was just something about being separated from that little being who had literally been part of me only moments before that made me sad.

Our nurse came in shortly after we pulled the curtain for some privacy to apologize. "I'm so sorry," she said. "They wanted us to leave the room, so they had to weigh him. I told you that we would wait, and I wasn't able to keep my promise!"

"That's okay," I told her as Maverick snuggled into my chest. "Really, it's okay."

"Thank you," she said as she turned to leave. "And congrats!"

"You'll never believe how much he weighs," Brad said to me, giddily.

"Ya?" I asked. At this point, I didn't particularly care.

"Guess!" he said with a cheeky smile.

Yes, Brad, I really want to play guessing games right now. How did you know?

I must have given him a look because he blurted it out right away: "Ten pounds, ten ounces!!"

"Wow!"

"Over two pounds heavier than Archer!" he said, his grin even bigger.

I was shocked. Now, since I had had my epidural, which involved being hooked up to an IV, I had received fluids into my body for over twelve hours. The baby also received these fluids, which I was told can have an impact on their birth weight. The baby's weight is more accurate around the 24-hour mark, at which point Maverick was around a pound less than his "birth weight".

"Ten-ten," Brad said, stroking Maverick's head as it nestled into me. "Our ten-ten."

And so, our chunky little fella had his new family nickname. Ten-ten. Ten-ten two-chins if you ask Archer.

We didn't have to wait too long in recovery before we were brought to our hall closet—I mean, room. Our doula and midwife said their goodbyes; it had been a very long day for them both. I was emotional saying goodbye to them. Blame the hormones if you want, but I was also emotional about saying goodbye to my midwifery team six weeks later at our last visit. They had touched my heart and my life so much. I hope they know how much I appreciate them.

Since I had suffered the third-degree tear and because I also had a bit of a fever while receiving the IV, the hospital wanted to keep me for two nights. I was especially eager to get home to Archer, but I think I did pretty well as a hospital patient that time around. I think it helped that we didn't have any outside pressure from out of town guests or other family. We chose to wait until we had settled at home to share the news of our new arrival.

I spent the second night in the hospital alone with Maverick as it made the most sense for Brad to get home to Archer and Eddie. He dropped Archer off at day care the next day and then came back to the hospital to pick us up. The discharge process went quite smoothly and my time at the hospital was pretty good overall. The nurses were fantastic and looking back on it I have no complaints about our stay.

We got home in the early afternoon and settled in before Brad left to pick Archer up from day care. I was so excited to see him! We chose not to have him come and visit us at the hospital so that we could have the time to be on our own with Maverick. There was also something special to me about Archer meeting his brother for the first time at our home. The hug that I got from Archer when I saw him was just what my soul needed. He had taken a bit of his frustrations with us for abandoning him over the weekend out on Brad, but I'm happy to say he treated me really well. He was kind to his baby brother and has treated him with love on the whole. There has been the typical preschooler stuff but he has accepted our newest family member with open arms ever since his arrival. We all have.

Sometimes when I watch Brad take care of the boys, I think about you and Jonathan. I like to think that Jonathan would have been that partner for you. I didn't know the guy, but I had planned to contact him while you were in South America, to see if he wanted to meet me. In a perfect world, he would have been the father of your children and your all, like Brad is for me. I can only envision your last moments if I remember that you were with love.

Being a mom is the most difficult thing I have ever done, second only to losing you. I never dreamed that I would be so lucky as to have a husband as perfect for me as Brad. Nor would I ever have guessed that I would be blessed enough to have two beautiful sons like Archer and Maverick.

I also never could have guessed that I would ever lose you, or how I would suffer because of it.

Most of all, I never could have guessed that I would persevere and come out the other side full of life, love and respect. Or that I am more than capable of it all.

The love that I carry from you is deep inside of me. I think that the longing I once had for you has manifested itself into love. I don't specifically think of you when I embrace how much I love my children or my husband, but I know that I learned from you what it means to choose love and let it be a positive guiding force. Your heart brought out the good that had always been inside of me. I wish you could see me now, at my best yet.

Your sister followed in your footsteps several years later, while she was a med student at UBC, by traveling to Bolivia and Honduras. I haven't had much contact with her myself, but thanks to Facebook and your mom I have been able to stay in the know somewhat. I can imagine the adventures you would have taken, in and out of the hospitals, through the mountains and with a variety of new and wonderful friends. I can imagine the abundance of stories you would have told. It's incredibly special that your sister was able to take that trip, both for herself and for you. Maybe one day I will too.

You and I never made it very far in our adventures together but I had always imagined a day when we would both be older and able to travel the world together. Travelling was such a big part of your life, and I yearn to make it a bigger part of my own.

A while back, the year after you disappeared, Brad and I went on a hike that was only slightly above our abilities. I say that with profound sarcasm—this hike was no joke. Your family and friends had planned a hike in your memory closer to Whistler that we weren't able to make it to, so we set off on our own, determined to make you proud. We were gone for the whole day and I tried to quit several times as we climbed Hollyburn Mountain. Brad cheered me on, constantly reminding me that we were doing it for you. I'm sure the hike would have been simple for you, just an everyday adventure. For us, however, it was a major challenge. It was July and being the inexperienced and naive hikers we are, we didn't realize that we would encounter snow at higher elevations.

I know that you were with me as we finally crested the mountain, breaking through the trees as we reached the summit. We had a beautiful 360-degree view of the surrounding mountains and could clearly see the Lions from our point at the top. You were there as Brad brought me into a giant hug.

I was sad but so unbelievably happy and proud of myself that I hadn't given up. I could see why you loved hiking so much. Beauty is at our fingertips and surrounds us from all sides in nature.

"We did it, babe," Brad said to me as I started to cry. "You did it."

"I did," I said through the tears. "Thank you."

He smiled down at me and kissed me there, atop the mountain.

"I couldn't have done it without you," I told him.

I couldn't have done it without you either, my love. Any of it.

With all the love that my heart possesses,

Anya

Acknowledgments

First, I want to thank my editor, Kristin, for her ideas, honesty and eye for the details. I feel that we worked really well as a team and my book would look nothing like it does today if it weren't for your insight and hard work.

A big thanks to my designer, Laura. Thank you for helping me bring my unique vision to life in the design of my book. You truly took what I said I wanted for the cover and brought it to life!

To the rest of my team at The Self Publishing Agency: thank you for being my cheerleaders from the very start and always supporting my writing with your positive energy.

For anyone that has suffered from abuse or loss of any kind, I hope you know that you are not alone. I have written about my experiences and how I have chosen to deal with them in ways that are truly my own. Everyone is entitled to do the same, whether a little or a lot, at any time that feels comfortable for them. I hope that my words have comforted anyone that has ever been through something similar.

To everyone that knew and loved Rachael, I hope you can feel her in my words and be proud that we knew such an amazing individual who will be forever missed. For a long time after her disappearance, I avoided listening to how anyone else missed her or thought of her, but that is no longer true. Please know that this is my account of my life and experiences, written for Rae. In no way do I mean to take away from how anyone else felt for her, or her value. There was more than enough of her heart to go around.

AJ, Ashley, Becky, Gina, Heather, Jaimie and Monika: thank you for your important roles in working with me to finalize this book. I appreciate the kindness in your opinions and I hope you all know how grateful I am for the time you took out of your busy lives to read my book before it was published. You are all my very special friends. Thank you for always being there for me!

For my family: we have an infinite number of memories together, most of which did not have a place in this book. The words that I have written do not mean that all of my childhood was bad, nor do they take away from the value I place upon our experiences together as they, too, helped to shape me into the person that I am today. And without all of you, I wouldn't have come as far as I have. Thank you for your love and support.

To my kids: I hope that you will follow my example and chase your dreams at every turn. May you always carry with you a piece of the innocent spirit you have now as children. Trust your gut and don't be afraid to take chances. Life is too short to play by the rules, but remember to always stay safe and come home for dinner every once in a while. The excitement I feel when I think about your potential could fill the earth infinite times over. I know that you have great things in you; stay focused and true to yourselves always.

Finally, I would like to thank my husband, Brad. May we forever share our souls when we glance deep into each other's eyes. And when we're old and gray, we can look through the pages of this book and remember how our love started. You are the reason why this book has a spine; there is no way I could put a price on what that means. *Til mountains crumble to the sea, there will still be you and me.* Fitting that the lyrics that shaped our relationship from the very beginning reference the mountains, isn't it?

Made in the USA
Lexington, KY
14 June 2019